BUT I AM
ONE OF YOU

BUT I AM ONE OF YOU

NORTHEAST INDIA AND THE STRUGGLE TO BELONG

Edited by

Samrat Choudhury
Preeti Gill

HarperCollins *Publishers* India

First published in India by HarperCollins *Publishers* 2024
4th Floor, Tower A, Building No. 10, DLF Cyber City,
DLF Phase II, Gurugram, Haryana – 122002
www.harpercollins.co.in

2 4 6 8 10 9 7 5 3 1

P-ISBN: 978-93-6213-857-6
E-ISBN: 978-93-6213-359-5

The views and opinions expressed in this book are the authors' own
and the facts are as reported by them, and the publishers are not in
any way liable for the same.

Samrat Choudhury and Preeti Gill assert the moral right
to be identified as the editors of this work.

Typeset in 11/14.7 Adobe Garamond at
HarperCollins *Publishers* India

Printed and bound at
Replika Press Pvt. Ltd.

From the mountains to the plains, from the rivers to the seas ... to all people everywhere who are struggling to belong

The detailed notes pertaining to this book are available on the HarperCollins *Publishers* India website. Scan this QR code to access the same.

Contents

Introduction

Peace, it seems, is always a bit of a shaky mirage in India's Northeast. Every time it looks like things are fine, something happens. We've had this experience twice in recent years.

In early 2019, we had a slim volume published.[1] It was called *Insider/Outsider: Tales of Belonging and Unbelonging in India's North-East.* When we started work on it sometime in 2017, those tales were meant to be reminiscences of an often bitter and undigested recent past—but, importantly, it was the past, not the present, and certainly not the future. It seemed then as though the region had turned a corner. After decades of unrest, there had been a period of peace and rapid economic transformation for seven or eight years, or more. Militant violence, by all measures, was down. 'Connectivity' was the new buzzword. 'Act East' was in the air. Fancy new hotels, stores and malls were sprouting. The romance of separatist insurgency, which had lured generations of youth, seemed to have lost its allure for the new generation entranced by the endless shiny new things that money could buy.

By the time the book was published in February 2019, that mood of buoyant consumerism had already begun to darken.

First the National Register of Citizens (NRC) came looming up into the lives of every resident of Assam. The scramble to prove through specified sets of documents that one or one's parents were legal residents there since before March 1971 began to create fresh turmoil in the state. The Citizenship Amendment Act (CAA) followed, and soon, Northeast India was back to seeing angry protest marches marked by sporadic violence. Tension was once again in the air. The hard-won peace had begun to evaporate. The question of insiders and outsiders, who belonged and who did not, had returned with a vengeance. It was in that changed milieu that our collection on the issue was published.

It was a timely and perhaps necessary attempt to break decades of silence on a difficult but vitally important topic. However, it was incomplete, as any such effort was bound to be. In the introduction to that volume, we had written, 'The only consolation is that completeness was never a possibility. Any anthology such as this was always doomed to be incomplete. The region itself is vastly diverse, with around 220 languages being spoken, and adherents of numerous and multiple faiths, and it would take an encyclopaedia in several volumes to bring voices from all these varied groups on board. Such completeness was obviously well beyond the scope of a book like this.'

Happily, this volume that you hold in your hands, which takes forward the incomplete work of the previous one, is now here. It is a book with a wide range of voices from across the states and communities of Northeast India. The pieces all examine questions of identity and belonging. These are difficult questions in a region with a history of decades of conflict between various communities. The mood and intention with which the issues would be addressed were, therefore, crucial: we were clear that we wanted truth and reconciliation, not a deepening of faultlines. We were looking for the light of mutual understanding between people from different and often opposite sides of various ethnic divides. The heat of atrocity propaganda, which is so much with us every day on social media, TV and even films, busily generating revenue for its purveyors, was something we wished dearly to avoid.

What we have here as a result is a collection of heartfelt and illuminating pieces by writers from across the region. Several of these are a mix of memoirs and essays in which writers from different sides of the various ethnic divides that so bedevil the region examine their own sense of self. The complexity and humanity of every human identity reveals itself, perhaps unconsciously at times, through some of these writings.

When we began work on this volume, it was again a time when things in Northeast India seemed to be getting better after a period of turmoil. The pandemic had ended, the agitations over the NRC and CAA had receded, and the limp back to 'normalcy' was on. Uncertainty still loomed over what would eventually happen in both those matters, and millions of lives remained suspended in the balance, but, for the moment, there was an uneasy calm. Then, suddenly, all of this changed in one of the states: Manipur. On the morning of 2 May 2023, the state was still a place where ordinary people lived normal lives. By 4 May, barely forty-eight hours later, it was on its way to becoming a war zone where the Indian Army, multiple paramilitary forces, the Manipur state police and heavily armed militias would engage in battle for months to come.[2] There is no end in sight even in early 2024, when these words are being written.

The core issue, once again, was and is the issue of insider and outsider—who belongs and who does not. Ranged on one side of this conflict are the non-tribal and predominantly Hindu Meiteis of Manipur, who claim to be indigenous inhabitants of that state. On the other side are the tribal communities, predominantly Christians, of the Kuki-Zo group of tribes, who also claim to be indigenous to the state—but often face suspicions of being recent migrants from next-door Myanmar, where a coup in 2021 triggered a civil war that caused several thousand refugees to flee to India. The Chin Hills of Myanmar were among the areas particularly affected by the war there, and a large proportion of the refugees were from the tribes known generally as

Chins, who have ethnic and cultural affinities with the Kuki-Zo groups of tribes of Mizoram and Manipur. While most of them found shelter in Mizoram, where they were given humanitarian aid by the local people and state government, their arrival in Manipur triggered fears among the two other major communities inhabiting the state—the Naga and the Meitei—that it would alter the demographic balance there.

Such fears are almost certainly exaggerated, but the Northeast has a long history of similar fears playing a pivotal role in the politics of state after state in the region through the decades.

The questions of who belongs and who does not, who is an insider and who is an outsider, has been a notable part of the region's politics for almost a hundred years now. The issue was being debated in the Assam Assembly, which was established in 1937, even before the independence and partition of India. At that time, what is now Bangladesh was still part of undivided India. The migration of peasants from there, which had been actively encouraged by the British administrators for decades—there was an enduring and widespread shortage of labourers in Assam, dating back to at least the 1840s—had turned in the decade of 1911–21 into a problem of plenty.[3] At the time, it was migration from one province to the next, within the same country, but it gave rise to political tensions in Assam, which were fanned by an inflammatory report in the Census of 1931 that raised a belated alarm about the migration whose volume had actually dropped sharply in the decade of 1921–31.[4] Assam's territory then included the Bengali-speaking Sylhet region, which is now in Bangladesh. The political contest in the province was mainly a three-way one, between the caste Bengalis, caste Assamese and the Muslims from the Brahmaputra and Surma valleys, both Bengali and Assamese. Linguistic and religious tensions, and perhaps a bit of 'divide and rule' by the British Raj, were at play. Anxieties about a change in the demographic balance grew.

Those anxieties, in one form or another, have remained the mainstay of politics in Northeast India since then. In Assam, they expressed themselves in subsequent decades through riots inspired by the goal of 'Bongal kheda' or 'drive out the Bongals', a generic term meaning outsiders that in practice tended to focus on Bengalis, both Hindu and Muslim. This gradually morphed into the powerful Assam Agitation of 1979–85 that ended with the Assam Accord whose aim was to detect 'foreigners' living illegally in the state, delete their names from electoral rolls and deport them. In Meghalaya next door, the capital Shillong was convulsed year after year by riots, most notably in 1987, 1991 and 1992, sparked by agitations that sought to drive out 'dkhars', meaning outsiders. The Mizo Hills, before the peace accord of 1987, had seen targeted killings of 'vais' or people from the plains. The 'vai' or outsiders were served quit notices by the insurgents. In the Manipur valley, the term for outsiders is 'mayang'. Records of conflicts between the Meiteis and the mayangs can be found dating back centuries, for example, in the royal chronicles known as *Cheitharon Kumpapa*.[5]

In the Naga hills, every Naga tribe—there are sixteen in Nagaland itself and an equal number outside the state—has its own language and ancestral domain. There, even a Naga from another tribe is an outsider in the area of a different tribe, but there are grades of outsider-ness. The outsider of greatest concern is one known locally by an acronym: IBI. It stands for 'Illegal Bangladeshi Immigrant'. Being called an IBI can have deadly consequences. For example, in Dimapur in 2015, a Bengali Muslim man from Assam accused of raping a local college girl in a hotel room—he claimed it was consensual sex for which he had paid money—was dragged out of prison by a mob and lynched in broad daylight. The crime of which he had been accused was heinous, but placards carried by members of mobs that had gathered before the lynching indicated that their fury had been compounded by the accusation that he was an 'IBI'.[6]

The idea of who belongs where, throughout Northeast India, is strongly associated with concepts of indigeneity. The indigenous are generally the ones with 'son/daughter of the soil' status, which gives them the birthright to live there as full citizens—they truly belong.

The rest, i.e., the not-indigenous, span a range of outsider-ness—from almost-indigenous to 'IBI' alien.

The commonly prevalent idea in large parts of this region has long been that the tribal is the indigenous insider and the non-tribal is the outsider. The 2023 conflict in Manipur has brought into sharp focus a reversal of this usual binary—here, it is the non-tribals, predominantly Hindu Meiteis who are claiming indigenous status, while it is the Kuki-Zo tribals who are facing the outsider tag. The other region in the Northeast with non-tribal insiders is, of course, Assam, where the key dividing lines between the insider and outsider have historically been language, followed by religion.

However, being of the 'right' religion and fluently speaking the local language are no guarantee of insider status. The issue of belonging is complicated further by a problematic notion: the notion of 'purity of blood'. Those of mixed ancestry, for instance, have to negotiate difficult questions of identity and belonging—a common experience in many societies, but one with a particular edge in contexts where such mixing is seen as impurity. Strangely enough, it is likely that this globally outdated concept, which went out of fashion following the global opprobrium brought to it by the Nazis, is actually new, at least in its present form, in this part of the world—like the idea of a nation-state.

In the old, traditional order, tribal societies had systems for initiating outsiders into the tribe through ceremonies and rituals. Khasi society, for example, had a system of inclusion called 'tang jait' by which new Khasi clan lines were begun, with full social approval, by children born of mixed marriages between Khasis and outsiders. There was also a custom called 'rap-iing' by which girls and women in the matrilineal Khasi society could be adopted into Khasi families whose female members had died.[7] In other words, while entry into the tribe was regulated by rules, the Khasi identity was not exclusively reserved for those of 'pure blood'. Ways for the assimilation of outsiders into the tribe existed even in other homogenous tribal societies in the region.

We have forgotten now that slavery was common across large parts of the world, including Northeast India, until about 200 years ago. What happened to the descendants of all those slaves, especially the ones of mixed lineage?

The coming of modernity to the region in late colonial times wrought a quick transformation of epic proportions. Ways of life that had continued with minimal change for several hundred years were suddenly rooted out in a matter of one or two generations. The paradigm shift was rapid and epochal. There are still a few tattooed Naga head-hunters alive today. They are now old men, but in their youth, they were witness to another way of life—every single aspect of which was utterly different from what it is today.

That world no longer exists.

The world of 150 years ago, not just for head-hunters but for all kinds of people from communities across the Indian subcontinent, was one without electricity, piped water, pucca roads and houses, modern toilets, bathrooms and even something as ubiquitous today as toothbrushes. There was, of course, no phone or television or internet. Everything about life, starting with its ordinary quotidian details, was different. Children very rarely went to school or adults to offices. Being educated was rare, the privilege of tiny groups of elites. Half the population—the female half—remained largely illiterate. Among the male half, there was no education for those considered low caste. People were ruled, for the most part, by local kings or chiefs, who often paid some kind of grudging tribute to a more powerful and distant ruler. Atop that hierarchical pyramid of kings and chiefs was Queen Victoria, Empress of India.

It was a world of kingdoms and empires and expanses of 'non-state spaces', mainly remote mountains and jungles between adjacent empires ruled by independent local chieftains. The concept of the nation-state was absent in that world.

The Merriam-Webster dictionary has the following meanings for nation-state:

a form of political organization under which a relatively homogeneous people inhabits a sovereign state
especially: a state containing one as opposed to several nationalities

This is, of course, completely different from the old idea of a kingdom or empire. An empire would extend as far as its arms would carry it. It was held together by the person of the emperor, typically fashioned by royal priests as some kind of descendant of God on earth, to whom the subjects owed their loyalty. Within that empire there might be people of a hundred or a thousand different nationalities, of diverse ethnicities and races, speaking their own languages, and having their own distinct religions and cultures. There might be a favoured religion or language, but homogeneity was not a requirement. Villages were expected to be homogenous; kingdoms and empires were not.

The recasting of that idea of how the world should be organized, which came in the wake of colonialism in Northeast India, has been very problematic in this part of the world. Firstly, the idea that nation-states should have borders as lines instead of zones of transition from one domain to another has wiped out the in-between buffer spaces and brought adjacent nation-states into direct conflict with one another. The territorial dispute between India and China is an example.

Secondly, the idea that all countries must be nation-states drove both Hindu nationalism and Muslim nationalism through the early 1900s. The idea that Hindus and Muslims are separate nations culminated in the partition of the British Indian Empire into India and Pakistan in 1947. The emergence of an international border between East Pakistan (which became Bangladesh in 1971, as Bengali nationalism asserted itself) and surrounding Northeast India has given rise to enduring problems related to migration, which have led to many a riot and agitation in the region through the decades.

Yet unresolved questions of who belongs, and who does not, also arose on both sides of the line from the drawing of an international border between India and Burma (now Myanmar). The idea of the nation-state, meanwhile, proliferated, along with the idea of the right of nations to self-determination. The result has been a long series of nationalist struggles for independence waged by various emergent nationalities in Northeast India since 1947. Thus, the Naga conflict is a struggle for the creation of a Naga nation-state. The Mizo insurgency in its heyday was similar. Other states such as Manipur, Assam and Tripura have seen powerful armed insurgencies as well, all intending to create some form of national homeland for a community that saw itself as a nation entitled to its own state. In some cases, the demand for such a state was not for an independent country but for statehood within India—for example, the Bodo and Garo struggles for Bodoland and Garoland respectively.

The current conflict in Manipur is to some extent a result of the same ideas of nationality and belonging playing out in what was historically a multi-ethnic kingdom. The three main ethnic groups there—the Meitei, Naga and Kuki—all have their own nationalisms with long and storied histories. Armed insurgent outfits of all three communities have waged protracted struggles against the Indian state in pursuit of imagined independent 'national' homelands. The maps of those imagined nations, not surprisingly, tend to overlap. The conflict, therefore, becomes a zero-sum game with no possible resolution that would be acceptable to all sides.

In a globalized world where there is, in truth, just one dominant global culture in many flavours—because there is only one modernity and, for all practical purposes, one economic system—the anxieties about losing one's cultural moorings and identity are heightened. It is, therefore, an entirely natural response to want to conserve and perhaps even assert, one's own identity. So far, so good … every community can conserve its own culture and identity without necessarily having to fight an armed struggle against another. Indeed, it can be done even without control of territory—Tibetan culture is largely conserved by followers of the Dalai Lama in India, who do not have a state or country.

The trouble with the idea of the nation-state, and its sub-units, such as states within the Indian Union, is that there is always an 'authentic people' and culture associated with each place who are seen as the legitimate owners of that space—the 'natural born insiders'. The corollary is that everyone else, by definition, is an outsider. Thus, the 'Miya' Muslim of Bengal origin in Assam is likely to be viewed as an outsider even if his or her forefathers migrated to Assam more than a hundred years ago. The Dalit Sikh in Shillong whose ancestors were brought there by the British during the Raj is an outsider four or five generations on. The Gorkha or Marwari whose forefathers arrived in the earliest days of colonial rule shares the same plight. The Kuki tribal, whose ancestors may well have been in Manipur for two or three centuries or longer, is also liable to be viewed as an outsider. The story of the Chakma tribal is similar. The Nepali and Bengali speakers, irrespective of religion, are liable to be seen as outsiders in Northeast India—and often assumed to rightfully belong in their 'national homelands' of Nepal, Bangladesh or West Bengal.

Yet, at a time and in a world where lakhs of people routinely migrate to other cities and countries for education and work, there are vast and growing populations of people who live outside such 'national homelands'. Entire communities of people from the Northeast have sprung up in Delhi, Noida, Pune, Bengaluru, Goa and several other Indian cities and states. Many second and third-generation kids of Northeastern heritage have grown up in those places. The experience of not feeling accepted as equal Indians because of their facial features, traditional food habits, or language and social norms more broadly, is a common one for many of them.

The insider in one place becomes the outsider in another.

The experience of simultaneously being both an insider and an outsider is thus part of an increasingly universal experience.

As readers who enjoy memoirs, personal histories and biographies, we believe that there is great value in these when we try to understand historical events that have shaped our worldview because they provide unique and intimate insights into the experiences and perspectives of individuals who lived through those events. The first-hand narratives in this book offer a personal and subjective understanding of history, complementing and enriching historical records. By the very fact that they are personal, often intensely and passionately felt subjective accounts, they provide an emotional context to historical events that may otherwise escape us. The fears, hopes, traumas and struggles faced by ordinary people as they live through significant events that disrupt their lives help to connect the reader to those events and make them all the more relatable and insightful. Often one gets diverse viewpoints and perspectives, more details, more nuance and more complexity that tends to get lost in 'mainstream' narratives. What we hear in personal stories, essays and memoirs—and we include here the ones in the present volume—is also unfiltered information and details that may not be found in 'official' documents. Most importantly, a volume such as this one provides a platform for voices that may have been silenced, ignored or overlooked.

By asking our contributors to write on the complex insider/outsider issue in a second volume, a follow-up to our first, we wanted to see where things stand today in states across the region. Despite the sweeping social and political changes in the country and in the Northeast, is there more engagement, acceptance and connectivity between disparate cultures now? Can we challenge the stereotype of the 'Northeasterner', who is viewed with 'suspicion' because of his/her distinctive features, eating habits, attire, culture and religion? In essay after essay, authors have tried to find a way forward, to be able to forge a connection, an understanding, by revealing their own angst, their own stories and their own histories, which have often been at the crux of these unyielding attitudes. By 'humanizing' their own and their community's histories, our contributors have helped us put faces to stories and events and view them with empathy and sensitivity. This makes their particular histories more vivid and relatable, especially when we look at areas where, even now, few from mainland India travel and fewer still record what happens on the ground.

The fact that Manipur has been in the throes of ethnic battles between the Meiteis of the valley and the Kuki-Zo tribals of the hills since May 2023 underlines these questions of identity, of who has greater access to government benefits and quotas, and rights to land. It underlines the faultlines, the chasms and divisions (some old, some newly created) that have taken many lives, destroyed homes and livelihoods. Yet, what amazes one is how nothing that the state and Central governments have done is enough to bring the battling sides to any understanding.

As you read the essays in this volume, not only do you get an idea of the many stories that exist side by side in the states of this region but also the feeling that these are all mirror images and reflections of one another. The simmering antagonism between communities, between majority and minority in the Northeast can be seen reflected in Delhi, Bengaluru and other metros, so similar in their dark and horrific detail. Let us try and contextualize the essays as well as connect them to make a 'story' of 'othering'.

Veio Pou, from the hills of Manipur, who has lived in the capital city, Delhi, for more than twenty-five years tries to address the 'everyday' experiences of being a person from Northeast India. While this is a thread that runs through the anthology because so many from India's 'peripheries' and borderlands come to Delhi to find education and livelihoods, opportunities that perhaps do not exist in their own home states, many are faced with hostility, harassment and discrimination. He feels that somehow the cosmopolitan space creates an atmosphere of living on the edge, which he did not feel even in a region that is stereotyped as a 'conflict' zone. For him, there is the ever-present fear in the everyday, a sense of not belonging, of being unsafe, vulnerable. Constantly overwhelmed by the question 'Where are you from?', only because he carries the physical markers that show him as belonging to a little-known part of India, he wonders, 'What does an Indian look like?' This very same question—what does an Indian look like—is one that is echoed in another essay by the Gorkha writer from Mizoram, Pratap Chhetri, who ascribes it to former Mizoram Chief Minister Lal Thanhawla. In his essay, Pratap talks about the history of the Gorkha settlements in the Northeast, which date back to almost two centuries, when the British first started expanding their territories.

Are minorities to always face xenophobia and prejudice just because the 'mainland Indian' doesn't know his or her own country? Why do they become targets of name-calling, of violence, and abuse—the case of Nido Tania, the young Arunachali boy brutally beaten up in Lajpat Nagar, a crowded part of South Delhi, so many years ago, is brought up in at least two of the essays in this volume. What pervades this essay and many others is a sense of longing for a beloved remembered home, away from the insensitivities of alienating spaces. Sangeeta Barooah Pisharoty's piece, 'Gaping at the Gaze', describes in detail the discomfort that a mere 'gaze' can create. She talks of the challenge the majoritarian gaze poses and how it can at once 'create' the other, pinning the outsider into the space of the Foreigner, who is always looked at with mistrust and suspicion. Ranju Dodum from Arunachal Pradesh says that identity is fluid and that *who* we are is often relative to *where* we are.

'Being different was a heavy burden to bear, frightening and confusing'—the minority is regarded as different and 'it's not a good kind of different but an uncomfortable different' is what Vatsala Tibrewalla writes, turning the gaze towards the outsider (the dkhar) in Shillong. She writes of her own experience as a fifth-generation Marwari in Shillong living in her ancestral home in the middle of the busy commercial Police Bazar. Going to school there, she was always acutely aware of being different—at the age of six she knew she did not fit in with her non-tribal, non-Catholic identity. The differences were stark and singled her out, invisible lines separated her from the others and forced them to remain trapped forever in their own silos. The violence of the 1980s and '90s, with bandhs, brutal killings, rapes and arson, poisoned her relationships. She writes, 'Assertions about whether one truly belongs to a place are most often based purely on ethnicity. The significance of having lived somewhere for an extended period is grossly underrated.'

In Easterine Kire's 'That Was My Hometown Too', we encounter her Punjabi classmate who remembers his growing-up years in Kohima where he always felt at home, where he spent his innocent days of youth, where people celebrated, ate and lived together, where there was a sense of community and ease and how all that was rudely brought to an end in the 1980s when factional killings, violence, threats, extortion and demands for money to fuel the 'Naga Movement' gripped the town. The movement was taken over by unscrupulous people who saw it as a way of making money, Easterine writes, and it was tough even for the locals to survive. Her Punjabi classmate rues the unpleasantness of the new order that forced so many to leave their homes, he grieves that 'the Kohima they knew had disappeared,' stolen by the new Naga nationalists who understood nothing of friendship and mutual respect. Kire's essay is a case in point of how the Punjabi outsider and the Naga insider were one until warring forces compelled them to part ways.

In another quest for personal identity, Indira Laisram writes on negotiating her Meitei Manipuri identity and constantly seeking affirmation because she grew up in Silchar, Assam, and was always aware of the subtle differences that existed between Manipuris who lived in Manipur and those outside it. Indira talks about the acculturation of minority communities to fit into the mould set by the majority, to take on the markers of the identity of the new homeland and become 'mayang' (the pejorative word used for someone from the plains beyond Manipur). She also writes about the multiplicity of identities, the interplay of belonging and unbelonging, which is something that has stayed with her. She has been the perennial outsider in Assam, Manipur, Delhi and then later in Australia. She has chosen to live a meandering life despite having to overcome language barriers and other obstacles. What the outsider resents most, however, is to be viewed as the other. She is an amalgamation (as are we all)—Manipuri, Indian, Australian.

There are brutal, inhuman ways of othering that some of our contributors write about. For his eighty-year-old paternal grandmother, a Partition refugee who has been left out from Assam's NRC, it is 'an unending Partition', says Abhishek Saha, as he describes her trauma. The preparation of the NRC was an unprecedented exercise of asking 3.3 crore residents of Assam to prove their Indian citizenship based on lineage, through documents and oral testimonies. The exercise cost the government a whopping Rs 1,600 crore, and when it was finally published in August 2019, it ended up stripping over 19 lakh people (including 7 lakh Muslims and 5 lakh Bengali Hindus) of their Indian citizenship. What this meant in terms of emotional distress, fear, uncertainty and shattered lives—by putting many on the Doubtful Voters list, rendering them potentially stateless since Bangladesh refuses to acknowledge them as citizens, placing thousands in detention camps and creating an atmosphere of fear and endless misery—is a sad commentary on how we treat our minorities. The parallel system of Foreigners Tribunals first appointed in the 1960s adjudicate on the cases brought before them and once a person is declared a 'foreigner' by an FT, she/he is liable to arrest and detention. As the 19 lakh excluded people wait endlessly to file their appeals to higher courts, they are in effect in limbo-land—their lives and citizenship uncertain.

Language is at the core of these questions of identity. The many riots in Assam and elsewhere in the country over the emotive subject of language have seen demands for detection, disenfranchisement and deportation in Assam, and both Patricia Mukhim and Subir Bhaumik refer to those in their essays. While Subir takes the case of Tripura, where the change in demographic balance between the indigenous tribal people and the Bengali refugees led to severe alienation between communities along with a huge violent backlash and riots, Patricia talks about the formation of the new state of Meghalaya, carved out of greater undivided Assam when the government tried to impose Assamese on the tribals of the Khasi, Garo and Jaintia Hills. The conflicts, triggered by inequality in access to land, assets and education unleashed some of the worst violence in Tripura in 1978 shortly after the formation of the Tribal National Volunteers and then again in 1988 in the run-up to the Tripura state assembly elections. According to Subir, the same thing happened in 1993 with violent attacks on Bengali villagers, abductions, rapes and arson. The movement for a separate tribal state has gained momentum now under the leadership of the present 'Maharaj' Pradyot Kishore Deb Barma.

Is the formation of new states and autonomous regions really the answer to the Northeast's complex problems? Patricia Mukhim describes the many problems that lie unaddressed in Meghalaya, despite the fact that the state was created in 1972 and is rich in natural resources and valuable minerals like limestone, uranium and coal. Without a concrete vision document to guide the policy of the state today, there is relatively little development or growth in the areas of education, health, land use, rail transport or mining there. In five decades, there is only one railhead in the entire state—the excuse to disallow rail transport is always the fear of the outsider, who may come in large numbers and overwhelm the tiny hill state. As in other parts of the Northeast, student bodies hold the people to ransom, creating an atmosphere of fear, and harassing dkhars, people from the plains, who are often blamed for taking away jobs, businesses and land. Communal tensions have flared time and again targeting Bengalis, Biharis, Marwaris and others. The demand to impose the Inner Line Permit, which will restrict the entry of plainspeople from the Indian mainland—this will hamper Meghalaya's economy, feels Mukhim—is a demand voiced with great vigour before every election. 'This is a state of unequal citizens. If "othering" means excluding people from the development trajectory that they have a right to, then yes there are about 90 per cent that make up this "other",' she says.

Nona Arhe's sensitive essay talks of the vulnerable group of migrant labourers in Nagaland, the lowly 'deshwalis' doing the most menial labour for the least compensation, their services needed for a wide range of jobs. Harassed and marginalized, they are never accepted as legitimate 'insiders' even if they have spent their entire working lives contributing to the state's growth and economy. They are often compelled to live and work in the shadows, hiding their grievances, afraid to complain, denied rights and freedoms, living in alien lands that they have made their home away from home. 'A sense of belonging comes from being accepted by and contributing to a larger group. A sense of belonging arises when an individual feels rooted and accepted by some community …' Obviously, there can be no sense of belonging if one is constantly being reminded of being an outsider, or the stigmatization and categorization it creates. Dominant narratives of fear and exclusion need to be replaced and changed—this is crucial in the Northeast as well as the urban conglomerates in the rest of India.

'Always the square peg,' writes Makepeace Sitlhou as she talks about her own identity as a Kuki in Manipur and two very strong assumptions about people from the Northeast that she carried: first and foremost, that they didn't see themselves as Indian (this was further compounded by decades of separatist movements in the Northeast states and brutal counterinsurgency measures unleashed on the common people by the security forces and, of course, the sort of treatment they continue to get in the 'mainland'); and second, because they were predominantly tribal. Her childhood years spent in secluded, sheltered army cantonments across India meant that her family was insulated from the extremities and uncertainties of the real world outside. She found this alienating and coercive in the sort of social expectations it placed on her mother, who was always expected to conform, to integrate with the dominant culture, but 'Only after living and reporting in Assam did I realize what it could cost a person to not belong to a place, in line with how the majority around them defines belonging.' She echoes many of us when she writes, 'I often think about these moments of what makes an outsider an outsider and who gets naturalized into becoming an insider …'

There are other stories of minorities and othering in the collection, each disparate and yet so similar. Teresa Rehman describes a Muslim-dominated area in Manipur's Imphal East district, Golapati, densely populated with clogged drains, unhygienic sanitation facilities and a paucity of drinking water. It is a community of Muslims, the Meitei Pangals, who make up 8.4 per cent of Manipur's population, who are seen as the 'other' even though they speak the same language, eat much the same food, and wear the same clothes as the other Meiteis. Rashmi Narzary's beautiful story-like essay talks about the Bodo's nagging sense of prejudice and deprivation—their forefathers have lived in Assam for countless generations but they are not Assamese, their language is different, and their story of being outsiders in their own homeland became even more exacerbated when the Assam Official Language Bill was passed in October 1960, forcing them to accept Assamese as their language. This led to riots and violence, with the Bodo Movement in 1987 bringing to the fore all the dissent and resentment, until finally with the creation of the Bodoland Territorial Region, with its headquarters at Kokrajhar, a sense of dignity and belonging was perhaps restored.

Ramona Sangma brings out the angst of another small community, the Garos of Meghalaya, where arguments regarding identity, of who is Garo, often do the rounds. They too face the usual discrimination, insecurity and name-calling when they travel out of their homeland. Back home, their rituals and traditions, their dress and food, the social structures of land ownership and inheritance become tourist attractions for visitors, something exotic and strange, creating distance and misunderstanding.

Hamari Jamatia's piece on fashion and politics draws upon the lives of some of Tripura's earliest women activists and leaders in a fascinating tale of how these women stitched together the past and the future with their sewing machines. She shows women's bodies as a cultural space upon which battle lines are drawn, the politics of dress where what you wear often rekindles pride in one's indigenous culture (we have seen this in the recent hijab debates where women are being told what to wear or not wear). By using their sewing machines these women brought back dignity to their culture by amalgamating their traditional rignai (wrap-around skirt) with the modern blouse that was worn by the 'respectable' women of the towns they encountered on visits. Tripura has the dubious distinction of being one of two states in the country where a migrant population has become the majority, owing to a severe demographic change, which was neither foreseen nor prevented by the leadership. The early indigenous leaders understood that it was important to safeguard their culture, identity and tribal lands and this was the first demand made by the Tripura Upajati Juba Samiti (TUJS). The women's wing was also created with this in mind—the belief that women can be powerful instruments of resilience and strength. Over the years the tribal and non-tribal have found a way to coexist but there are bursts of communal tensions and violence every once in a while. There is a wonderful story Hamari tells of how her mother and other women activists went to Delhi to meet Mrs Gandhi, the then Prime Minister, to apprise her of the ground situation in Tripura and how they connected with her woman-to-woman.

An interesting, somewhat unusual conversation between Karma Paljor, a Bhutia from Sikkim, and Naresh Agarwal, a fourth- or fifth-generation Marwari who also belongs to Sikkim, harks back to a simpler time when 'community was based on friendship, kinship and location'. The vexed question of Sikkimese citizenship (which had been offered to everyone in 1961 by the Chogyal[8] and which many Marwaris chose not to take up), comes up: 'If you have lived in a place for 120–130 years, why are you still being called an outsider? How many generations does it take to be considered an insider?'

The fifth essay in this book is one that we want to end this introduction with, for it is a personal account of a momentous journey where a young child of eleven sees her house burning, the streets of her hometown deserted, the family's printing press and pharmacy burnt—a reality that has been part of people's lives in many of the states of this region. This story is set in Aizawl, Mizoram, the year is 1966 and the little girl is Margaret Zama, who is returning home from her boarding school in Assam. She reaches her street, which is unrecognizable. Her father sees her alight from the bus and comes running—the family has been staying in the home of a close political colleague. Most families had already fled Aizawl at the start of the Mizo National Front (MNF) insurgency, remembered in Mizoram as Rambuai, meaning 'troubled land'. Margaret's family, too, flees on foot to a nearby village from where they watch their town being bombed by the Indian Air Force on 5 and 6 March 1966.[9]

The Mizo story is one of rage, resistance, retribution and reconciliation, as are so many of the others in this anthology. To read each essay is to open yet another window to the land and its people, to see where the problems lie and how best to move forward, to acknowledge them and search for solutions, knowing the vulnerabilities and delicate handling required. We would like to thank each of our contributors for sharing their stories so honestly and openly, and Swati Chopra, Siddhesh Inamdar, Tanima Saha and the entire team at HarperCollins India, for taking these stories out into the world.

Samrat Choudhury and Preeti Gill

Negotiating My Manipuri Identity

Indira Laisram

He looks every bit the woman. Even the voice. Amid the vast expanse of the paddy fields, the makeshift stage is the nucleus of the village theatre scene, where instinctive actors like him enact roles with passion. The audience is captivated.

In this Meitei village in Assam, the 'shumang leela' is a regular cultural import from the neighbouring state of Manipur. A traditional form of open-air theatre, the shumang leela uniquely has an all-male cast. The men adeptly take on female roles with an infectious likeability.

As a child, spending my winter holidays in my paternal village of Ramnagar Tuko in Silchar in the Cachar district of Assam, the shumang leela transported us to a world where the actors and the arc of the plays left an impact. It brought us cultural cues from a homeland I had not seen until then.

I used to look forward to those cultural nights. I remember with particular vividity the intonation and accent of the actors, quite different from the Meiteilon or Manipuri language I speak.

It was perhaps then that I started developing a certain internal narrative about the subtle differences that existed between the two kinds of Meiteis—those settled in Manipur and those in Assam, both states part of Northeast India. Despite its subtlety, it was a narrative that questioned my sense of belonging and would shape my sense of self.

I knew I was a different Meitei; my accent was somewhat sing-song and Meiteis from Manipur looked at Meiteis like me from Assam as 'somewhat different'.

There is, in my perception, a lot of Bengali influence on Meiteis settled in Cachar. These days, influenced by popular Hindi television serials, some married Meitei women even wear the mangal sutra (necklace worn by Hindu women signifying their marital status), sindoor and the sankha pola (red and white bangles unique to Bengali culture and worn by married women). It makes them look more 'mayang' (non-Manipuri) than the Meitei women in Manipur. Many even wear the phi (shawl-like garment worn with the phanek or traditional sarong) differently.

Several stories are told about how Manipuris came to settle in Assam. In the case of my own family, according to the account of my uncle, Laishram Tejamani Singh, a retired government officer, my great-grandfather Laishram Hingonchaoba Singh fled Manipur during the Burmese invasion of the kingdom—the Awa Lan (Burmese War of 1819–26). The war marked seven years of devastation.[1] My great-grandfather, a popular pung (drum) player who had many disciples, settled permanently in Silchar after leaving Manipur.

Other historical circumstances, such as marital alliances between royal families, trade and commerce and battles of succession between claimants for the Manipur throne, also led to migration, according to researchers. H. Basanta Kumar Singha of the department of sociology, Maibang Degree College, Assam, notes that those events give grounds to believe that the beginning of the Manipuri settlement in Cachar occurred much before the eighteenth century.

In navigating my identity as a Cachar Meitei, the awareness of being 'othered' came from close to home. In the eyes of the world, I was a Manipuri, but the question 'where are you from' would remain a perennial one.

I was born and brought up in Shillong, Meghalaya, but my ties to Silchar, where my grandparents from both sides and extended families lived, constantly reminded me of the multiplicity of my identity—a multiplicity sowed in parentage as well as location. I was a non-resident Manipuri, a bit of an outsider in my own moorings, someone who felt more at home in Shillong.

Ironically, Shillong, too, has a history of resentment towards outsiders. I remember the long spells of curfew in the late 1980s—school education was disrupted for almost a year in 1987—as the local Khasi Students' Union (KSU) agitated for the extension of provisions of the Assam Accord signed in 1985 to Meghalaya. Key among those was the identification and deportation of all illegal foreigners, particularly immigrants from nearby Bangladesh. The KSU wanted the same for Meghalaya.

The protestors' ire came to be primarily directed against the local resident populations of Bengalis, Nepalis and anybody who appeared 'dkhar', the Khasi term for non-Khasis. Appearance counted for a lot; looking like a dkhar could mean getting attacked on the streets. My youngest uncle was cautioned by the family not to venture out those days because he looked like a dkhar.

The Manipuri equivalent of dkhar is mayang. In calling someone a dkhar or a mayang, we were making a distinction between who we were and who they were. But, of course, such distinctions come with the potential to cause conflicts.

For some, this is a ubiquitous issue in the region. A few friends who have left Shillong for good reminisce about the good old days, but their memories are tinged with sadness. In the final analysis, they felt they never belonged.

A Bengali teacher friend, who spent her entire life in Shillong but moved out to another state a few years ago after retirement, tells me a classic story. 'To collect the cheque for a grant we received because of a proposal I prepared single-handedly, I was told by the managing committee to not go or send my office assistant, who was from the Hajong tribe. Instead, they wanted me to send my Khasi accountant because he was a local.'

She adds, 'I was the principal of a special school, yet its only contractual employee. Everyone else was regularized. I pulled that organization out of the dumps in the eight years I served there. But who cares? I am a dkhar.'

Even at the political level, the exclusion extends, with non-tribals being barred from voting in district council polls in the Khasi and Jaintia Hills. Friends who've lived for a long time in Shillong love the town and the community, but in private conversations admit to the experience of being 'othered'.

Growing up in Shillong, I saw the outsider issue festering before my eyes. Yet, somehow, I felt a sense of safety. I suppose it had to do with belonging to the local majority (the racial stock of East Asian appearance), despite being in a place and a region where many different peoples and cultures converged.

The diversity of Shillong meant friendships with people from various backgrounds, beyond Manipuris. My neighbourhood had Manipuri, Bengali, Assamese, Khasi, Nepali and Bihari families. I attended the midnight mass for Christmas with my friends, enjoyed the Hindu festivals of Durga Puja and Diwali, and went to my sister's Assamese Muslim friend's house during Eid.

Looking back, those years were enriching as I felt a sense of oneness in that diverse place. Yet, there was also an internal conflict. Why did being a Manipuri feel less intimate to me?

I looked at the Shillong Manipuri Students' Union with a bit of trepidation. At the old Manipuri Rajbari in Shillong, the home of the erstwhile Manipuri royal family where a few families like ours from Silchar lived and where the students often gathered for meetings, we were considered outsiders occupying the palace compound. Two of the four families that lived there actually had ties to the royal family. We had been custodians of the land for decades, but I could sense a constant politics of 'othering'.

So in my coming-of-age story, there was an interplay of belonging and unbelonging as a Manipuri.

My uncle, who lives in our ancestral home in Ramnagar Tuko, believes that the 'othering' of Cachar Meiteis, if it exists, comes from people who do not understand the real history of Manipuris. He argues that scholars have acknowledged that Manipuris in Cachar are 'pure Meiteis', even in terms of language usage. This perspective makes sense to me as we use some archaic words in Cachar in our daily conversations, such as 'olangba' for feeling hot or 'pay' for umbrella. The latter, in Manipur, is commonly called 'chatin', similar to the Bengali word 'chata'. Often, friends from Manipur do not understand the terms we use.

My first visit to Manipur was as a journalist in 1998, to cover India's general elections. I enjoyed the freedom of being a stranger in a land where everyone spoke my language but, at the same time, I dreaded conversations, especially formal ones. I didn't feel judged but, perhaps subconsciously, I was carrying inexplicable guilt for being an 'impure' Meitei, a 'mayang macha' (non-Manipuri child), as described by a relative because of the way we spoke—our language interspersed with words of English, Hindi and even Bengali. As I made my way across the state with the help of local friends, revelling in new-found friendships, I could feel my perspective of being the outsider change.

However, there was a lingering discomfort from the presence of the Indian Army. With checkpoints every few kilometres, I could feel the underlying tension between the army and the general population. It always felt like an untoward incident could be around the corner.

Some parts of Manipur fall under the jurisdiction of the Armed Forces Special Powers Act (1958), granting the Indian Army the authority to maintain a continuous presence in 'disturbed areas' of the state and subjecting all civilians to effective rule by martial law. Human rights organizations, like Front Line Defenders, have reported that, 'Under this Act, thousands of Manipuri civilians have been detained, jailed, tortured and extrajudicially killed by the armed forces and associated paramilitary forces.'

Women and students in Manipur have long been at the forefront of protests for the removal of AFSPA. After decades of protests, it was finally withdrawn from the Greater Imphal area in 2022 but continues to hang over other parts of the state.

Imagine the army knocking on your door in the middle of the night, escorting you out with impunity and offering no promise of a safe return. That is the power AFSPA grants the army.[2] For decades, it has played a significant role in perpetuating one aspect of the insider–outsider divide—that between the Northeast and the mainland—in the region. AFSPA may have various interpretations, but to me, its most obvious implication is that it is laden with stories of army excesses, thus perpetuating the insider–outsider conflict.

In my role of covering the elections and visiting polling booths, I spoke to a few jawans or soldiers, who, surprised by my Hindi, were friendly. Many of them hailed from northern Indian states and were clearly 'outsiders to the ethnic and social fabric of the state'. The soldiers did not speak Manipuri and the Manipuris, non-tribal and tribal, were less conversant in Hindi. With Bollywood movies banned in the state by insurgents to stop the state from becoming 'Indianized' more than twenty-three years ago, there is little incentive for comprehension of the language.

~

The Northeast in its entirety feels like home to me—safe and familiar.

I moved to Delhi in 1993 after completing my MA in English literature from the North-Eastern Hill University, Shillong. Delhi was a destination for thousands of students like me for further studies or job opportunities. I went to study journalism and subsequently worked there. It would be my home for seventeen years, even though I would remain the perennial outsider falling into the category of 'yeh log' (these people).

Ethnic lines in Delhi are well-defined.

My previous fleeting visits to Delhi involved staying in one of the Northeastern state government houses such as Meghalaya House or Manipur Bhawan. These bhawans cater to students, tourists, government officials and others who visit Delhi for work, leisure or medical treatment, offering not only accommodation but also regional cuisine in their canteens.

Obviously, until I moved there, I didn't know what it was like to confront life on a daily basis as a resident. A big city is always intimidating for small-towners. Delhi is huge. I was told by well-wishers back home to be 'suspicious of anybody and everybody'. I believe that is the usual handed-down advice for freshers.

The asperity of that advice would have served me well initially, had I heeded it. The first time I went house-hunting in a snobbish south Delhi suburb, not only did the auto-wallah, whom I had paid in advance for a few visits, dupe me—he sneaked away after the first drop—but the landlady refused point blank to rent out to single women.

I had not realized that trying to find a house would reveal how absurdly parochial the society in Delhi is.

Single women, I would later find out, was not so much the issue; it was women from the Northeast like us. The hypocrisy at the heart of the rental business in Delhi at the time revealed itself. Everyone would promise something on the phone, but upon meeting in person, they would back out.

After a long, futile search, I ended up spending the first year with north Indian family friends who were very accommodating and helpful.

But I didn't want to overstay my welcome. Finally, with their local assistance, I found a place for myself. We had a discreet understanding that I would not meet the landlord. My local friend acted as an intermediary and delivered the rent. This became an oft-repeated story with other houses.

Social scientists have observed this polarity between people from mainland India and those from the Northeast. In a 2014 news article in *Hindustan Times*, Dr G. Amarjit Sharma, professor at Jawaharlal Nehru University's (JNU) Special Centre for the Study of North East India, was quoted as saying, 'People from the Indian mainland experience a dichotomy in their relationship with those from the North-East. On one level, they rent out their houses to them and enter into business relationships, but because their lifestyles and cultures are different, they feel threatened. Not everyone, even when educated, has the courage to allow for diversity.'[3]

I came to realize that we Northeastern women arouse a lot of resentment because of the 'stinky' food we eat, the way we dress, the boys who visit our houses, and, in some cases, the lack of knowledge of Hindi. We are stereotyped as 'women automatically available'. The kabadi-wallah or trash collector once had the nerve to ask me if I had only empty liquor bottles to dispose of—as if all I did was drink. And how can I forget the neighbour who, peeved at my dog playing for a bit outside, yelled, 'Take him in. I know what all goes on inside this house.' We were three Northeastern women professionals living together at the time, each with odd working hours—one worked with an airline company, another at a call centre and I was working for a news organization. But our professional credentials did not matter.

Looking back, I can't help but feel what a precarious life we led. One night at 3 a.m., I heard the doorbell ring and, a few minutes later, the sound of a motorbike scooting off. It was apparent that we were a target of harassment. Another time, we found obscene photos shuffled under our front door. It took a week to identify the perpetrator, who turned out to be the neighbour's young son.

Practically all strata of people in Delhi seemed to have negative stereotypes about us.

My favourite subject of conversation with my girlfriends was typically the dating scene. It seemed very clear to me that my Northeastern girlfriends who were dating men from the mainland were never going to have success stories. Unfortunately, that turned out to be true for many. One girl who was dating a Punjabi boy saw a glimmer of hope after she was invited to a family function. But her hopes fell flat as she learnt later that the would-be mother-in-law had categorically told her son he could marry anyone except the Northeastern girl. It was a world of prejudice she couldn't escape.

This is not to say that all interracial relationships were or are not successful. However, the traumatic stories that I witnessed reinforced the distinction between them and us.

I wish I could explain how being called 'Chinky' crept into my Northeastern sensibility. If I think of this as a flippant remark, nothing more than some cheeky people having fun, then it is a very thin conception of racism. Where racism occurs and recurs, it is the work of people who focus on differences in looks or colour, exploiting these superficial traits to perpetuate prejudice and division. Not surprisingly, in 2012, the Ministry of Home Affairs recommended recognizing the use of the word 'Chinky' as a criminal offence under the Scheduled Castes and Scheduled Tribes (Prevention of Atrocities) Act with a punishment of up to five years in jail.[4]

The Northeastern population in Delhi is huge. In rock concerts and other major events, they turn up like a unified force—all different yet the same. Delhi seemed to know little about this community. In this persisting environment of differences, I was one with the Northeast. I was the insider, or perhaps slipping into the affectations of being Northeastern to comfort myself.

In many ways, I also felt very cosmopolitan. My friendships, several of which I cherish to this day, extended beyond the Northeastern groups. Funnily enough, this gave me immunity as an insider–outsider in a city divided by classism, racism and more.

With my Meitei compatriots, I became the universal sister. This new-found identity was reinforced by my working status. I saw the perennial 'where are you from' question dissipating in Delhi, bound by a strong sense of allegiance to the community rooted in birth. Responses to how I spoke my Manipuri began manifesting in an interesting way; I was looked up to. For me, this thwarted any immediate discrimination. This was my Manipuri identity gaining traction.

At the same time, living in Delhi, I was meeting Manipuris and other Northeasterners who felt they never really belonged. They had suffered several direct discriminations and specific experiences from mainland people, enough for them to say they were going back home after a point in time.

A 2019 article in *The Times of India* says there was a drop of over 25 per cent in the number of people from the Northeast going to Delhi in the decade between 2001 and 2011.[5] Nonetheless, you cannot escape the ubiquity of Northeasterners in Delhi—those who have chosen the place despite language barriers and other obstacles to living there. What they did not choose, however, is to be viewed as the other.

I stayed put in Delhi for seventeen years for professional reasons. At work, I often got a laugh from the fact that people couldn't pronounce my surname well. Laisram often became Lassi-Ram or Lazy-Ram. I didn't feel like an outsider in this space, but it was an issue that was perceptible in negotiating my Indian identity because I was assimilating at the same time. The journey towards assimilation can be hard—if you are not from the Hindi-speaking parts of India, try getting your Hindi grammar and accent right!

The one conclusion I can draw from my years of living in Delhi is this paradoxical feeling of belonging and unbelonging at the same time. I share a love-hate relationship with the city. It has given me valuable friendships and a sense of belonging at one level. Yet, when I wander through the city, its lanes and bylanes, even years later, there is the feeling of being an outsider that invariably creeps up.

That feeling comes from deep in my soul. On a recent visit, I was in Old Delhi soaking in the magical winter air when I was met with not just one but too many 'lecherous' looks. I had to adopt the Delhi gait, which among us women is a self-defence style with our bags held against our chests. Perhaps one could interpret these incidents as big city encounters for every woman, irrespective of background, but they connect me instantly to the vulnerabilities of earlier days experienced in this city. They come between me and Delhi.

Various academics, while writing about the gaps in perception that prevail between Northeasterners and non-Northeasterners, argue that the gap is shaped by the process of 'othering' that happens from both sides.

It is a never-ending struggle of trying to build a bridge instead of a wall. Noted American novelist Toni Morrison beautifully summarizes that, 'Othering whoever has othered us, in reverse, is no liberation—as cathartic as it may feel.' I couldn't agree more.

Very recently, on a trip to the southern city of Bengaluru, I visited a shop run by Northeasterners. There are many such small enterprises now catering to the thousands of Northeasterners living there. Some of these shops even sell fresh river snails and other indigenous food. I noticed two sari-clad women walking into the shop actually muttering, 'Oh, it's a Chinese shop,' before turning to leave. Immediately, I corrected them politely, 'Not Chinese but Northeast Indians.' They smiled and left.

But in the space of an hour, another local gentleman walked in and bought singju, which is a Manipuri salad made of fermented dry fish, vegetables and herbs. It needs orientation to develop a taste. Curious, I asked the gentleman if he liked it. 'Yes, I need one every day,' he replied.

Two contrasting incidents. The women made me think about this huge gap in understanding or knowledge of India among Indians. Even in 2023, at the time of writing this, the Northeast is still not familiar territory, or so it seems. However, the latter incident was a balm on the richly unsettled topic of the outsider.

~

Moving thousands of miles away from home to Australia in 2009, I didn't carry the naivety of thought that racism and classism would be things of the past. It was the year when Indian students suffered alleged racial attacks in that country—the news of which made nationwide headlines in India. Ironically, when such attacks happen within India, they seldom make it to the front pages. News coverage of the Northeast in mainstream media has, in any case, always been 'granular'—not in the sense of detail, but because there are only a few grains of coverage.

By the time I arrived in Melbourne in 2009, it had a sizeable number of Indians—thanks to Australia's educational policy that linked it to migration. Because the country was facing shortages of chefs, cooks and hairdressers, thousands of students from India came to enrol in those courses that provided an easy pathway to permanent residency (PR).

Among them, the question of PR is a pertinent one. I happened to travel to Woolgoolga in New South Wales, home to the first Sikh gurdwara in Australia, in 2010. There, I met gurdwara volunteers who, upon learning that I was Indian and relatively new to the country, didn't inquire about my background but instead asked, '*PR ho gayi?*' Have you got your PR? As immigrant experiences go, the precarity of their visa status made them obsessive about permanent settlement in the new country. They immediately established a kinship with me, assuming I was in the same boat as them.

Melbourne felt like a thriving multicultural city—full of Indians, Chinese, Greeks, Italians, English, etc. Like others, I was lost in a sea of anonymity. For a moment, it seemed the insider–outsider conflict was losing its relevance, or, let's say, it appeared inconsequential. We were all strangers trading small talk on a journey called life.

Friendships in this big city were hard to come by in the beginning.

The new wave of Indian immigrants saw a mushrooming of grocery stores and Indian restaurants. When I did meet Indians who, like me, were willingly marooned far from home, I looked for a spontaneous connection over food, language and other shared commonalities.

Working with community magazines provided me with opportunities to engage with diverse groups of Indians. However, whenever I disclosed to them that I hailed from the Northeast, the majority—save for a handful—would respond with a perplexed look, as if pondering, 'Where?' The Northeast is not even in the imagined construct of the real Indian identity. My Northeastern roots did not stand in a different relation to the 'mainstream' Indian culture, but I felt like an outsider once again. For a brief spell, I toyed with the idea of telling some of them I was also raised a Hindu, but assimilation of that kind is not my thing. Religion is a private matter.

Once, I went to interview an Indian lady for a story. When her husband opened the door, I introduced myself in Hindi. He asked me how despite being Chinese, I could speak Hindi so well. He was just one of the many who, for the life of them, cannot fathom that India also has millions of people of a different racial stock.

For immigrants, owning a house (for some Indians, multiple houses) is realizing a part of their Australian dream. This should connect them to the people around them, but most move within their own circles. In many social gatherings, I have seen that my Australian husband is the token White guest. Regarding Australians in general, a friend once said, 'These people are not like us.' Clearly, their allegiance is with people who speak the same language and to the world they left behind. So, you find expat groups of Punjabis, Rajasthanis, Gujaratis, Kashmiris and so on. When it comes to belonging, the question of culture and the problems of assimilation intertwine.

On a good note, we have contributed significantly to Australia's cultural capital. According to the Australian Bureau of Statistics, the Indian population has grown from 592,000 in 2018 to 660,000 in 2019, an 11 per cent increase.

The few Northeast immigrants, a minuscule fraction, have their groups too.

Despite once feeling like an outsider in Delhi, my current role as someone deeply involved with a community magazine for the Indian diaspora positions me as a community insider. After fourteen years in Australia, I think a lot about how I can move beyond all these inner identities that still surface in my social spaces. The 'where are you from' question, which was there in Shillong, Delhi and even Imphal, remains a constant in my life.

In today's globalized world, researchers emphasize the undisputed need for developing cross-cultural understanding. I do believe that we need to engage more with each other, irrespective of our backgrounds— breaking down boundaries of culture, race and social class. One can be anchored in one's community but still keep the doors open for others.

I have my culture and my Meitei clan, but that is one of the many identities I assume. I perceive myself as an amalgamation—Meitei, Indian, Australian.

If you look into the depth of things, it becomes evident that the process of 'othering' is a persistent phenomenon. I notice numerous parallels, such as the way some queer friends experience othering or how certain communities are perceived as the 'other'. It is wrong to efface somebody's identity.

What will eventually give us immunity to the insider–outsider conflict? I'm not so conceited as to claim that I have the answer.

The world is a perplexing place.

Always the Square Peg

Makepeace Sitlhou

Mohammad Sukkur Ali (name changed on request) was not home the day two officials from the border branch of Manikpur police station came on a 'survey' visit to his village in Bongaigaon district. Dressed in plainclothes, the officials started asking the residents for their documents. The year was 2007 and it was the first time village residents recalled seeing someone from the border branch come to their village to make an inquiry.

'I showed him the 1966 voters' list, which has our grandfather's name on it,' his brother told me. That day, only the brother was at home with their maternal cousin. 'But they asked for a certified copy, which I didn't have.'

The police officials offered to save them all the trouble in exchange for Rs 50. The village residents said the officials also took cash from them as reimbursement for the expenses incurred on food and travel in coming all the way to their village, located deep inside Manikpur subdivision. The cousin and a neighbour, who subsequently passed away, however, had to sign on a blank piece of paper before they were relieved by the officials.

'I can only read and write my name so I didn't have the faintest idea what paper I was signing,' said the cousin. The whole incident was dismissed as routine police harassment and forgotten into oblivion for the next eight years until one not-so-fine day in June 2015.

Again, two officials from the Manikpur border branch came by, this time with a notice in hand. Ali, a government schoolteacher of the Assamese language, was at home this time and as the only lettered person in the family, received the notice. Without any reason or qualifier, the notice from the Foreigners Tribunal 1 in Bongaigaon said that he, his brother and their mother were suspected to be illegal foreigners and that they must immediately report to the FT to prove their citizenship. The state had challenged their citizenship and the burden of proof was on them, which meant that they had to produce every evidence to prove they were Indians. The state didn't owe them probable cause to doubt their status.

I met Ali and his family for the first time in 2019 while researching a report commissioned by Amnesty International that was investigating the functioning of the Foreigners Tribunals. If you have been nerding out on the NRC in Assam, an exercise that ambitiously aimed to identify 'illegals' in the state based on documentary proof, you probably know where this story is going. The tribunals are quasi-judicial courts. Detailed reports on their functioning have quite conclusively shown them to be both arbitrary and biased. Depending on who you speak to, the NRC has been similarly described.[1] There are people for whom neither papers nor linkage has ensured a place on the list.

Supporters of Assamese identity politics (who have a historically fraught relationship with the Bengali language and East-Bengal-origin settlers) argue that the NRC exercise was poorly executed by a Hindu nationalist government determined to appropriate a legitimate regional cause towards their goal of othering only the Muslims.[2] The right wing (which runs the government) touts the narrative that while many Hindus were left out of the NRC, a lot of 'illegal Bangladeshi

Muslims'[3] made it to the list by using fake documents, and the entire exercise needs to be reattempted now that the Citizenship Amendment Act (naturalizing Hindus) is in place. For mainland Indian liberals (with rare exceptions such as Yogendra Yadav), most of whom came to know of the NRC only after the CAA was passed, the NRC might as well be the right-wing government's version of Nazi Germany.

My homecoming and reporting stint in the seven states of the Northeast coincided with the NRC and a rise in right-wing nativist nationalism. As a person belonging to the Thadou-Zo tribe, better known as Kukis, of Manipur I came with the baggage of two very strong assumptions about folks in the Northeast: first, that we didn't see ourselves as Indians. The decades of separatist movements and counter-insurgency in all the states, not to mention how different we looked from mainland Indians, what we ate and how we lived (in addition to how we've been treated by them) indicated that we were coerced to be a part of the country. But in our heart of hearts we never accepted it, nor could we ever 'integrate'.

And second, because we were predominantly tribal—living and warring amongst our own and wandering on our own—we never really recognized borders drawn up by Sir Cyril Radcliffe (who never travelled to India either before or after his quick border-drawing trip in 1947) per Hindu and Muslim majority populations. We were barely 'civilized' enough to own land (even if we were tilling it), let alone draw borders that separated commons from private entities, except informally acknowledging the territory of various village nations.

So, as the hoopla and outrage around unchecked illegal migration in a neglected part of the country—or its obverse, outrage over the BJP using Assam as a Hindutva experiment laboratory—unfolded, I was flummoxed at how 'my' people were suddenly so sure of their documents, identity and indigeneity. Didn't everyone come from somewhere unless you can prove your lineage from a local Stone Age ancestor? How many families have proof of their ancestral residency or migration from more than a hundred years ago in this land? If we are calling to identify foreigners living amongst us, what does that make us?

It all came to a head on Facebook when a Bengali friend demanded to see documents of an Assamese, who was correcting anyone who'd (mis)understood the NRC to be a xenophobic exercise. To my utter surprise, the Assamese posted a photo of her great-grandfather's name on the ledger of a tea garden he managed at the time. The document was from the late 1800s. My jaw dropped as I followed the thread where both former friends, who met in journalism school, were at each other's throats simplifying their stances on a rather complex subject. She argued that the NRC was one of the historical reparations long due to all the martyrs of the Assam Agitation of 1979–85—people who laid down their lives to protest uncurbed immigration, following which the state spiralled into three decades of darkness. To him, it was yet another blow to the Bengali settlers, who had already suffered through the language movement in 1960 and the 1983 Nellie massacre during the agitation.

But that photo made two things very clear to me. One, families and residents in Assam who had been privileged across generations were nothing like the tribals I'd long seen them in kindred spirits with. They were well-documented because they were privileged. Two, an exercise undertaken to single out post-1971 settlers from the land that became Bangladesh that year was going to have a devastating impact on many more vulnerable communities and populations. Unfortunately, I wasn't wrong.

~

Fifteen years ago, I met Russell Peters, the famous comedian of Indian origin, in New Delhi on his very first tour in the motherland. Peters was one of those first internet sensations whose stand-up act on racial stereotypes and growing up in Canada as an Indian immigrant had gone viral in the early aughts on The Pirate Bay. After the show in Delhi, I waited outside the venue, eager to meet him and get a photograph. There were no other fans around except me, my brother Lalmoon and my best friend from college, Lara, who is from the Philippines. When he finally stepped out, wearing baggy denims paired with a white shirt and white sneakers, he was taken by surprise to see there were still some fans hanging around the back of the venue. The fans didn't look 'Indian' as he might have expected. He came closer to greet us and let us have the reward that any fan most wishes from a celebrity they love—a picture with them.

'Where are you guys from?' he asked.

'Filipino,' said the college friend, who wore a near-perfect look of an 'Asian nerd', complete with glasses and acne. He made a joke about Filipinos that I don't recall now.

Peters then turned his gaze towards me and my brother.

'What are you guys?' he asked, before quickly guessing, 'Chinese?'

My brother and I shook our heads and swiftly corrected him, breaking it to him that we were, in fact, Indians. He was in disbelief, a reaction we were used to for the better part of our lives. I imagine we were the first people from the northeast part of the country, not too far from his family's ancestral place in India—West Bengal—he'd ever met.

'Oh, so you're Chindians,' he quipped, in his signature comedic routine of cultural crossbreeds of Hinjews (Hindus and Jews) and Jalapeños (Hindus and Filipinos).

It was the early 2000s and the bar for jokes on race was extremely low. But Peters spoke to a generation of Indians, South Asians and immigrants of colour who grew up abroad. Oddly enough, he spoke to us too, my brother and I, who were growing up away from our home state—so different from the rest of India it might as well be another country.

~

We were similar yet different from everyone around us. Although surrounded by army 'brats' like us, who otherwise belonged to different parts of the country, my brother and I always knew that our culture was very alien to the mainstream Indian sensibility and style. Cut off from the civilians, life in army cantonments is insulated from the extremities and uncertainties of the real world outside. We attended our own army schools, shopped at the canteens that exclusively supplied groceries and alcohol to army families, and had our own water supply and a sprawling ventilated space to walk, play and dine in. The cantonment is a city within a city, strictly regulating and monitoring who comes in, when, how and to meet whom. Cantonments have always been the object of both contempt and envy among neighbours. In Delhi, the temperature drops down several degrees when you enter the cantonment. Water was never in shortage, even in the peak of summer when the rest of the state was struggling to make ends meet. Back in the 2000s, Chief Minister Sheila Dixit once took a potshot at army officers for wasting water washing their cars. My father, like many officers around him, just brushed it aside as sour grapes. The army always takes wasteland and develops it into an oasis in an efficient way, he would say. 'Seeing us flourish, local politicians start heckling us, but the truth is that they're just incompetent compared to the army,' he reasoned.

As blissful as that life is, it is in equal parts alienating and coercive in its social and economic expectations of its residents, especially of those coming from the officer class. While I fondly remember my childhood as a treat—safe open spaces, lots of kids around to make friends with and weekly parties where delicious snacks and cold drinks were served—for my mother, it was not as great. As a twenty-four-year-old woman who grew up in Manipur, having only lived in Shillong (where she completed her postgraduate degree) and visited Delhi, Mumbai and Goa up until then, she barely had a clue about what she was getting into. My mother grew up in a liberal family where her choices or clothes were not subject to interrogation. In the cantonment, she had to quickly ditch the pencil skirts that were considered too bold in exchange for sarees though it revealed her midriff. She was smart and fairly well-exposed for an average Indian woman of her age but was somewhat ambivalent about her career choices, something she regrets to this day. As a reasonably attractive woman, she tried her luck to become a flight attendant and was considering taking the civil services exams. But she never got a call back from Indian Airlines (she suspects it's because she sent pictures of herself wearing thick glasses) and my father popped the question before my mother made good on her plans to move to New Delhi for coaching to crack the civil services exams.

My mother hated the army culture and social life. She found it stifling with all the small talk, formal pleasantries and rank-based hierarchical structure. People were friendly (or not) based on your husband's rank and posting and the gendered segregation in parties was nothing like what she was used to. Carrying on the Victorian values of the British Army, women who drank at the bar were considered unsightly. In fact, women who drank were unsightly—only the men were expected to drink. Many women, she said, would drink out of steel glasses. For someone who was already alienated in terms of language and culture, she did more than her best to fit in. It wasn't for herself as much as for her husband, whose career also depended on how well (and frequently) he entertained his seniors and mingled with his contemporaries. The entire family, including the kids, had to be in on the act. But while many families did this for better postings and a higher rank, for my family it was a shot at integration. We were always the outsiders, something I was yet to be fully aware of, who had to fit into the culture of the dominant majority that we were surrounded by. In my twenty years of growing up in army cantonments, I've been a part of celebrating more Hindu rituals and festivals than holidays from any other religion. Not once do I recall going for iftar during Ramazan, something that only hit me many years into my adulthood.

But we were also nothing like our country cousins in the hilly district of Churachandpur (that we affectionately call 'Lamka' in the local dialect) in Manipur. In our home state, my brother and I shared no common ground with the adults or kids whose lives were so different from ours and who spoke a language that was familiar yet alien to us. I had no understanding or appreciation of how they survived, or even thrived, living with routine power cuts, militancy, curfews and young people dropping dead like flies from drug overdoses. Back then, all this was just too homogenous, too decrepit, too country. Like in a true Pavlovian understanding of human behaviour, we were rewarded for playing the good minority in a foreign land, while being mocked and criticized for being terrible natives in our own land. In pursuit of giving us a better life and ensuring we could fit among second- to third-generation officers' families, my parents were not militant enough to pass on their language and culture to me and my brother.

In a progressively globalized world, this sort of quandary is hardly new. People in similar situations have been called many things: American Born Confused Desi (ABCD), Third Culture Kid (TCK), Immigrant. None of these labels help to blunt the consequences of being different.

Thanks to my East Asian features, I've been taken to be a domestic worker in Delhi Cantonment, mistaken for an escort in Defence Colony, treated as a cultural curiosity to be bullied and poked fun at in Army Public School, Dhaula Kuan, and viewed as a 'loose' character by some of my professors at Delhi University. In Bengaluru, a cosmopolitan city of tech parks that I escaped to for some respite after years of battling racist jibes and stereotypes in the Hindi heartland, my race/ethnicity immediately came to be profiled a month after I made the big move. Overnight, some 10,000 residents from the Northeastern states left the city in panic, mostly by trains in August 2012.

They fled based on rumours circulating on WhatsApp that come Eid, the Muslims in Bengaluru would avenge the deaths of Bengali Muslims killed in clashes with Bodo tribals in Kokrajhar, Assam. A few stray incidents of racial profiling and harassment, which is fairly normal for Northeastern people in mainland cities, added fuel to the fire. There were also images of dead bodies from another country and context that were circulating on Facebook and WhatsApp on the need to avenge what the Bamars had done to the Rohingyas in Myanmar, which had led to their first exodus in 2012.[4] Two isolated and distant events thus had ramifications in Bengaluru—an up-and-coming metropolis that offers jobs to lakhs of working-class migrants and students pursuing higher education—because people (whether Bodos or Bamars) from Northeast India and Southeast Asia share East Asian features.

I was working from my tiny bedroom in the middle of the night, planning the editorial cycle on some sustainability theme for the digital magazine that had brought me to the southern Indian city, when news of the exodus went viral online and all over television channels. I was in shock like everybody else. It had barely been a month since I'd moved to Bengaluru and had just started to make friends. Most of those I knew in the city were people I had just hung out with occasionally or met at parties. None of them checked in on me to ask if I was all right, including an old friend in the city with whom I had just rekindled a friendship. The fear and paranoia were so high at the time—and being stuck in my apartment only exacerbated it—that I had impulsively posted on Facebook about understanding what Jewish people went through during the Holocaust.

The old friend, who never checked in on me, was correct to tell me off on the tone-deafness of my post considering there had been no targeted incidents reported in the city. I felt stupid but also isolated and alienated by his comment that cared to correct the political implications, without ever addressing the emotional insecurity behind it. I just put it down to his lived experience as an Assamese, who could pass off as any other Indian or South Asian, and couldn't empathize with a tribal from the region.

I thought about this a lot over the years and then I saw a movie a couple of months ago that hit the spot. *Passing*, a film based on the 1929 novel by Nella Larsen of the same name, explores the racially fraught nuances of racial assimilation in America. Two African American women, who grew up together on the wrong side of the tracks, live entirely different lives as adults. Clare, the one with lighter skin, passes off as a White Caucasian (and is married to one) living a pristine life among White folks in the Upper East Side, while her childhood friend, Irene, lives in a Black neighbourhood and is married to a Black man. Through Irene, Clare rekindles her connection with the Black community, attending their dances and events. The ease with which she can fit into both worlds, while Irene nervously hides under a hat in White areas, was remarkable to watch.

It is this fitting-in that I never had the privilege of until I arrived in Northeast India and, funnily enough, in the US. In the Indian mainland, I would constantly fight off the racial biases or fetishization associated with women from the Northeast. It is why my parents drilled down the need for people like us to always look presentable, speak English well and confidently assert our socio-economic class as hailing from an officer's family. Due to my education and class, even though I couldn't avoid profiling and discrimination, I could still work around the scale and veracity of it.

However, you can overcome race and ethnicity, or caste in India, only so much with class privilege and education. Despite being widely applauded by friends and English teachers for my command over the language, I've had senior journalists gaslight my ability with the language and its prose.

In a 2010 interview for a job at a veteran journalist's publication, the journalist pointed out several grammatical errors in my curriculum vitae. At one point, she was 'correcting' my spoken English in the interview ('as do I' is wrong, it is 'so do I'), which irked me into asking why she had even bothered to call me if she deemed me so unworthy. She said that she wanted to give a chance to people who came from 'far-flung regions of the country'. When I told her that I was a city girl, she continued her condescension to say she wanted to make her office more 'colourful'. I was so demotivated by that very first interview fresh out of university that I didn't gather the courage to apply to another magazine or newsroom until much later. And this was despite having worked and interned in media houses.

Cut to ten years later, I was working on a very important long-form story on the history of the Naga Movement. I'd written to another veteran journalist whose reportage from the Northeast I had long admired. We were already connected on Instagram, where he had left very encouraging words in my DM on more than one occasion when my stories came out. But when I did speak to him for my interview and later emailed him a playback of his quotes, there was a sea change in his demeanour, which began with slights on my understanding of the subject before it devolved into a full-blown insult. His trust had 'depreciated', he said when he declined to participate any further, even schooling me on how I should quote from his published books. This happened only a while back, by which time I was already a seasoned journalist of many years, who already had a couple of awards under her belt. My editor saw this sort of self-aggrandizing behaviour as typical of upper-caste male chauvinists, especially in the national security beat. I saw it as yet another casteist/racist infliction that I'll possibly deal with for the rest of my life. In the US, where I was attending the Arizona State University on a Fulbright fellowship, my colleagues admired both my writing and speaking prowess, even if it took them a little while to get used to the accent.

The unfortunate part of my trauma is not as much contempt towards these individuals but the generalized resentment that I've developed against people they represent—upper caste, qualified, privileged and entitled. The ones who have never had to deal with such insults to their dignity and humanity as no one, ideally, ever should. Oh, how I envy how normal their lives must be.

Understanding who I am and where I belong, to date, remains the most sensitive if not triggering subject for me. The answer to where I'm from is difficult to explain and often goes into a monologue that I'd rather not get into. Most parts of India think I owe my origins to one of the East Asian countries. 'My people' back home think I'm very 'kol' (in Kuki-Zo dialects) or 'mayang' (Indian, as in South Asian). My brother and I were once mistaken as South Koreans in our hometown in Manipur. Whenever I travel outside or meet foreigners, I have passed off as some third-world Asian, Asian American and, more recently, Polynesian (thanks to my protruding love handles).

But class also affords me the privilege of a fluid identity, only afforded to the English-speaking elites who can move cities and countries without needing to fully immerse in the grassroots of the local culture. We call ourselves 'global citizens' and whatnot, but ruefully decry our rootlessness.

Only after living and reporting in Assam did I realize what it could cost a person to not belong to a place, at least not along the lines of how the majority around them define belongingness. I came to live in Assam to report on the Northeastern states with my baggage of being a native outsider along with my lived experiences in the Indian 'mainland'. I was someone who was never seen as Indian because I didn't pass as one. Assam showed me people who never will be accepted as Indians, merely because of their ethnicity, mother tongue and religion.

Ali and his family's case went on for about a year after the notice was delivered. In 2016, his brother and mother were declared Indians but Ali was declared a foreigner of the post-1966 stream and his name was removed from the voters' lists for ten years. Under Clause 5 of the Assam Accord, persons who came between 1 January 1966 and 25 March 1971 are to be deleted from the electoral roll for ten years.

Ali said that while all three of them had submitted their grandfather's name in the 1951 NRC list, the lawyer failed to mention the submission of this affidavit only in Ali's 'written statement', a petition filed by the person under trial making their case for citizenship. The FT order said that the 1966 voters' list does not do much in terms of proving his legacy before 1966.

In accordance with the rules, Ali was forced to register with the FRRO in Bongaigaon under the Registration of Foreigners Act, 1939, and the Registration of Foreigners Rules, 1939. In the form seeking registration under 6A of the Citizenship Act, 1955, the date from which he is 'ordinarily resident in Assam' is given as 1970, which was also noted as his year of birth at an address in Bangladesh.

Meanwhile, his matriculation certificate, which was submitted to the FT and a part of his written statement, says he was born in 1980.

'As part of the formality, I was taken to an FRRO office where I was asked for my address in Bangladesh but I have never been to Bangladesh. The police wrote down an address and told me to corroborate it if anyone asked. When I refused, they threatened saying the police would take me away,' he says.

The FRRO officials wrote 'Village Koraimari, P.S. Gaibandha, District Rongpur, E/P' as his address in Bangladesh, which was also noted as his place of birth.

When he filed an appeal in the high court, the bench asked for a re-examination of his case as well as that of his family, who had earlier been declared Indian citizens on the grounds that only one family member couldn't be a post '66 foreigner.

Ali believes the Bongaigaon FT member was not in favour of declaring any Muslim an Indian. He said that the FT member had grilled him for four hours on the stand. 'He asked me if I have a birth certificate, PRC certificate, my grandfather's name in the voters' list as well as his constituency name and voter serial number. I answered all his questions,' Ali said. However, in the FT opinion, the member had written that Ali could not answer questions about 'the death of his grandparents' and 'was unable to say voter serial number, holding number and polling station number of his grandparents'.

'I remembered my grandfather's serial number: 99,' Ali says, 'I counter-asked him if he knew the serial number of his grandfather in the voters' list?'

His brother said that the same FT member had taken a very threatening tone with him. 'He kept asking me where in Bangladesh did I come from. I denied having any connection to Bangladesh and that I was born and brought up here just like my parents were but he kept pressing on,' he says. His mother was similarly coercively asked questions about her village in Bangladesh. The member spoke to them in Hindi, a language only Ali was conversant in.

Ali alleged that before the final opinion, a lawyer asked for a bribe of Rs 4 lakh on behalf of the FT member for a favourable outcome. 'We even gave them Rs 2 lakh that a relative had arranged for,' he confesses.

The family has spent all their life savings, a total of Rs 6–7 lakh. 'We've sold two bighas of our agricultural land and the rest was kept under mortgage. That is also lost now. I had to leave my job at the local Assamese-medium school, where I taught for eleven years,' Ali says. In 2018, when he stood trial for the second time, the FT member (a different one) asked him the serial number of his grandfather in a particular voters' list. But Ali knew the serial number in a different year's voters' list. 'I couldn't answer that but counter-questioned whether he could remember the serial number of his grandfather in any voters' list,' he said.

On 18 May 2018, Ali, along with his brother and mother (who had earlier been declared Indians), was declared a foreigner of the post-1971 stream.

Subsequently, he filed a writ petition in the high court that year. In his bail application, Ali submitted an affidavit from his cousin attesting that the three family members were residents of their village and that the police officer who took his signature as a witness did it under the pretext of 'verification of population' in the village.

Further, the cousin said that he had never recorded any statement before any police officer of the border branch with respect to their nationality, nor did he ever say that either of them had come from Bangladesh.

The address noted in the affidavit as the place from where Ali and his family were accused of coming, lifted from the inquiry form submitted by the Border Police officials in 2008, is 'Gaji Nogapara, P.S. Islampur, Dist–Moimonsingh, State–Bangladesh'. This is markedly different from the one listed in the FRRO form.

For three months, Ali along with his mother and brother went into hiding to avoid the Border Police who had come to take them away to a detention centre. Once they got bail from the high court, they returned home, but Ali quit his teaching job.

'I need to have a free mind to teach young children,' he says. With frequent visits to Bongaigaon and other places for his documents and to meet lawyers, he could no longer devote his time and energy to his students and didn't want them to suffer.

His cousin has been living with guilt for unknowingly putting his relatives through such extenuating circumstances that have psychologically and financially drained the families.

'I have known them since their father and their father's father, so I was very hurt to see my name being used against them,' the cousin says. 'But I don't know anything about these papers and documents, so I don't know how to fight for them.'

Ali claims that only persons from the minority community are getting notices in his village, where Hindus and Muslims have otherwise been cohabiting amicably. The foreigner cases have left them feeling alienated.

'My son spends most of his time at our neighbour's place,' he told this reporter in April 2021. 'Since he was six, he has been practically living at their place. He just comes home to drop his backpack after school and then in the evening to study a bit.'

Bhanu Baishya, a single woman in her fifties whom Ali endearingly calls baideow (sister), took care of his wife and kids when the rest of the family went into hiding.

'She [Ali's wife] did not keep well that entire time. We were tensed and worried if her husband and others would come home,' Baishya told this reporter. 'I didn't allow the son to go to school, afraid that someone might say something to him.'

Ali routinely monitors the cases in his FT, noting the regularity with which the present member declares foreigners, while also keeping track of the judges hearing foreigner cases in the high court. Aside from speaking to the local media, he had approached the local AASU unit as well as the minority morcha of the state BJP for assistance. This level of vigilance and follow-up would ordinarily be out of reach for most others in his village.

Navigating this legal quagmire would be intimidating for an average college graduate in India, let alone the largely semi-literate or illiterate persons in Assam whose citizenship has been brought under scrutiny by the state. Moreover, a process wherein the person under trial is seen as guilty until proven innocent, or a foreigner until proven Indian, has been criticized by the United Nations' Special Rapporteurs on freedom of religion or belief; on minority; and on contemporary forms of racism, racial discrimination, xenophobia and related intolerance. They stressed that the burden of proof should be on the state, particularly considering 'the discriminative and arbitrary nature of the current legal system in Assam'.

'My mother and brother would have just died if I wasn't around to do all this paperwork. If I was declared a foreigner despite all this, I can't imagine how difficult it must be for someone who's barely literate.' Ali shudders to think what would have happened to his mother had she been in a detention centre, where more than thirty detainees have died—the last one just weeks into the nationwide lockdown in the first Covid-19 wave. 'She's scared to even step out of the house now, paranoid that the police will come for her,' Ali says.

~

In mid-2017, I quit my job at Amnesty International in Bengaluru with the mission to relocate to Guwahati, the gateway city to India's Northeastern states. Up until then, I'd travelled all over the eight states, following my dad's appointments in the military and visits to the extended family in Manipur during the summer/winter breaks from the late 1980s to the early 2000s. But the only place I had ever lived in the region was Shillong—the first-ever cosmopolitan hub in the Northeast.

Owing to its erstwhile status as the capital of British-era Assam, the hill town was a sprawling education hub thanks to missionary institutes and a melting pot of outsiders, both South Asian and Anglo-Saxon foreigners. After Independence, the town became a platform for tribal students to pursue higher education decades before anyone had access or the courage to go to Delhi. Typically, these students would be from socio-economically well-off backgrounds and serious about their studies. My grandmother finished her matriculation from St. Mary's in the 1950s (her father was a clerk in the British administration) and about three decades later, my mother was the first woman from the Zo tribe to get a distinction in her master's degree from North-Eastern Hill University.

Understandably, I have a much deeper attachment to Shillong than I ever could muster for the place that I 'originally' belonged to. In fact, if you speak to (almost) any millennial kid from the region, they would probably have a special relation to the town, having either grown up there even if for a few years, or visited for family vacations, a school or sports competition or attending university. But how (or if at all) cosmopolitan Shillong truly is, depends on who you ask. Like any place in India or the world, the city is segregated into neighbourhoods of middle-class Khasis, poor Khasis, rich Khasis and Assamese, Khasis and Pnars, Garos, mixed tribes, Mizos, Nepalis, Mazhabi Sikhs, business-class Punjabis, Marwaris, Bengalis and working classes from across the board.

As a tribal and a military kid, I could traverse through all neighbourhoods, enjoying the natural sense of belonging with the indigenous tribes and the army privilege allowing my family access to the bureaucratic class and upwards. For the ten-year-old me, and the adult version too, Shillong is where I felt at home with the diversity of tribals and non-tribals as my friends, with whom I'd enjoy spending my Christmas and Diwali in equal splendour.

Coming home, after all these years of living in major Indian cities and travelling to all the places where I'd fancied working or studying, was kind of like reparations for me. Not because I had any wounds or injustice to attend to, but to really understand who I was. The cousin I'm closest to described it as my longing to get back to my roots and I, who only had a vague idea and more assumptions about where I come from, couldn't disagree entirely. But I knew that I'd always be the square peg, never quite the right fit in a round hole. While I can adapt like a chameleon anywhere, I remain everywhere an outsider looking in.

This myth of a cosmopolitan Shillong was severely challenged on my first reporting assignment in May 2018, when I'd finally settled in Guwahati. My mother and I had just unpacked our boxes and belongings accumulated by my parents over my father's career of thirty-five years all over India and Cambodia. I had barely got my bearings together as a person, let alone as a reporter, when I received a call from an editor in New Delhi. She wanted me to cover the riot-like situation that had broken out in neighbouring Shillong, roughly three hours away from where I lived. The sceptic in me initially dismissed it as yet another conflict between the dkhars (which literally translates to 'people from the plains' but over time became a slur since it racially profiles South Asians) and the territorial Khasis.

Not wanting to sound ignorant of local news, I frantically started making a few calls, before I ended up talking to Samrat Choudhury, one of the editors of this book. Like me, Choudhury grew up in Shillong but in an earlier decade when the anti-outsider sentiment was high in the state. Building on the back of the movement for separate statehood, organized campaigns and attacks against Bengalis, Nepalis and other 'outsiders' quickly followed. From his memory and lens, the trouble stirred up this time was unlike the same old story.

It was the first time I'd even heard of a place called Punjabi Line in Shillong or that there was a Dalit Sikh community who had been living in the city for more generations than most of us from other states or even from other parts of Meghalaya itself. While reporting this story, I met community members who recounted how the targeting became progressively worse once they started getting phased out of their sanitation jobs, which they had been originally brought there to do by the British. The introduction of septic tanks and upgraded safety gears meant that the local tribals started vying for these otherwise unspeakable jobs. Some of my Khasi friends didn't agree with me when I said that the Punjabi Line was under siege, as they felt for the local mobs who had violently clashed with the central security forces that were brought in to rein them in.

Covering these stories constantly challenged the set narratives I held of these places and their people. There have been moments of utter disappointment, like learning that the Mazhabi Sikhs couldn't apply for jobs under the scheduled caste category because Meghalaya hadn't listed them as such. These moments brought to light the hypocrisy amongst the Northeastern tribals—we who have protected and defended our entitlement for reservation and concessions under the scheduled tribe category to death.

But there were also moments of quiet solidarity and humanity. I probably was the first reporter to gain access to the Punjabi Line, which was being protected like a fort after petrol bombs were thrown inside, burning down some of the houses tightly spaced with the rest of the shanty. My first point of contact there was a Khasi lady, sitting in the same packed Sumo cab to Shillong as I was on that morning. She overheard my several calls to people looking for a way in and put me on to a Punjabi doctor who was in touch with the residents. I never got my co-passenger's name, but it must have taken a resilient form of humanity to supersede the jingoistic nationalism that nativity can guilt you into.

I often think about these moments of what makes an outsider an outsider and who gets naturalized into becoming an insider, juxtaposed with my own 'global citizen' sense of identity and my history. For someone who has been accused of not knowing where she comes from, I have often retorted that I'm hyper-aware to a point where I can't stop finding common ground and differences with others.

Although Russell Peters thought we were 'Chindians' all those years ago, I'll always remember the words he left us with: Stay Black.

Edgy in the City

Veio Pou

Whenever people ask me, I often tell them that I've been living in Delhi since the previous century. Somehow, I enjoy the split second when there is an incredulous look on the other person's face until the realization dawns on them that the new century is just over two decades old. Sometimes, it feels like I've overstayed in the city, without really intending to hang on this long. By and by, the city has become my home for more than half my lifetime, beginning with university life to working and living on as a family man. Through this piece, I shall try to address the 'everyday' experiences of being a person from Northeast India in the capital city of the country. From what I've seen, the city has undergone considerable transformation in every sense, including its demographic composition, of which the Northeast population now forms a fair size. There are various dimensions to understand this inflow of migrants from a far corner of the country.

Undeniably, the pursuit of higher education and the search for job opportunities become the main 'pull' factors to the metropolitan cities; and the absence of the same in their respective states remains the major 'push' factor.[1, 2] The turn of the century saw an upsurge of young Northeast migrants in the big cities, especially with economic liberalization paving the way for them to venture into various service sectors—retail and hospitality industries, multinational companies and other private enterprises. Earlier, they were only a visible minority on university campuses and as employees in government sectors. With time, many have made the city their home. And yet, often, the 'city of refuge' for Northeast migrants is not quite the safest or free of conflict. There are still undesirable things that make many of them feel unsafe—from the various kinds of discrimination and harassment to being treated as 'outsiders'.

Thankfully, today, many mainlanders are well-aware of the northeastern region of India, so one does not really need to explain at length to tell them about the place, the people and their culture. But the problematic projection of the region as a troubled periphery or a conflict zone continues to haunt the psychological make-up of people living outside the region. Regrettably, the media and other dominant narratives, including the state and the quasi-state agencies, continue to typecast the region in those terms and, therefore, many people's opinions are shaped by such images. At the same time, there is no denying the fact that many young people do leave their place of birth in the Northeast 'to escape the violence and militarization in their respective homelands and states'.[3]

The perpetrators of violence are often both the state and non-state agencies, and the consequences of living under a sustained period of political instability leads to a structural breakdown of the social, economic and educational institutions, thus resulting in a greater 'push' factor for leaving the native land in search of livelihood or education. Nevertheless, most of the eight states that comprise the Northeast are quite peaceful now. One may say, therefore, that there is a relative 'normalcy' in recent times. Yet, the image of the Northeast as a conflict region is still imprinted in the minds of many. Often the disruptions in the region are in the limelight of the mainstream media, as though there is nothing else there that is newsworthy. I suppose this is also true of a few other regions like Jammu and Kashmir and the

Naxalite insurgency-affected areas of central and eastern India that are sensationalized beyond lived reality.

I remember working on a project with some students under the Delhi University's Innovations Project, for which I was planning to take them on a trip to the Northeast because it had to do with understanding cultures and languages. This was meant to be an exposure trip. The majority of the students were from various states of north India and were initially excited about the trip, but when the time came to finalize it, most of them dropped out one by one after being persuaded by their parents that the Northeast was not a good place to visit. I had to cancel the trip since it was meant to be a team project, much to the disappointment of two students from Kashmir who were quite excited about the trip. This was about ten years ago, and I sincerely hope that perceptions about the region have changed to some extent in the minds of people since then. It is in situations like these that I realize Oscar Wilde was right when he said, 'Most people are other people. Their thoughts are someone else's opinions, their lives a mimicry, their passions a quotation.'

Growing up in a region that was typified as a 'conflict zone', I never felt fear the way I feel living in the largely 'migrant' city of Delhi. Somehow, the cosmopolitan space creates an atmosphere of living on the edge. Oddly, there is a sense of being constantly in conflict with the world around. This was when I realized that within the meaning of 'conflict' the feeling of 'fear' is deeply embedded. Where there is conflict, there is always a haunting sense of fear. For me, I confront fear at several levels of the everyday. First, at the individual level, I'm often made conscious of my Northeast identity, a minority from a fringe of the country. The sense of not belonging is terrible, especially when it is imposed on you! Second, at the family level, I'm often petrified about their safety, especially the innocent ones, perhaps something that finds resonance with many parents in the city because of so many unsavoury happenings. Third, there is anxiety at the community level. By this I mean, the tendency to find Northeasterners in the city huddled in a particular locality or crowd somewhere is suggestive of their sense of security when they have a sense of familiarity. I shall try to unpack these points as we go along.

'Where are you from?'

Generally, a person's identity is deeply rooted in where one belongs. Sometimes this sense of belonging is a given but in an increasingly fluid urban space, there is also the impression of choice that comes into play. Believe it or not, even after all these years in Delhi, I still face the difficulty of being accepted as a person of the city despite accessing all kinds of rights, including the electoral franchise. I am still asked 'where are you from?' when out on the streets or meeting new people. When I answer factually, saying, 'I'm from south Delhi,' they ask the same question a second time with stress on 'where'. Then I understand that they wish to know which state I belong to, if not which country! Thankfully, today most people's mental map of India includes a region called the Northeast; but when I was a student, I often got into endless bouts of explaining that Manipur or Nagaland are not somewhere in China or Thailand! This is the experience of many people from the Northeast, especially those with predominantly East Asian features. Some years ago the governor of Arunachal Pradesh, P.B. Acharya, while commenting on the general ignorance of the Indian public about the region, made an outrageous statement that caught some attention. He said, '…the people of India know more about America than the Northeast.'[4] I believe it was not an outlandish statement but that it points to a truth that needs redressal and not dismissal. I can only hope that people are more informed nowadays.

However, even after locating the states of the region as part of the larger Indian imagination, another trouble remains—the acceptance of being from Delhi. Can a person from the Northeast belong to the city? One may say, it depends on how the individual approaches the question. But the question 'where are you from?' certainly has the aspect of 'exclusion'. I don't see such questions being asked of my friends, be they from Himachal Pradesh, West Bengal, Bihar, Rajasthan or other states. So I've now come to conclude that most people's understanding of Delhi is of it being a place devoid of people who look 'like' me. What I mean is that I continue to meet more people who are willing to consider me 'not' from Delhi than those who would accept me as one who has made Delhi his home. Hence, over the years, I've come to the conclusion that it would be easier for a person from across the north-western border of India to pass off as an 'Indian' in the capital than for a person from the Northeast to be accepted as fellow Indians. Given the nation's geographical size and diversity, it seems quite possible for many groups to pass as other nationalities. I say this from the vantage point of being from a region with porous international borders. Just as cheap Chinese goods and illegal drugs get easy access through some of the favourable entry points of the region, the nationalities of people are also blurred. Even as the population of Northeast people grows in the capital city, another challenge looms large because they remain a visible minority owing to their physical features, which Sanjib Baruah calls 'a battle over images'.[5]

This, then, begs the question, 'What does an Indian look like?' For a country like India, it's difficult to project a single image of Indian-ness, even though there are concerted efforts to create a sort of homogenous entity. The mind-boggling cultural, linguistic and ethnic diversity defies all such attempts. Yet, despite valid concerns raised against creating homogeneity of the Indian identity, there are zealous proponents of such ideologies from time to time. Perhaps we're living through a period of their dominance right now. However, this is not something new. I think for a long time now, some ideas of India seem to have sold better across the world. I remember my relatives in the US would often say that people there wouldn't believe they were Indians; instead, they were treated as East Asians. So, clearly, elsewhere too, there seems to be a unique image of an Indian. Perhaps the debate around identity will take different shapes and sizes.

While this goes on, I'm reminded of a powerful poem, 'What Does an Indian Look Like', by Cherrie L. Chhangte, a poet from Mizoram who critiqued the much-hyped notion of India's diversity because it seems to provide lip service only. While lamenting that minorities are often 'sidelined, side-tracked, side-stepped', she ends on a satiric assertion:

I am a curiosity, an 'ethnic' specimen.
Politics, history, anthropology, your impressive learning,
All unable to answer the fundamental question—
'What does an Indian look like?'
—An Indian looks like me, an Indian is Me.[6]

Where is home?

Quite often, I find myself concerned about the safety of my family members. Unfortunately, even after staying in a neighbourhood for so many years, I do not really know others who stay in the vicinity. It feels strange, but this appears to be the case with most people. You just don't know people around—no interactions, no socializing. Everybody is busy with their own life, work or other stuff. But there is also an uneasiness to being friendly because sometimes your friendliness can be misread. Perhaps the fear psychosis has gripped the social mindset to such a point that one is reduced to isolation. Or perhaps it's an exceptional case with me/us feeling 'unsafe'. As a parent, I don't let my kids step outside the door on their own, forget about letting them go down the building or on to the roadside near the building to play by themselves. When I was growing up in the hills of Manipur, we were always out on the streets with friends. Our parents were least bothered about our whereabouts, which is not to say that they weren't concerned about us—but, instead, that used to be a socially conducive environment for children and the parents didn't need to panic. The last time we went to visit my birthplace, one of my kids asked,

'How is it that everyone knows you by name?' There was puzzlement in that question—a sense of incomprehensibility for the young mind. Needless to say, it springs from their own experience of growing up in the city where we often shield them. Yes, certainly, there is a difference in the milieu of the locality. But it nevertheless made me ask myself if the city creates its own fear syndrome?

I remember once I forgot that it was time to pick up my daughter from her school. My wife happened to call just about that time and upon realizing it, she became really panicky. You can imagine what might be rushing through the mind of any parent in that situation—the 'what ifs'—which can make you lose your heartbeat till the time you have your child right in front of you. The paranoia can be quite deadly! Sometimes, looking from a little distance, I muse at the impatience of parents/guardians who wait at the school gates to pick up their wards. Their focus is quite acute as they look through the stream of kids flooding out. At times, the rush to pick up their kids is quite amusing, as though someone else would grab their children before they could, even though they hold their parent/guardian ID in their hand. Of course, one can understand the anxiety of parents as undesirable incidents get reported once in a while—of kids being kidnapped right outside school or other unwelcome events involving kids. After all, why take chances? That also explains the heightened security measures in school vicinities, mostly by school authorities.

I think big cities like Delhi harbour a sense of danger at multiple levels. There is the fear of the unknown that can strike you anytime, which haunts life in the city. And for a visible minority like the Northeasterners, the anxiety of being reduced to an 'easy target' adds to the fear even more. Almost on a daily basis they, especially the women, are teased on the streets, directly or indirectly. At times, it becomes obvious that predators try to take advantage of their vulnerability or 'outsiderness'.

I remember an incident that disturbed our family for a long time. My adult niece was groped and her purse was snatched as she was heading back from the vegetable market in the neighbourhood. She was merely walking down the regular route around 8 p.m. and was barely 200 metres from home when a couple of men emerged out of nowhere and tried to drag her away. Thankfully, she bit the hand of one of the attackers and ran home. Strangely, no one came to her rescue. She was too traumatized to speak about it for some time and swore never to go out on that route again. Of course, we called the police helpline and registered a complaint, but the culprits had vanished. What bothered me deeply about the incident, among other things, was the indifferent attitude of the passersby. This incident took place not very late at night and it was on a usually busy route. I was quite baffled by the general reluctance of the public to help the victim when an incident was happening right before their eyes. Perhaps the fear of being implicated in the case kept people away.

I've realized that it can be quite dangerous to be helpful, even though, yes, there are still a few good people around. Once, my car was hit by a drunk biker. I was angry and stepped out to confront the fellow but he 'acted' quite hurt and was bleeding from one of his fingers too (I didn't realize he was acting until sometime later). Even though he was clearly in the wrong, my anger quickly gave way to pity on seeing the injury. We (I was with a couple of others) offered to help and he didn't resist, until he saw a few of his own people around. He happened to be a local hero, or should I say a goon? Suddenly, he screamed and shouted that my car had hit him, instead. Within seconds, before we realized what was going on, we were outnumbered. One can imagine the mob mentality. That fellow was all normal then, with no sign of being hurt. As the one who was in the driver's seat, I became the main target of the mob—shoved by a few and slapped by a woman. There was no way of arguing our way out. Thankfully, that evening, a sensible guy from the local gym (as we noticed from his clothes) became our saviour. He was truly godsent. Rather than seeking compensation for the damage, we considered ourselves lucky not to be roughed up badly that day. Did we make a mistake by not calling the police right away and ignoring the 'injured' fellow? How would the local people have reacted if we weren't of a 'different' appearance? These are questions that will, perhaps, remain unanswered.

Home away from home?

Studies have shown that the global population is increasingly concentrated in cities and that the Global South will see maximum urban growth.[7] Delhi is an example of this exponential growth and it is expected to be the world's most populous city in less than ten years.[8] Despite yearly grievances of extreme pollution and weather, the capital city continues to attract more and more people. A multicultural cauldron of a city, it has already ushered in a sizeable population from the Northeast too. In a timely study, Dolly Kikon and Bengt G. Karlsson observed, 'In the last decade, the migration of indigenous youths from the uplands of Northeast India to metropolitan cities across India has become one of the most significant social and economic transformations of the region.'[9] Yet, the Northeasterners in the city tend to get huddled in particular localities. Colonies closer to Delhi University's North Campus, like Indira Vihar, Nehru Vihar, Gandhi Vihar, Vijay Nagar, etc., have always seen a high concentration of students from the region. Likewise, Moti Bagh, Humayunpur (Safdarjung Enclave), Munirka, Kishangarh and a few other localities in south Delhi have been favourites of both students and working professionals. Many of these areas have become 'mini-Northeasts' with shops and eateries run by Northeasterners dominating the small locales. The sense of feeling secure—with familiar faces and foods around—seems to be a key factor in the creation of these Northeast localities. In this sense, there seems to be no difference in why and how ghettos sprout up in many growing cities across the world. Of course, Indian cities are not new to being surrounded by slums, except that these new colonies by 'migrants' from different parts of the country live a relatively better life economically, socially and politically.

Duncan McDuie-Ra offers another angle to the city favouring the Northeast migrants, 'The neoliberal transformation of Delhi is creating spaces of engagement between Northeasterners and the Indian mainstream.'[10] The factor of globalization helps in understanding this perspective. Since global spaces exemplified by the emergence of upscale shopping malls require global services, the Northeast labour force seems to fit into the role of ubiquitous internationalism. Besides, the typically 'non-Indian accented English spoken by most Northeasterners, especially those from the hill states' played to their advantage in being employable in other professional sectors, too, particularly the call centres'.[11]

Yet, despite the conducive environment for the Northeast populace to find their home in the city, somehow there seems to be a difficulty in finding acceptance. Often, they're faced with racial prejudices and discrimination from the general public. The unfortunate case of a young man from Arunachal Pradesh, Nido Tania, in 2014, sparked a wave of protests and demonstrations not just by the Northeasterners but also by various social and human rights activists. The aftermath of the incident saw the setting up of various state mechanisms to provide safety for Northeastern people. Even educational institutions were directed to set up nodal officers to address the issue. Today, the Delhi Police also has a dedicated unit, Special Police Unit for North-Eastern Region (SPUNER), to provide safety and security measures for people from the region. With such mechanisms in place, one can say that things have grown much better in recent times, even if it is far from being completely safe since prejudices are deep-rooted. It is encouraging to see many organizations that work tirelessly to address these social problems. One such organization is the North East Support Centre & Helpline (NESCH) initiated by the lawyer Alana Golmei, which has been of huge help to the Northeasterners.

Even with many measures in place, different forms of racial discrimination are faced by people from the region. According to the report of the M.P. Bezbaruah Committee formed after Nido Tania's death, 86 per cent of Northeasterners experience discrimination in some form or the other. The Covid-19 pandemic, especially its first wave, added to the woes of the Northeasterners in various parts of the country—being called 'corona' or 'virus' alluding to the first emergence of the pandemic from China. Even as the whole nation saw the heartbreaking images of migrant labourers fleeing cities on foot, the young working population of Northeasterners in the cities also took the same route of heading back to their hometowns but with 'an extra baggage to carry back to their homes—"bitter memories" of racial discrimination.'[12] Since that retreat, many did not go back to their previous place of work or cities even after the pandemic was over, for obvious reasons.

Despite all the fears and insecurities of living in the city, I would still be considered fortunate to be able to drive to work or other places, thus avoiding many unwanted circumstances on the road or in the crowd. Most Northeasterners working in different service sectors have to deal with prejudices or biases on their daily walk or ride to work and fight stigma or victimization on a routine basis, all because of the jaundiced mindset among many. Needless to say, there is a huge lacuna in sensitizing the larger public about the nation's people and culture. Perhaps, a historical fault line lies at the core. Identifying the problem of ethnocentrism in a multicultural and multireligious country like India, Nobel Laureate Amartya Sen rightly said, '… even when we are clear about how we want to see ourselves, we may still have difficulty in being able to persuade others to see us in just that way.'[13] Seeing others as we see ourselves is quite challenging, let alone loving others as we love ourselves.

Unfortunately, globalization also creates its subalterns and generates conflict situations between groups even within the nation-state, particularly with the emergence of new minorities in the newer urban spaces. As Arjun Appadurai puts it, because 'minorities' are often 'produced in the specific circumstances of every nation and every nationalism', they also become 'scapegoats in the era of globalization' and thus 'have always been targets of prejudice and xenophobia'.[14] In a similar light, therefore, there are visibly new forms of violence unleashed at different levels on the minority Northeast population in the city, from harassment by landlords and being taken undue advantage of by employers to facing racial slurs in the everyday. Such experiences also pushed them to be huddled up in small pockets of the city, creating 'mini-Northeasts' in an effort to feel at home.

Certainly, there is a general sense of solidarity among the diverse communities of the Northeast when it comes to fighting against racial discrimination or violence against them. Perhaps this kindred feeling is also shaped by the fact that they are often categorized together as 'outsiders' in the vocabulary of those from other parts of the country. The deep-rooted insecurities of their everyday struggle led them to find common ground in the vastness of a city that can be intimidating. Just before the Covid-19 pandemic hit, I was invited to deliver a lecture at the Indian Institute of Technology, Jammu. As I was preparing to talk about my 'everyday experiences' of living in the capital city, I came across an interesting piece in *The Indian Express*, which was at the time running a series on the rehabilitation of the Kashmiri Pandits. That day, the article was titled 'Three words that haunt the Kashmiri Pandit migrants—home, livelihood and safety'.[15] I thought that summed up the existential reality of the community in focus quite well. But for many of us, those three words capture our everyday reality. Our quest in life is very much for a place to call 'home', a 'livelihood' to keep us going and the 'safety' of an environment to live in peace. And yet, they are often quite elusive. The absence or the uncertainty of those basics of life drives us to a point of fear.

The journey of survival

Back in the 1980s and '90s, when I was growing up in a typical small hill town in Manipur, the notion of fear was largely personified by the camouflage uniforms of the Indian Army patrolling up and down the highway or the speeding convoys, with dust trailing the olive-green trucks. Now, living in the city, those earlier images are completely absent from my current imagination of fear. But many young people leaving the land of their birth have similar memories, especially those who have seen protracted violence and militarization in their homelands. And so, relocating to cities is also metaphorical of their effort to start life afresh—'It is a journey of survival, leaving behind the histories of armed struggles and massive human rights violations and a corrupt local state structure …'[16] Despite the physical move to a greener pasture in the big cities, with its well-paying jobs, there is often a longing for home—the idea of home that they have left behind, which is attached to their heart like an unbroken umbilical cord. However, there is also the realization that things haven't changed much since their leaving. So, in essence, there is a nostalgia tinged with doubts about returning to their place of birth. Kikon and Karlsson quite appropriately sum up that mixed feeling with these words: 'There is always a sense of home and a longing to go back, but at the same time, many of the indigenous migrants do not see themselves at home in the highlands of Northeast India. Anxious about being unemployed, the violence, and the corrupt system, and having no desire to do farming, they continue to move further away from home.'[17] It's a sad picture to paint—'to move further away from home'—but that's the reality for many Northeasterners.

I believe my experience is a shared one with many who have left the beautiful hills of the Northeast in pursuit of a better life, only to realize that it's as much of a struggle in the city too. Life brings its challenges. For many years, I have looked for opportunities to head back home or somewhere closer to home but without many prospects. I'm just one of those who desires to go back to the land where clouds meet the hills, but a future tinted with uncertainties forces me to hit the brakes. I hope, however, that things will get better. Like in all conflict situations, the only thing that drives away fear or reduces it is 'hope'. And it is this hope that keeps me going even now in the city. Where there is hope, there is the certainty of a peaceful future. I shall persevere in hope!

Of Begums and Lailas

Teresa Rehman

A woman inhabits many lives in her lifetime, as the saying goes. Dr Anis Iraqi's steel almirah at home pops with a colourful chaos of fineries from multiple cultures—phanek, mekhela sador, dokhona, salwar kameez, sari and even a pair of jeans. Her closet is a pointer to the countless social realities she has lived in her life of over four decades. Her quest for financial and social stability made her shed the comforts of home and hearth and shift out of her home state, Manipur, to neighbouring Assam. In the process, she had to unlearn many old practices and habits of food, dress, language and beliefs and pick up new traits, traditions and allies.

'Oh, are there Muslims in Manipur?' Random acquaintances and colleagues usually hurl this question at her. A barrage of friendly enquiries follows, leaving her amused and awkward. Many assume that she is a Hindu married to a Muslim. Oblivious to the politics of displacement and migration, Anis, in her forties now, still feels a 'moment of emptiness' when she thinks of 'home'. She is a thoroughbred Meitei Pangal and her 'home' is suffused with the pervasive reek of dried fish, the comforting clatter of rickshaws on the broken narrow streets, the irregular line-up of rich and poor houses in her leikai (locality), the familiar lilting call of the street vendors, fooling around with cousins. It is a place of walks on rainy evenings to her grandmother's house, lazy afternoon conversations with her aunts and grand-aunts, sneaking out to watch the latest films and the ubiquitous call of the azaan (Islamic call to prayer).

When asked where 'home' is, Anis's reply is immediate and emphatic— 'Golapati'. A full-fledged Golapati of her girlhood lives deep within her. A typical Muslim area in Manipur's Imphal East district, Minuthong Golapati (better known as Golapati) is a densely populated area with clogged drains, unsanitary conditions and a paucity of drinking water. But it is still 'home', a place where her parents lived, died and are buried. It is a place she trusts. The snug winding streets, trees, lamp-posts, the masjid gate, the street dog fights, the corner store where she got her trinkets, rings, nail paint and earrings, her mother's old school friend who is now a vegetable vendor, the exhilarating ride to college on her Kinetic Honda, the chaotic traffic snarls, the squawk of her pet parrot lovingly called 'Macha Tombi' (sweet little girl) and all other sights and sounds of her childhood tug at her heartstrings.

Her community, Meitei Pangal or Muslims from Manipur— scattered in different places around the Imphal valley like Lilong, Hatta, Golapati, Kshetrigao, Yairipok and Thoubal Moijing—have often been vilified and stereotyped as uncongenial and regressive. According to the Census of 2011, the population of Meitei Pangals was 2.4 lakh, which makes up 8.4 per cent of the total population of Manipur. There are several theories about the settlement of Meitei Pangals in different parts of Manipur, which go back centuries. The Manipuri royal chronicles known as *Cheitharon Kumpapa* record the settlement of Pangals in Manipur, who had been captured after an attempted invasion of the kingdom, in 1606. They were given servants and land for sustenance by King Khagemba (1597–1652 CE) and were gradually integrated into Manipur's polity. They have contributed immensely in various fields of the state, such as polity, economy, socio-cultural and administrative affairs, from the seventeenth century onwards. The Manipur Muslim

Pangal Historical Society has made a list of the Meitei Pangal soldiers who took part in the 1891 Anglo-Manipur War.[1]

There are nonetheless vulnerabilities and prejudices that come with the tag of 'Pangal'. Anis got used to those quite early in life. Disturbing memories often fade away with time but some episodes stick in the mind. She still remembers the time when as a young high school student, she used to go for private tuitions with her elder sister, Shireen Nesha. As they stepped out of their locality, they faced catcalls from young boys lurking at the street corners. The boys used to jeer at them with jibes of 'Laila' and 'Begum'. 'Hey, Laila, spare us a smile.' 'Where are you going, Begum?' Anis found those remarks derisive and unsettling. She recoiled into her private microcosm. She had to gather her wits while crossing that road again. She says, 'It affected my self-esteem. I was both nervous and alert and used to sweat profusely. I walked briskly. I wished I did not exist. I felt like something was wrong with me.' Though her mother reassured her and urged her to ignore such comments, she realized that there was an incongruity.

She was the 'other' though she spoke the same language, relished the same food, wore the same attire, performed Manipuri dances, went to the same school and recited the same poetry as her Meitei friends. She waited for Cheiraoba, the beginning of the Manipuri new year, when her mother made a variety of traditional dishes, including a few fish items. As a child, she used to accompany her mother to her maternal grandparents' home on Ningol Chakouba, an occasion when married daughters are invited for a feast. 'We used to wait to open the gifts that my uncle gave our mother,' she says. Anis's nickname is 'Memton', a common word for the youngest child. Her best friend was also lovingly called Memton. She called her mother Ima, just like her best friend referred to her mother. Like all young girls of her age, she too swooned over Manipuri pop singer and heartthrob Sadananda. She hums a romantic song of Sadananda's that is close to her heart, *Purnima oina leigadaba* (Your face resembles the full moon). 'I have attended his concerts. He is also an actor, and I never miss out on his films.

When I was out of Manipur, the first thing I would do when I went home was to find the CDs of his latest films and watch them. Now, his songs are available on YouTube,' she smiles.

On the surface, the Pangals engaged with everyone at various levels, at school and in college. It was customary for her friends to come home and gorge on Eid delicacies like pulao, korma and sewaiyan. But the imperceptible divide was always there. 'We could discern a difference in school, college and among friends. We were unrelenting. We followed the tide and sometimes fought our way. My defiant mother was a fighter too. We emerged stronger but it left behind a palpable sense of dejection,' says Anis.

Anis credits her boundless energy to her mother, Samsun Nessa, who was a daunting personality. She had no creeping frailty and was a role model in the entire family for her grit and resoluteness. 'My mother always earned her own money. She wanted us to be self-reliant. She did not want our energies to be sapped by household chores only. We knew we had to achieve,' Anis says, with her characteristic mixture of humility and firmness. Her mother was among the first few women from Manipur to be trained as a health educator at New Delhi's Lady Hardinge Medical College in the early 1960s. One of her maternal aunts studied at Guwahati's Cotton College and worked as a teacher in Imphal. The community leaders threatened their maternal grandfather that they would stop his family's hookah-paani, meaning that they would be ostracized, if he allowed his daughters to go out and study. But her grandfather insisted on going ahead with his daughters' education. This inspired others in the community to educate their daughters too. There were also other women in Anis's close-knit family who inspired her. One aunt was a midwife who told her stories about the traditional methods of childbirth; and she learnt basic budgeting from two other aunts who have stalls in the all-women Ima market.

Her mother worked as the lady health visitor in the state's Health and Family Welfare Department and later retired as an extension educator from the same department. After retirement, she set up her own pharmacy. As a child, Anis saw her office-going mother gingerly balancing her Kinetic Honda through potholes and garbage strewn on the roads in her neighbourhood. Her mother used to wake up at the crack of dawn, offer namaz and browse through local dailies like *The Sangai Express*, *Poknapham* and *Amrita Bazar Patrika*, an English newspaper published from Kolkata. After preparing breakfast, she would set off for office. She would usually wear a sari to office, though she wore phanek at home. She would not cover her head or wear a hijab while going to office. There were very few working women in Anis's community back then. Samsun's role was to provide nursing care and maternal and child health facilities to women in urban and rural communities. She was in charge of family planning and used to counsel and encourage Muslim women to go for a tubectomy or use contraceptive methods. 'This also led to a wrangle with the community and religious leaders. They even imposed social sanctions, popularly known as hookah-paani bandh, on any women who used contraception. My mother herself went for a tubectomy after she had five children,' Anis says.

Peace is fragile in Manipur. The year 1993 was the turning point for Anis's family. On 3 May 1993, riots broke out, in which more than 140 Meitei Pangals were killed.[2] Both Shireen and Anis were in high school then. They could not go to school and their mother could not go to office. 'Whenever I think of those days, I get goosebumps. There was a total shutdown. There was a constant fear as people were killed and thrown in the river, houses burnt and property destroyed. Both guns and machetes were used in the attacks. The dead bodies of a mother and child were stuck together and they had to be buried together. We had to face scarcity of food,' Shireen says. Every year, Meitei Pangals observe a commemoration day on 3rd May. The stifling fear still lingers. 'Our heart misses a beat when we talk of the 3rd of May,' she adds.

They survived the riots unscathed. After completing high school, it was time for Anis and her sister to pursue their goal of becoming doctors. The sisters could not get admission in institutions in their home state despite their best efforts. So they enrolled in and completed their BSc degree from GP Women's College, Imphal. Their mother, meanwhile, had got some information about degree education in the Indian system of medicine. Finally, Anis got through the Government Ayurvedic College in Guwahati in 1997 under the Manipur quota, and Shireen followed her the next year.

Eight years after the two sisters left home for greener pastures, there was an important development for their community. Conceding to the demands of various Meitei Pangal groups, the Manipur state government decided to reserve 4 per cent seats for the community in state services and professional courses in the year 2006. 'Women, however, continue to lag behind in terms of education and thereby economic empowerment. There is a high drop-out rate, especially in the rural areas, and few venture out to urban areas for education,' adds Anis.

From a childhood in Imphal surrounded by kindred, Anis moved in 1997, alone, to an unfamiliar Guwahati. Initially, she was disconcerted. The fast-moving traffic startled her. She gained confidence gradually and adjusted well with the anonymity that comes with living in a big multi-cultural city. Guwahati had always been a stopover when the family travelled to Delhi and other parts of India. Her brothers had done their schooling in Lucknow. Their father had thought it would accord them better opportunities and keep them away from volatile situations back in Manipur.

All through that period, it was their mother who had stood like a rock with them. She was always edgy about her two daughters' future. Quite ahead of her times, she did not want them to be confined to domesticity and marriage. She fought for them with her husband, who insisted on getting their daughters married early. Anis harks back to her mother's advice: 'I don't care whether you get married or not. But I want you to study as much as you can and stand on your feet. You should not be dependent on anyone.' This was quite remarkable in a community that restricted women's mobility and prioritized marriage for their girls. Her father, however, was opposed to the idea of them venturing out to study in a different state. He used to be grouchy even when they came home for vacations. Although he was finally happy after they graduated from college, his biggest regret was that he could not get them married in his lifetime.

Both the sisters got married after their parents' death. Anis gets emotional, 'My father did not live to see both of us get married. I feel sad that my mother is not around to see how we are living her dream.' Her husband, who was her batchmate in college, is her constant companion and helps her in everything she does—on the domestic and professional front. She decided to tie the knot with her batchmate despite family opposition. 'My eldest brother has still not reconciled to the fact that I did not marry a Meitei Pangal. He has strong ethnocentric views. He is more of a Meitei than a Muslim. He and his family did not attend my wedding, which was held in Guwahati,' she smiles. Shireen, however, got married to a Meitei Pangal man in a match arranged by her brothers.

Life as a student in Guwahati was not easy. The tedious journey back home, a distance of almost 490 kilometres by road, took her twelve to fourteen hours by bus on the iffy highway. 'Sometimes, we were stranded for hours due to landslides. I had travelled alone several times. There was a constant fear as we were travelling through an insurgency-ravaged terrain. I used to be tense and my family members were anxious till I reached the outskirts of Imphal,' she says. Guwahati was a more secure second home but she had to grapple with other worries. Her friends spoke in Assamese in the college hostel. 'I used to ask someone to translate it for me. In the class, too, the teacher taught in Assamese,' she rues. She also had to learn Sanskrit for the first time. 'I struggled a lot with Sanskrit, parroting from seniors' notes, and somehow managed to pass the first year. We were not ragged much as we did not know the local language,' smiles Anis.

Both the sisters became first-generation doctors and both found work as rural doctors in different parts of Assam. Before she could make sense of the dichotomies of 'outsider' and 'insider', Anis found herself transported to a distant, unfamiliar setting. Now, she tries to fit in with the formal yet unrehearsed life she leads, complete with handling complicated delivery and accident cases, organizing vaccination camps, cleanliness drives, a girl child week, tubectomy and vasectomy camps and various medical trainings. All of these are after she is done with her daily namaz, cooking, cleaning, dusting and sending her children to school with incredible efficiency. Her two sons go to the nearest 'good' school that is 30 kilometres away.

As a rural doctor, she lives in tune with nature. An early riser, she grabs a few moments of solitude each day. 'Life has been kind to me,' she says as she tends to her small kitchen garden in the backyard of her government quarter in Kokrajhar district, Bodoland Territorial Region (BTR), Assam. She grows all kinds of vegetables and fruits like bottle gourd, green chilli, cabbage, potato, cauliflower, guava, starfruit, jackfruit, gooseberry and jujube. She grows turmeric and ginger throughout the year. It is her own little haven. Surrounded by paddy fields, the government quarter is her home now. Her workplace is just 50 metres away. She shares a symbiotic relationship with her hospital staff and local people. Her patients call her 'doctorni baideo' or 'madam'. A local celebrity now, Anis is invited to birthdays, weddings, festivals and public events. She even wears the dokhona, the traditional attire of the Bodo community, on special occasions.

With a smattering of Hindi, Assamese, Bodo and Bangla, Anis handles her patients with finesse. At home, she converses in Hindi and Assamese with her two sons and husband, who is from Assam. Whenever she longs to speak to someone in her mother tongue, she makes long-distance phone calls and video calls to her friends and relatives back home. 'Who doesn't know Hindi these days?' she questions. A movie buff, she picked up some Hindi from television and Hindi cinema. The last Bollywood film that Anis recalls watching in Imphal was the Bobby

Deol starrer *Barsaat* at a hall called Jina Cinema. Now, the hall has been pulled down to build an educational centre. Hindi films have been banned in Manipur since 1998, after a diktat from a militant group. Korean, English and Manipuri films have taken over from Hindi films now. 'I have not watched Korean films. Manipuri films are quite good. But a lot needs to be improved in terms of quality and content,' she says.

A great believer in the usefulness of having hobbies, she enjoys crafting, gardening and trying out new recipes from YouTube. Married to a man from Assam, her kitchen is more cosmopolitan now. She loves food and cooks whatever her children relish. But she misses the typical Meitei cuisine like eromba, singju, uti, hangam, kangshoi and champhut. 'Most of these dishes are boiled food and are hot and pungent as we add a lot of chilly. My husband can't stand the smell of dried fish. Most of the time, I have to eat it alone. Though I have all the ingredients in my kitchen cabinet, I don't want to cook something that I can't share and eat,' she rues.

Like a child, Anis is curious about everything. Her keenness to learn new things keeps her on her toes. She loves learning new languages and about new cultures. Maybe it brings her momentary relief from anxiety and yearning. She misses Manipur and her home all the time. 'I have been adjusting all my life. From a city life, I have now settled into a rural life in Assam. I am happy, though I am *dil se Manipuri* (a Manipuri at heart),' she says. Whenever she sees a Bodo woman weaving, she remembers her aunt, who is an adroit weaver and used to weave phaneks, enaphis and gamchas. Anis is now learning weaving from one of her office staff. 'I find the Bodo weaves absorbing. I find weaving therapeutic. The threads on the loom seem to connect me to home,' she says. She had also picked up knitting, embroidery and stitching from her mother. Her industrious mother had a knitting machine and used to take orders for cardigans and pullovers. As a tribute to her mother, Anis still embroiders her pillow covers, tablecloths and handkerchiefs.

Anis is the lone female doctor in this far-flung area and so female patients prefer to consult her, especially with their gynaecological problems. 'There are times when patients run away from big hospitals fearing a Caesarean procedure. We have to handle impossible cases under unthinkable conditions. Sometimes, I have to handle three to four childbirths in a night,' she says. Apart from attending to the gynaecological problems of adolescent girls, she is always ready with a quick tutorial on the physical and psychological changes that come with menopause. 'My patients share a very good rapport with me and bring fresh organic vegetables, fruits and even milk as gifts almost every day. I feel blessed,' she beams.

She has earned respect now, something her mother always wanted for her daughters. She feels honoured when she is asked to hoist the national flag at her health centre on Independence and Republic days. Growing up in conflict-torn Manipur, under the shadow of AFSPA (1958), she understands what fear means. She feels a sense of quiet peace, dignity and freedom here. 'When we were very young, we celebrated these days in school. But things changed gradually. Manipur reminds us of curfews, protests and general strikes. There was an unofficial curfew there as soon as dusk set in,' she says.

She talks about her mother with a mixture of affection and awe. Her mother engaged them in thoughtful conversations and encouraged them to read books in their mother tongue. 'We used to read storybooks. My best-loved folk tale is "Eta Thaomei". It's about a wise old woman and a thief. I have also narrated this story to my kids.'

In Manipur, every locality has women's groups or Meira Paibis who take to the streets against social evils and injustice. Meitei Pangal women, too, are part of these Meira Paibis and other clubs and organizations that fight against drug abuse and alcoholism. Though her mother was not a member of the local Meira Paibi, she did a lot of social work. There are many community organizations of the Meitei Pangal women—the Muslim Chanura Development Organization, Kangleipak Muslim Chanura Marup, Ushoipokpi Tharaurok Women

Development Organization and United Muslim Women Development Organisation (UMWDO)—who work for women's empowerment. Historically, Meitei Pangal women were active in the Nupi Lan or Women's Uprising of December 1939.[3] Over thirty Meitei Pangal women took part in the uprising against the Manipur maharaja's policy, supported by the British, of exporting rice to other states, which led to inflation and a rice shortage in Manipur.

Most often, religious clerics hold sway over Anis's economically and educationally marginalized community. Her parents were devout Muslims and had even performed their hajj. She and her siblings were trained in the Quran and the tenets of Islam in their early childhood when they went to the madrassa at the local mosque with other kids. When she and her sister grew older, her mother engaged a religious priest also known as 'Miyazi' or 'Miyasahab' who taught them the scriptures. True to the tradition of their family, even today, Anis maintains daily discipline and makes time for her namaz five times a day.

Both sisters long to be at 'home' on Eid. They often plan ahead and travel to Imphal. Shireen is effusive when she describes the resplendent Eid in her locality, 'Eid celebrations are special there. It is probably the grandest Eid in Manipur. It feels like Delhi or Mumbai.' Groups of fervent youths spend days putting together the Eid decorations. Being a part of the Eid committee also makes them feel like bigwigs. Moreover, it's a respite from their mundane jobs as petty traders, salesmen, lawyers, teachers, carpenters and rickshaw pullers. The resplendent Eid gate is a badge of honour for those young boys.

Eid is also a celebration of life, a time to meet relatives and cousins. The celebrations start five days in advance. Makeshift stalls of modish garments, knick-knacks, trinkets and accessories are set up in the evenings and are open the entire night. This is unusual in a state like Manipur where practically everything closes after dusk. 'Women and children come out to do last-minute shopping. It goes on till dawn. The locality is alive with celebrations the entire night. It's a new trend. It was not there when we were kids. It's like a carnival with the silvery streamers and tinsel strings all over the street,' gushes Shireen.

The evening before Eid is filled with crackling laughter and the frenzied chatter of kids. Vendors from Bengal and Bihar sit in a row on the footpath under the bright halogen lights. Girls sit in a line, pick and choose the colourful glass bangles, and the bangle seller slides it over their delicate hands. 'It's a lot of fun. All night the girls apply henna on each other's hands. We cook curry and sewaiyan the night before. Only the pulao or biryani is made in the morning,' she says. There is no open space for a sprawling Eidgah. The Eid namaz is done in the mosque, which has multiple floors and can accommodate many people. After namaz, people go around in groups and visit homes.

'Isn't she looking elegant?' asks Anis as her fingers slide over an old black-and-white photograph of her mother in a dance pose while wearing customary Manipuri dance attire. Contrary to stereotypes about Muslim women, Meitei Pangal women take an active part in cultural activities. 'My mother had a zest for life. She used to perform a Manipuri dance on stage. She had learnt it from her dance teacher in school. I, too, danced in my school and college functions. I had even won medals for our school,' explains Anis. In March 2019, women and young girls took an active part in the religious songs and naats in the two-day international conference in Imphal on 'Manipuri Muslims: Past, Present and Future'. Even qawwali was performed in Meitei by female artistes at the event, which was organized by the All Manipur Muslims (Meitei Pangal) Welfare Association, Imphal.

Anis has a never-ending to-do list whenever she is in Imphal. She knows the nooks and crannies of the city. She hops on to her brother's Kinetic Honda and goes to the market, meeting friends and relatives in her fast-changing city. She makes it a point to visit her only surviving paternal uncle and other relatives who live in Keirao Makting, her father's ancestral village. She also goes to meet her mother's relatives in Hatta. Her social engagements also include dawats (invitations) at the home of one relative or the other. 'I ask them to make only traditional Manipuri food for me,' she grins. Walking on familiar streets is a joy for Anis. She loves Keishampat market, where she can pick up goods like electric rice cookers and pans, blankets and cutlery imported from Myanmar, and she buys local fruits and dry fish from the Ima market.

Anis and Shireen have become role models in their locality now. 'When we go home, people say that we are an inspiration. Parents give our examples to other daughters as two diligent sisters who broke many glass ceilings—left home for higher education, are earning well, got married and have families of their own now. They shattered the myth that girls bring a bad name to family when left alone,' beams Anis.

Back in Assam, the sisters regularly visit each other though they live many miles away. Shireen lives in a government quarter in Kamrup Metropolitan district. Shireen, too, has adapted well to the mixed population of the Assamese, Tiwa and Garo communities around her. She, too, handles emergency and accident cases apart from other routine duties.

Shireen is the only person who can slow down the unstoppable energy that so envelops Anis.

They have a striking alchemy. Shireen is more than a sister. She is Anis's mentor, guide, philosopher and keeper of secrets. Mention her name and Anis softens, 'I have a very good rapport with my sister. We have never fought with each other. We share our little joys and sorrows. Before taking any important decision, we consult each other. We speak to each other almost every day. We talk about our daily life, professional life, domestic squabbles and family life back in Manipur.'

The only solace Anis has is that her sister is in Assam. 'Geographically, she is far from me but still she is in Assam. Otherwise, I would have been all alone. I fear that if she shifts back to Manipur then I will have nobody to call my own in Assam. There are things we can't share with our husbands or brothers. She is my support system. My mother used to always remind us to stick with each other, even if we got married and led disparate lives.'

Shireen's life is more cohesive as her husband is also a Meitei Pangal from Hatta, Manipur. Hatta is the locality adjoining Golapati and so her in-laws' place is at a walking distance from their ancestral home. Her husband is a post-graduate in commerce and has worked at several places, but now he runs his own business. Shireen, too, has a small kitchen garden in her government quarter. Shireen's two children speak in Meitei, but Anis speaks to her children in Assamese. When the cousins meet, they speak in Hindi and English. Their children like going to Imphal and share a loving bond with their relatives there. 'We have a fond relationship with our nieces and nephews back in Imphal. They, too, look forward to meeting us,' says Anis.

Anis is destined to settle down in Assam, her husband's home. She still thinks that Shireen is more mature and can handle any kind of situation. 'I was afraid because I was marrying out of the community, but my husband supported me. I am grateful to my mother for urging us to go for this professional degree. It has helped us lead honourable lives,' says Anis.

Shireen, however, has made up her mind to spend her post-retirement years in Manipur. She also hopes to go for hajj. 'I don't feel at home here. I am not at peace,' she says. Resettling in Manipur will be tough as few people know her as a medical doctor there. 'But, as usual, I will have to adjust,' she says. Moreover, she wants to die among her dear ones and be buried near her parents. 'I don't know what destiny holds for me. For instance, my father-in-law had come to visit us and then the Covid-19 pandemic lockdown happened and he passed away suddenly. He had to be buried in Guwahati,' she narrates.

Their community has seen rapid changes in the past few years. Young people have it all—chutzpah, attitude, talent, confidence, imagination, guts. They are more conscious about their life and career than the sisters were in their time. They are opting for professional courses and are relatively more devout. They have started wearing more overt symbols of their religion like the hijab. 'It is a global phenomenon,' Shireen explains. She is happy to see that the young generation is using many online forums like YouTube and Facebook to share information about the community. 'It gives us a glimpse into the changes happening in the Manipur we left behind,' she adds.

Anis celebrates daily, with every meal and in every prayer, the life of quiet dignity she lives today. She has a curious bond with memory. She hoards objects, photographs, curios, old clothes of her children and even their school notebooks as keepsakes. She refuses to let go. She feels deeply connected to old things. She holds her mother's old phanek and becomes pensive, 'I hardly wear it now. But it's the only reminder I have of my ima and Manipur.'

Samsun Nessa, Anis' mother, performing a dance on stage at Lady Hardinge Medical College, New Delhi, 1962.
Photo courtesy of Anis.

The Journey Home

Margaret Ch Zama

I studied at St. Agnes' Convent, which was run by the Catholic nuns of the Congregation of Sisters of Our Lady of the Missions. It began as a boarding school for girls over a century ago in 1918 in Haflong, a small hill station that became the district capital of Dima Hasao, formerly known as the North Cachar Hills District of Assam, after Independence. As I recall, Haflong was connected to the rest of the world by dusty and narrow winding roads. There was also the Northeast Frontier Railway, which in those days was a narrow-gauge line with two small railway stations—Lower Haflong and Upper Haflong.

In 1961, when I was not even six years old yet, I arrived into that world of a remote convent school life. The memory of that day remains strongly etched in my mind even today. I still remember the porter leading the way uphill from the train station—he was drenched due to the torrential rain and bent with the weight of my school trunk and holdall (canvas bedding roll) on his back—grunting with the effort, the muscles of his short, stout legs wet and glistening in the rain. My eyes fixed on his rough bare feet as I followed him in a raincoat and oversized gumboots, trying not to stumble on the steep slippery path. With my father following behind, I managed to negotiate the makeshift little bridges as the rainwater gushed swiftly below. I also recall the numerous rail tunnels and old bridges that spanned the deep ravines we crossed all the times we travelled by train to school. I remember my elder brother, Sammy, who had joined St. Agnes' a year earlier, laughing and crouching low on the floor of the train with me each time we passed through a tunnel or crossed one of those narrow viaducts, while Dad laughed at our antics. It made the long journey so much more fun.

I remember Haflong as a serene little town in the 1960s, except for the noisy marketplace and the town's only cinema hall, Haflong Talkies. In 1918, Nicholas Beatson-Bell, then chief commissioner of Assam, had taken up the task of draining the marshy malaria-infested swamp around the newly established convent school. That, in turn, led to the creation of the lovely Haflong Lake, which is still considered the most beautiful lake in the hills of Assam. This winding artificial lake with its wooden arched bridges gave the town a quaint, whimsical look and character, which, to me, seemed to have come straight from a storybook. Our Sunday walks along the meandering lake escorted by the nuns, were occasions we looked forward to. We were made to walk in pairs and keep in line, wearing our Sunday dresses or sometimes our Sunday navy blue uniforms along with our red berets.

I remember an incident during one of those walks, when a senior girl accidentally dropped one of her shoes into the lake while bending over one of the wooden bridges, and of course, she started to cry. The nun in charge was furious with her. There was nothing that could be done about the unfortunate shoe that had sunk into the depths. I am not sure till date at whom all of us girls were twittering and giggling—the angry, red-faced nun or the poor girl crying. We returned to school with her walking barefoot and holding onto her remaining shoe. Such were some of the few exciting incidents that added spice to our otherwise routine boarding school life.

One of the mysterious secrets we girls at school longed to discover was whether the nuns were really bald under their well-secured headpieces, which had a stiff lining topped by a finer veil, sometimes black and sometimes white, which hung down to their waists. As though that was not sufficient cover, they used to even wear a stiff white broad band across the forehead—so all that was revealed of their open face was a triangle. The removal of that stiff band later must have been such a welcome relief. In any case, if a small scandalous wisp of hair ever escaped the cover of the veil and was sighted, we would notice it soon enough and try to slyly spy it, before the nun would hurriedly push it back out of sight. That obsession never really left me. One day, as we were playing basketball, Sister Scholastica, who was young and quite tall, joined the game enthusiastically. During the fast-paced game, amid loud shouts and laughter from the other girls watching the game, just as Sister was about to score a basket, I as a defender of the opposite team 'accidentally' pulled off her veil. Well, there stood Sister on the court with her very short cropped hair exposed, laughing her head off as she quickly adjusted her veil with clips and we continued the game—no reprimand, no punishment and, of course, no shaved head. As a Catholic myself, I have continued to be associated with nuns and priests of every hue and from every culture all my life and they always enjoy hearing this little anecdote of mine. Times have, however, changed after all these years, and much of the mystique that surrounded the nuns then has sadly disappeared today.

I think one of the most exciting things about studying in a convent boarding school was without a doubt the end of every school year. With our final exams over and report cards received, that was the time for packing up to go home for the long-awaited winter vacations, after spending the better part of the year behind convent walls and high hedges. Taking down our dusty school trunks from the store room shelves with the help of friends, sunning out our musty holdalls, then folding and packing our clothes and belongings with great care, exchanging little knick-knacks with close friends, circulating autographs, promising to remember each other forever, and then, of course, the tears as each boarder left when a family member arrived to escort them home—these are all indelible memories still etched in my mind today. We would crane our necks and attune our ears to each ring of the parlour bell, yelling out names and bidding our goodbyes. Those of us who were from Mizoram were not too large a contingent, so we often went home in small groups usually in a Willys Jeep belonging to one of our families. That was also how we often returned to school after the winter vacations.

The Jeeps were sturdy, versatile and road-worthy. It required great expertise to arrange the school trunks and beddings of four to five of us in one Jeep. Space had to be allocated for the spare tyre and petrol jerry can as well. Since there was no rain in December, the canvas hood of the jeep would be rolled towards the front, so that we children could sit atop the open Jeep as it were, cushioned by the many holdalls. Entering into Mizoram would perk us up and, standing up in a row while holding tightly onto the jeep brackets, we would sing our hearts out with joy and excitement. By the time we approached Aizawl, our entire bodies and clothes would be covered with thick dust from the long journey, making us almost unrecognizable—but that only served to add to our excitement. As we passed the Durtlang tunnel amidst shouting and laughter, our joy upon seeing the twinkling night lights of our hometown was indescribable.

~

The journey home, 1966

My journey home from school in 1966 was very different and unlike any of the previous ones. Back then, I was an eleven-year-old who had just passed class six. My mind draws a complete blank now as to who escorted me back home that year and how. Our usual group had been escorted by their families to other destinations, having left Aizawl temporarily to take up residence elsewhere due to the outbreak of the Mizo National Front (MNF) uprising in Mizoram on 1 March that year. Since us kids were away from home at boarding school when 'Rambuai' (the land's troubles) started, none of us really understood the insurgency issue. Nor did we realize the extent of the damage and human suffering that ensued because of the conflict. I vaguely remember being told about it by some of the senior Mizo girls at school and being shown a newspaper that carried a photo of my father on the front page, who had gone to meet with the Central government in Delhi. I was young, puzzled and also somewhat frightened; I felt shy and, therefore, suppressed my curiosity to know more. My father Lawrence Ch. Chhunga was an MLA in the Assam state government and President of the Mizo Union Party, the first political party of Mizoram established in 1946. He was one of the more prominent political leaders at the time who played a crucial role on all fronts during that dark period, negotiating between the Central government and the underground.

Though I can't recall the first part of the two-day journey from Haflong to Silchar, what I remember very clearly about my homecoming that year was my arrival in Aizawl by bus. It was already evening and very quiet, with no one to be seen out on the streets. There was probably a curfew in effect though I wouldn't have known about that anyway. As the bus entered the commercial hub of the town, Dawrpui Veng, I looked out of the bus window and immediately noticed that things were no longer the same—I saw all the shops and houses along the main street were burned to the ground and there were blackened remnants and pieces of debris strewn around everywhere. As we drew near our family shop, my eyes saw only blackened remains of what was once a thriving pharmacy that used to be manned by no less than seven to eight salespersons at a time. As for the family-run printing press on the ground floor below the pharmacy, all I saw were the two large printing machines, dark and sooty. That press was a part of my childhood years, a place where I used to stand in fascination, gawking at the printing process and listening to the steady clanking of the machines, watching the round plates move back and forth receiving blank paper and bringing back printed ones, the black grease that fed the machine paddles, the young men and women crouched over their tables with their fingers deftly picking out and arranging the tiny letters and numerals, or khawl ha (teeth of the machine) as it was called, and placing them on trays. Though I did not know it at the time, the model of the press we owned was what used to be called a letterpress, which was manual and very laborious.

The bus kept driving on as I continued to look over my shoulder until the sad scene disappeared out of sight. Looking back today at that particular experience of mine as an eleven-year-old adolescent, it can best be described as something strangely surreal and tragic. It drew no tears from me at the time. I was alone and the impact of the shock and pain was probably internalized by me, due to which it remained unshared for a long time. The unfamiliar address that I clutched in my hand was 'Pu Hrangaia, E.M., Khatla Veng'. When we finally arrived at that destination, the bus driver dropped me by the side of the road and continued on his way. As I waited in the quiet dusk with my school trunk and holdall beside me, looking at the house situated some distance downhill from the road, I noticed a curtain move inside the house and soon its door opened as my father came running up, followed by my younger brother. As my father put his arms around me, I heard him softly say, 'You have arrived home safely.'

Pu Hrangaia, though not related by blood, was more than a close friend and political colleague of my father. He was also an executive member (EM) of the then Mizo District Council. He offered shelter to our large family because we had become homeless overnight after our home at Sarawn Veng was burnt to the ground by a man identified as belonging to the Assam Rifles paramilitary force, whose barracks were not too far away from our home.

A mass exodus of families from Aizawl had taken place in the initial days following the first sounds of gunfire and swirling rumours that bombs, too, would be dropped soon. Families had panicked and fled town haphazardly to the outlying villages and forests. Others with more resources had loaded their vehicles with whatever they could carry and fled to places outside Mizoram such as Silchar, Shillong, Kohima and even Haflong, to name a few. Our family, too, had fled town without any fixed destination at first. My mother recounts how the family made their way by foot downhill towards Chite rivulet, then uphill to Zemabawk on the outskirts of Aizawl to the east and further on uphill to the adjoining village of Beraw, where they spent a couple of nights. At the time, my youngest sibling was just a year old and still being breastfed. It was from there at Beraw that my family watched the aerial bombing of Aizawl, situated across the distant hills, by the Indian Air Force, on the 5th and 6th of March 1966. There were loud cries, great wailing and weeping from the crowds who stood and witnessed it all. From Beraw, my family made its way further towards Sesawng village, situated forty-two kilometres east of Aizawl, and finally put up with our relative Pu Chawimawia. After sheltering there for a month, they returned to Aizawl to their new shelter, which was to become their home for the next year and a half—the residence of Pu Hrangaia at Khatla locality in Aizawl.

Initially, my father, too, had gone with the rest of the family up to Sesawng. But he had returned to Aizawl after about two days with four adult members of the family to keep our house at Aizawl safe from looters and troublemakers. The irony, of course, lies in what I have already narrated earlier. My father returned only to witness our house being set on fire the very next afternoon by a man from the Assam Rifles who was supposedly drunk, but unquestionably armed and dangerous. All efforts to deter the man failed and as he was armed, the others watched the house burn down, while my father went to the AR Commandant to report the incident. Our home was a stand-alone house with a large compound surrounding it, so there may have been some truth to the rumours that the man had received directions from some unknown persons to torch our home.

~

My father and paternal grandfather remain my heroes till date because of some of the extraordinary things they faced with sheer grit and determination during that difficult and dangerous phase of our lives. Yes, there were some events that I witnessed as a young adolescent during that time that affected me a lot, and the lessons those events taught me continue to remain crystal clear. What were they? There weren't many, but I can share some of them here. Providing shelter for our large family could not have been an easy task for anyone. There was my grandpa and grandma, my father and mother, nine of us children by 1966, with two more who followed later. At any given point in time, there were also no less than eight to ten members of our extended family who were part of the retinue as well. The group also included Ni Laii (Aunt Laii), who was called 'aunt' by all, children and adults. She was deaf, difficult and ever at odds with us children. She was a constant thorn in my mother's side too. Being a poor orphan, she had been adopted as a young child by my grandpa and was, thus, a permanent family member long before us children came around.

Imagine the housing problem faced with such a huge family sheltering in a congested wing of Pu Hrangaia's house, which was meant to serve as a large Assam-type kitchen for his recently built house. That space and an adjacent room in their main house was where we managed to survive for over a year and a half. As for the sleeping arrangements, there were two double beds that were occupied by my grandparents and parents respectively. There was a single bed on which my younger siblings slept, while the smaller ones somehow fitted in with our grandparents and parents in their beds. The rest of the family slept on the floor, which meant that if one wanted to visit the bathroom at night, one had to carefully tiptoe in the dark through the sleeping figures on the floor. On one such night, when I got up to use the bathroom I noticed a burning ember in the dark. I was frightened at first, but soon realized that it was my father sitting on a chair and smoking a cigarette. Since it must have been well past midnight, it struck me that my father must have had too much on his mind and in his heart for him to sleep. I felt a surge of sympathy as my young mind filled with questions like how often did this happen to my poor father and who were these people who caused him so much pain and woe? Later in life, I learnt more about other issues related to the troubled history of the Rambuai and my father's role in the never-ending negotiations between the Central government and the underground, despite the constant threats to his life. I would often recall that lonely night of his I had witnessed and retained it as an unshared secret for a long time.

Much has been written about the Rambuai, even as more narratives continue to creep out of the woodwork. I don't think I can even begin to describe what life must have been like for the ones in leadership, particularly for my father who somehow kept his sanity amidst the clash of both internal and external conflicts and tensions—within the underground, within his own party and with the government of India as well. It is to his credit that throughout that period, he never brought home political baggage. Our home continued to be full of loud noise and happy laughter with never-ending funny stories that continue to be told to this day.

Never one to say die, Grandpa almost immediately set up shop in the Treasury Square area, not too far from Pu Hrangaia's house, after we moved there. Before long, the little pharmacy began to do good business and Grandpa's already established reputation as a humanitarian and trustworthy compounder continued to grow. I used to enjoy helping out in the small shop during my school vacations, watching life get back to normal and people gradually getting on with their lives again. That was not all—Grandpa eventually organized family and friends to help rebuild his pharmacy at Dawrpui Bungkawn at the same spot where it had been razed to the ground, by salvaging whatever he could from the burnt remains of both the old shop and our house at Sarawn Veng. After Grandpa completed it, half the family moved with him and Grandma to live on the ground floor of the pharmacy. The rest of the family remained with my parents at Pu Hrangaia's house. Everything was makeshift and whatever my family had at that point was shared or given by relatives and other families to us—pots, pans, bedclothes, clothes, basic furniture, etc. The ground floor was small and, therefore, still quite crowded with insufficient room to place beds and other pieces of furniture. I remember there was a large wooden cupboard without doors that served as storage for all the bedclothes during the day and served as a largish bed during the night, when pulled face down onto the floor.

In retrospect, my journey home from school in December 1966 was the start of a different kind of life for me. Spanning the years from my adolescence to teenage years, I grew to appreciate my family more. Though it took some years for Grandpa and my father to initiate building another home for the family at our ancestral plot in Sarawn Veng, the temporary makeshift ones in between were all interesting and happy homes. Though we had so much lesser, materially, we had so much more as the family was together. It was during those times that I learned a sense of sharing and inclusion of those other than family.

The aftermath of the 1966 MNF uprising and the ensuing famine created new social problems, such as the homeless poor and people struggling to put their lives back together after losing everything. Our house, especially the one at Chandmari (before the one that was yet to be built at Sarawn Veng), was like a temporary home for whoever needed shelter and food. One of our neighbours even called our house, disparagingly no doubt, a zawlbuk or male dormitory at the time. To illustrate the variety of house guests we had to put up with I shall share the stories of two of them. A holy man by the name of Pu Chawngkupa would stay for weeks on end before deciding to move out elsewhere, then would come back again when it suited him. He used to take his morning bath at around 3 a.m., after which he would beat his little drum, facing the east and singing praises to God in an off-key and eerie low-pitched voice with a strange pronunciation of words. No one was permitted to complain, laugh or ill-treat him in our house—it was forbidden by Grandpa and my father.

Another one of our more colourful house guests was Kutbuli, which translates to 'one without hands', a condition she said had been caused by burns when still very young. She was a heavy built woman who was homeless after she had left her village to roam and beg in the streets of Aizawl. She used to carry a large em, which is the traditional Mizo bamboo woven basket meant for being carried on the back with a woven strap resting on the head. Her em used to be filled to the brim with her possessions. She was a difficult woman given to angry rantings and foul language whenever she suspected us children of trying to steal something from her. My mother eventually noticed that some of our utensils had gone missing, which were eventually found tucked inside Kutbuli's big em. Getting caught infuriated her so much that she left in a huff, cursing my mother aloud from the road above. Her behaviour was always loud and dramatic. Despite all of this, she was treated well in our house and permitted to sit with us during mealtimes when she would loudly demand that only well-cooked rice be served to her, so that she could scoop it well into her mouth.

These stories make me laugh today when I remember them. I am grateful I got to learn what generosity of the heart meant in our household, thanks to our elders who demanded no less from us children.

Note:

To understand the context of some of the things that I have shared in this brief non-fiction narrative, understanding the meaning of what family meant to us is important for the reader. It goes something like this: my paternal grandfather may best be described as a patriarch and a disciplinarian with some really strong principles that we had to follow and respect, chief of which was total obedience to his word, respect for elders and care for the less privileged. My grandmother did not say much. Her thoughts and fears for the family remained hidden behind her unsmiling face. She was dutiful, the pillar behind my grandfather. My father was an only son whose priority in life since his student days was Mizoram and its future, nothing more, nothing less. There was no room for compromise even when his life was at stake. That was his life, his politics. So how did he manage to still be a good father to such a large brood of children? It was with the help of the team with him—my grandpa, grandma and, of course, my mother. My mother, a slight, unassuming and brave woman, stood with my father with absolute loyalty and devotion—for how else could she have cared for him single-handedly during his eleven-year struggle with Alzheimer's, and in the aftermath of the Rambuai that fell on him during its darkest period, and during the immense task of building a team from scratch for the first Ministry of Mizoram under the status of a union territory (1972–77). Besides all the above, I must also mention the large extended family that lived with us under the same roof at any given point in time, which comprised relatives and non-relatives, cutting across all age groups.

Chronicle of the 'Visibly Invisible':
The Gorkhas in Northeast India

Pratap Chhetri

Lance Havildar Padam Lal Gurung. Rifleman Jaharsing Thapa. Rifleman Harkaman Gurung. Subedar Parmansing Lama. Jemadar Thane Buro Thoki. Rifleman Buddhiman Thapa.

The names ring no bells. History does not remember them. Yet, they did play a role in the grand theatre of history and their names are etched in stone in memorials or cemeteries maintained by the Commonwealth War Graves Commission (CWGC) in France and elsewhere around Europe. They were among the thousands of Gorkha soldiers who died during the First World War—but they were not, as anyone familiar with Gorkhas might assume, from Nepal. Their homes were in Northeast India. This essay is about people like them, who continue to inhabit Northeast India.

The terms Gorkha and Nepali are often used as synonyms, but they are not synonymous. Gorkha is the name of a district and a hill in Nepal from where the kings of Nepal once ruled. There are diverse identities within the larger Gorkha identity, which itself is a small part of the even larger and far more diverse Nepali identity. There are further complexities in the terminology of the Nepali identity. The word Nepali is used in general for speakers of the Nepali language, which includes the citizenry of Nepal and Indian citizens who speak the same language. In recent times, citizens of Nepal have started using the term Nepalese to refer to their nationality, perhaps to distinguish it from the language. Gorkha as a term (spelt by the British as 'Gurkhas') initially connoted the soldiers recruited by the East India Company after the Anglo-Nepal War of 1815. The bulk of those soldiers had links to the Gorkha Durbar in the district by that name in Nepal. The Gorkha identity continues to represent the martial aspect of the Nepalis through the almost 4,000-strong brigade of Gurkhas in the British Army, the seven Gorkha regiments of the Indian Army that have more than 40,000 Gorkhas both from India and Nepal, the small but elite Gurkha contingent of the Singapore Police Force, and the specialist Gurkha reserve unit from the brigade of Gurkhas who guard the ultra-rich Sultan of Brunei.

The Indian Nepali-speakers, to distinguish themselves from the citizens of Nepal, have been using the term Indian Gorkhas or simply Gorkha, more conspicuously after the Gorkhaland statehood movement in the hills of Darjeeling during the 1980s. Further, our ethnic group is also the product of a long assimilation process between two great racial groups—the Indo-Aryans and the Mongoloid Kiratas. The majority of Indian Gorkhas are spread in the northern sub-Himalayan belt, which encompasses Jammu and Kashmir, Uttarakhand, Himachal Pradesh, Darjeeling and its adjacent foothills of north Bengal known as the Dooars, Sikkim and Northeast India. Soldiering was an ancient tradition in these lands. Long before the recruitment of Gorkhas by the British, warriors from these areas were joining Mughal and Sikh forces. Those who joined the Mughal forces were known in Nepali as Munglane, and those who joined the Sikh army of Maharaja Ranjit Singh in Lahore were called Lahure. Even today, people in Nepal sometimes refer to Indian Nepalis as Munglane and Gorkha soldiers as Lahure, irrespective of their homelands or the armies of which they are a part.

It was the same soldiering tradition that brought the Gorkhas to Northeast India almost two centuries ago. The British expansion into the region during and after the Anglo-Burmese War of 1824–26 used a large number of Gorkha soldiers to stave off the Burmese challenge and to colonize and administer the region in the following decades. The Lushai Hills (now the state of Mizoram sandwiched between Myanmar to the east and south and Bangladesh to the west) was one of the last frontiers of British colonization in Northeast India. Even though there had been a punitive mission to the region in 1871–72—the Lushai expedition—it was only after the Chin Lushai expedition of 1889–90 in Myanmar and India that the Lushai Hills formally came under British control. With the setting up of forts at Lungleh (now Lunglei, the second biggest urban habitation in the state) in 1889 and Aijal (now Aizawl, the capital) in 1890 and the stationing of British forces in these places, soldiered exclusively by Gorkhas, our history in Mizoram formally began.

The colonial administration also encouraged the migration of Nepali farmers, herdsmen, wood-cutters and labourers, particularly from eastern Nepal, to kick-start and develop the oil, coal and tea industries in Assam, and forestry and dairy farming in Bhutan, Sikkim and across Northeast India. For the expansion work as well as the smooth functioning of the administrative and military machinery, the British needed masons, mail-runners (known in the Mizo Hills as Dak Pu), chowkidars to man the halts (bungalows), cart drivers, etc. A lot of Gorkhas were hired for these jobs. It was these people and the retired Gorkha soldiers who became the first Gorkha settlers in Mizoram.

My maternal great-grandfather, a rifleman of the then Lushai Hills Military Police Battalion (now the 1st Battalion Assam Rifles) headquartered at Aizawl, was one of those soldiers. Before his retirement, he also saw action in a distant war. Drafted as support soldiers to bolster the Gorkha regiments in various theatres of the First World War, four pre-1917 military police battalions based out of what was then Assam made their way from one of the British empire's remotest corners to the battlefields of France between the late autumn of 1914 and the spring of 1915. They fought alongside those legendary regiments in Europe in that epic war. Great-grandfather was fortunate for he did not end up as a name etched in stone in a faraway land. He returned, but perhaps the traumatizing experience scarred his mind, because he left the Lushai Hills Military Police to take up service as a chowkidar in one of the inspection bungalows of the Raj.

My maternal grandmother's first husband and her brother lost their lives during the Second World War, though they were recruits from Nepal. She was married to her second husband—my grandfather—as a 'parcel' bride. Very often, these simple men—soldiers and labourers—working to earn a living far from home didn't have the luxury of courtships, so their relatives would simply bring them brides from Nepal. Neither husband nor wife would have seen one another before the marriage ceremony. Another uncle from my father's side who died during the Burma Campaign is commemorated at the Rangoon War Memorial.

Some of my relatives still serve in the Assam Rifles, India's oldest paramilitary force. It is an amalgamation of several forces raised by the British in colonial Assam. Other forces such as the Assam Light Infantry and Sylhet Light Infantry eventually became parts of some of the celebrated Gorkha regiments. They were all a part of the various nineteenth-century expeditionary and punitive missions into what was terra incognita for both the British and the Gorkha soldiers alike.

For close to two centuries, we have called this part of the world our home. It is the only home we have and we know. Yet, we are often branded as foreigners; stereotyped as chowkidars, darwans and other menials, and called names such as Bahadur, Kanchha, Daju or dkhars, vais and mayangs—the last three all rather loaded terms for outsiders in the Khasi, Mizo and Manipuri languages respectively. Yet, we continue to live proudly as children of an all-embracing Mother India.

I have realized that developing a thick skin helps in negotiating the insider–outsider complexity. Sometimes, a bit of humour also comes in handy. For instance, a colleague of mine has this habit of saying jokingly that I am the only 'vai' in the office. I shoot back telling him that early historical writings on and about the Mizos refer to only three communities: sap, the English; vai, the plainspeople and the Gorkhas. I also remind him that his surname is a common Kuki, rather than Mizo, surname. He nods grudgingly but takes no exception whatsoever. My work entails using quite a bit of written and spoken Mizo; but having studied Mizo for just two years, I sometimes mistakenly use words with the end letters missing. My diligent colleagues make it a point to iron out these inadequacies and in the process polish my writings. The result of all that editing is that once a state minister remarked to some of my colleagues, 'Your non-Mizo colleague writes much better Mizo than some of you.'

With my ancestors having lived in the hills of Mizoram for more than a century, generations of us have known no home or hearth other than Mizoram. When it first dawned on me that I belonged to a non-indigenous community and was perceived as an outsider, it hurt. But when I look back at my lived experience of more than three decades of navigating the waters of exclusivity, there have been storms—yet my ship sails on, for the welcoming harbours of inclusion are aplenty too; one just needs to anchor at the right spot.

My first experience of 'othering' happened at an age when I did not quite understand what it meant. I was in Shillong, a city that to this day I call my second home. The year was 1987; I was in class four. Waves of communal riots between the locally dominant Khasi tribe and 'outsiders' were targeting the Indian Nepalis and Bengalis of Meghalaya. I was then a student at a now-defunct school run by a Malayali-Bengali couple. As the unfortunate months marked by seemingly endless curfews unfolded, my father could not make it to Shillong to pick me up. Everyone who could get out left; eventually out of the nearly 150 boarders, only me and five other children remained. Then one day I got a bad toothache. A visit to the dentist became unavoidable. The principal, the Malayali husband, had to take me on his Chetak scooter to the hospital. Before embarking on that potentially dangerous trip, he warned me twice, 'If anyone asks you what community you are from, say you are an Assamese. Do you understand? Don't say at all you're a Nepali.'

I nodded obediently. Fortunately, we did not run into any mobs.

It was only years later that I understood what a harrowing time the principal would have had if someone had stopped us and asked me the question 'Hey you, which community?' that I now take pride in answering. Yes, I am a Gorkhali and an Indian Nepali—a fourth-generation Indian Nepali living and working in Mizoram, one of the only three states in India with a tribal Christian majority. I take pride in this because I embody the spirit of India—I represent plurality and resilience. In today's India replete with majoritarian chauvinism, I am a different kind of minority.

One of the many disadvantages of my position became clear to me when I was in class nine. In 1992, the Mizo Zirlai Pawl, the powerful Mizo student body, launched protests in response to the government's allocation of five seats among the twelve MBBS seats allotted by the Central government to Mizoram to non-Mizo students whose parents were serving in Mizoram. The protest quickly took a dangerous turn; to stop it from taking a communal shape, the government cancelled the allotment. The daughter of one of India's most famous IPS officers (now retired) who was then posted in Mizoram was among the five affected non-Mizo students. Rather than relinquishing the seat, the officer flew overnight to Delhi lock, stock and barrel and admitted her daughter to one of India's premier medical colleges there. Years later, I came to know that all that effort, and the precious medical seat, had finally gone to waste: the girl had dropped out of her course. As a young lad of fifteen who had aspired to become a surgeon, the politics of reservation was beyond me; but I grasped the simple fact that I would not get a medical seat.

Two years later, another incident shaped my understanding further. In September 1994, a Mizo was mercilessly murdered in Silchar in the Barak valley of Assam. In retaliation, non-Mizos living and working in Mizoram were targeted by mobs. In a single night, unruly mobs went around town burning down all non-Mizo shops and business establishments. Our little shop survived. It was saved by our Mizo neighbours who did not allow the mob to touch it. I still remember squinting through a small hole in the corrugated iron sheet door of our shop and looking at the mob frenzy unfolding just outside. The next day, fearing that things might escalate, our Mizo neighbours advised us to stay overnight in a quieter place, away from the market area. That night, our refuge was the house of my father's Mizo friend. Our families were so close that his wife even breastfed one of my younger sisters when she was an infant. Both the patriarchs have passed away, but we the present generation continue to nurture the relationship forged by our parents almost five decades ago.

We got nothing but benevolence and unconditional love from our Mizo landlord and his wife too. His property, our rented home, was in a prime location. Many prospective tenants eyed the premises and expressed their willingness to pay much more than what we were paying. Our landlord always turned them away saying we were his family. My father addressed him as Ka Pa (father) and his wife as Ka Nu (mother). Both of them doted on me and my elder sister. They even chose Mizo names for me and my elder sister, and lovingly called us Mama and Mami. We addressed them as Ka Pu (grandpa) and Ka Pi (grandma). We were their tenants for thirty-four years. Long after we had moved to a house of our own, we continued to visit them around Christmas, bearing gifts. We were never sent back empty-handed—cakes or Mizo delicacies would invariably be handed as return gifts.

The greatest gift we received from them was the gift of acceptance.

Usually, Mizo funerals, or for that matter funerals in Mizoram, are very well attended and the photo sessions are an elaborate affair. Once, my father had gone to attend a funeral in the landlord's family.

Seeing my father in the family group photo, a woman asked about the different face in the group, that of my father. Ka Pi remarked jokingly, 'Oh, he is my husband's son from another wife, he is our son.'

In 1966, when Mizoram plunged into insurgency, some Gorkhas supported the Mizo separatist leader Laldenga and his cause. The Mizo National Front supremo is said to have issued special instructions to his followers to not treat Gorkhas harshly. He also issued an appeal to Gorkhas, famed for their soldiering qualities, to join the ranks of the MNF. Some did. Others provided arms training.

That tumultuous spring, there was an air of unease in the small hamlet of Neibawi, known to its residents as Egharah Mel (Eleventh Mile). The settlement comprised about thirty or so Gorkha families, most of them engaged in dairy farming. My grandfather had been transferred to the PWD inspection bungalow there a year earlier. They knew that something was going to happen; Indian Air Force fighter jets had strafed the town of Aizawl, then under rebel control, over seventeen kilometres away. Grandma was cautioning the eldest of her five children to not venture into the forest to collect firewood. Around midday there was a loud commotion and cries of '*Bahar niklo, bahar niklo*' (come out). Most of the menfolk had by then run off to the nearby forest to hide, sensing that either the MNF or the Indian Army would round them up. Only old men, children and womenfolk remained in the village. The heavily armed soldiers from the Jat Regiment who had entered the village collected all the remaining men and forced them to lie down on the dirt track. One of the junior commissioned officers shouted in Hindi, 'Tell us where the MNF people are or we will drive this vehicle over you!' The men explained to the JCO that they were not Mizos, nor were they sympathizers of the MNF, but the JCO and his men still did not believe them. Most of the women and children were crying, but two elderly women stood stout, brandishing kukris.

Suddenly a young Gorkha officer, a major who had just arrived at the scene, rushed forward. He was able to stabilize the situation. The Gorkha officer, who happened to be one of the sons of Independent India's first head of the Assam Rifles, Colonel Sidhiman Rai, explained to the men the gravity of the events that had unfolded in the past week and advised them to leave their homes and move to refugee camps in Silchar.

As soon as he left, some of the Indian Army men went to the area where the women were huddled and tried to pull two young girls away. It was the two old women with their kukris who stood between those men and the girls. The soldiers did not venture further and left after setting some thatched houses ablaze. Once the high-pitched drama was over, everyone gathered around and made plans to leave their houses. That night the men, including my grandfather, came back. News had now arrived that the Indian Army was marching up to Aizawl from Silchar and transport would be provided by the administration to people who wanted to leave. My mother and her siblings, as instructed by Grandma, carried just a change of clothing each, which she bundled up in one of her three saris. The next morning everyone untied their cattle and goats and shooed them into the forests. That afternoon my mother's family and everyone from the village left for Silchar in two trucks, where they would remain for two months. Little did they know the fate that awaited them on their return. Everything would be gone!

About twenty Gorkha men joined the ranks of the MNF in those days, with many more providing logistical support.

The Lunglei Post of the 1st Assam Rifles fell into the hands of the MNF due to the actions of a Gorkha JCO, Subedar Akal Singh Gurung, who was pro-MNF. He and some Mizo non-commissioned officers created confusion among the Assam Rifles troops who thought a ceasefire had been ordered and laid down their arms. As many as seventeen Gorkhas joined the MNF from this unit. Subedar Gurung was later court-martialled and discharged. Man Bahadur Karki (his Mizo name was Zokailiana) was an active member of the MNF and later served with the Z Battalion of the MNF as both the security guard and medical aide of Laldenga. Bal Bahadur Limbu (Zohmangaiha), a jawan of the Gorkha Rifles who was involved in the recapturing of Champhai Post by the Indian Army, helped eighteen captured MNF volunteers escape. He joined the L Battalion of the Mizo National Army, the military wing of the MNF, and was later imprisoned in Aizawl District Jail from 1974–77. Kalu Singh, Nepali vernacular teacher at the Government Mizo High School in Aizawl was invited by Lalnunmawia, the then vice president of MNF to make an appeal to the Gorkhas of Mizoram to join and help the MNF cause. The appeal was made and distributed among the Gorkhas. A 'shoot at sight' warrant was issued against him by the 1st Assam Rifles and he was arrested on 15 March 1966. He was released on 6 April 1967, after being interned in various jails of Assam.

These Gorkhas are hardly mentioned in Mizo writings about the MNF.

It is only recently that interest has been evinced by the Mizo academia about our sufferings. At an International Seminar in 2012 on village grouping during the Mizo insurgency, I was asked by one of the organizers to act as an interpreter as a last-minute arrangement. I agreed to interpret on one condition, that I be allowed to speak about the sufferings of the Gorkhas during the MNF insurrection. There was pin-drop silence in the hall as I recounted my mother's experience of those troubled years. It was a story that no one had heard.

Almost 25 per cent of the Gorkha population did not come back to Mizoram after the insurgency. Most settled in Assam. Almost fifty years later, many of them came to Mizoram to collect documents to prove their legacy during the NRC exercise in Assam.

Before 1966, some localities in Aizawl had a majority Gorkha populace. Even the names would sound alien to young ears. Today's Zotlang was called Sriman Tilla then; Dinthar was Survey Tilla; Tuikual was Gairigaon; Hunthar was Patharkhani; and Vaivakawn was Kasibhanyang. The Lushai Hills District Cover compiled by Major

A.G. McCall during 1938–39 mentions that there was a Gorkha panchayat in Aijal and there was one for 45th Mile Dwarbond Road settlement, near Thingdawl. That settlement was set up by the British to accommodate Gorkha pensioners. Besides these, a lot of Gorkhas were chowkidars in the bungalows that dotted the main roads from Silchar to Aizawl, Aizawl to Lunglei, Aizawl to Champhai and elsewhere.

The population of Gorkhas, which in the 1951 Census was 3,468, increased by only 4,218 people in seventy years, to 7,686—the number of permanent Gorkha settlers as per the Gorkha Census of the Mizoram government in 2021. The growth rate of the Gorkhas has been negligible and insignificant. The Gorkhas of Mizoram are unable to match up to the standards of their Mizo brethren due to their social, economic and educational backwardness, but they have contributed in whatever small ways they can to the state.

Our forefathers pioneered wet rice cultivation in Mizoram. The wet rice fields in and around Champhai town are a legacy of the Gorkhas. Dairy farming is another economic activity that was established in these hills by the Gorkhas. Today dairy farming is an important source of livelihood among the Mizos. Living amicably, we have shared the pain and the angst of the twenty years of strife that enveloped Mizoram from 1966 to 1986. We have equally, too, shared the joys and successes of our Mizo brethren. We applaud the successes of footballer Lallianzuala Chhangte, weightlifter Jeremy Lalrinnunga and hockey player Lalremsiami whenever they have brought laurels to Mizoram.

The majority of us still profess Hinduism. Taking a cue from the organization of the church, we have strangely imitated them. The upkeep and common code of practice for the Gorkha temples is drawn by the Central Gorkha Mandir Committee, much like how the Mizoram Synod administers the Presbyterian Church (the largest Christian denomination in Mizoram). On Sundays, all Gorkha temples organize an hour-long worship service, with separate worship services for children where they are introduced to the tenets and practices of Hinduism. We have introduced the singing of bhajans when vigil must be observed overnight at bereavements and have taken into our fold other noteworthy and unique Mizo funerary practices. An hour-long condolence meeting is held till the shraddh ceremony or chokkhine as we call it. The dead are taken in coffins for cremations and not on bamboo mats. Some of these practices would definitely not have the sanction of Hindu communities elsewhere—but they are our practices, for there is no central authority in Hinduism, syncretism being all pervasive.

The Gorkhas who have settled in the various states of Northeast India have embraced the cultures of tribal societies, so much so that some of them have completely been assimilated into the tribal way of life and culture. Such assimilation is perhaps not seen on a similar scale in other communities who have settled in the region. The result: a Gorkha from Mizoram speaks Nepali with a distinctive and hilarious Mizo tone; the Gorkha lady in Shillong is more comfortable in the jainsem then she is in the phariya sari; without a taste of iromba, for the Gorkha of Manipur, his meal is incomplete. As for the Gorkha from Nagaland, his brethren earned the admiration of the Nagas for the rebuilding of Kohima town in the aftermath of the Second World War and for their contribution to the Naga cause. This is attested to by the fact that the leadership of the separatist government of the People's Republic of Nagaland/National Socialist Council of Nagaland established a 'Gurkha Affairs' desk to look after the affairs of Gorkhas in Nagaland.

In Arunachal Pradesh (when it was still NEFA), in 1962, 200 Gorkha pensioners of the Assam Rifles and their families settled in the strategic tri-junction of India, China and Myanmar, which was then an uninhabited Indian territory and which has today become the town of Vijaynagar (one of the country's hardest areas to reach, requiring a difficult trek of ten days through dense jungles and inhospitable terrain). In some of the present-day states such as Nagaland, Mizoram and Meghalaya, in the early 1900s, Gorkha populations rivalled local tribal populations in what are today the cities and towns of Kohima, Aizawl, Shillong and Tura.

Today, Gorkhas are largely accepted as a part of each state's legacy and history in some form, owing to several factors—cultural, societal, religious and even anthropological. Despite the grudging acceptance sometimes bordering on alienation, the displacements, disenfranchisements, evictions, intimidations and occasional non-existence in government records, their sufferings and tribulations hardly mattered. These were not much documented or known about. Having developed thick skins over the majority–minority discourses, the indigenous and non-indigenous narratives and the migrant–foreigner tags, Gorkhas of the Northeast continue to eke out their existence in the only home they have known. They are the 'visibly invisible'. The stories, experiences and ordeals of the Indian Gorkhas of Northeast India, or for that matter the Indian Gorkhas from the rest of India, have hardly found space or expression.

The stories and tales of the struggles, triumphs and despair of Gorkhas in each of the states of Northeast India have similar strands of exclusion and alienation yet differ in their nature and are unique to each state depending on the relationships Gorkhas have forged with the dominant majority in the region. Except in Assam and Arunachal Pradesh, where they comprise 1.91 per cent and 6.60 per cent of the state population respectively, in the rest of the Seven Sisters, the Gorkhas are a micro-minority. During the pre-Independence era, a Gorkha Brahmin (Bahun), Chabilal Upadhyaya, rose to be the first President of the Congress party's Assam Pradesh unit on its formation in 1921. Gorkhas continue to have political representation in the legislative body of Assam and have even sent parliamentary representatives to the Lok Sabha in the past. In Manipur and Meghalaya, for many years there was one constituency each (Mawprem in Meghalaya and Kangpokpi in Manipur) that generally elected a Gorkha as a member of the legislative assembly of the state. During the union territory-hood of Mizoram, a

Gorkha was nominated as an MLA. But that's not the case anymore in these states.

The redrawing of the Mawprem Assembly Constituency as South Shillong robbed the Gorkhas of Meghalaya of their representation, while in Manipur, the dwindling numbers of Gorkhas in the Kangpokpi constituency perhaps sounded the last bell for the electoral representation of the resident population in that state. It is a population that has been there for well over a hundred years. In 1891, Subedar Niranjan Chhetri, a former British soldier of the 34th Native Infantry, was sent to the gallows by the British. He had joined the Manipuri Prince Bir Tikendrajit in his war against the British.

The only state in Northeast India where Nepali-speaking Indian Gorkhas have a significant political representation is the eighth and last state to become an official part of the region—Sikkim. They form the majority there, and the state has had Nepali-speaking chief ministers for decades. The case of Sikkim and of Darjeeling—which are geographically separate from the Seven Sisters and closer to Nepal—are different, and beyond the scope of this essay.

Sometimes I am forced to ask myself, where, really, is my home? Where do I truly belong? What does the future hold? These thorny questions may never have answers, yet they must be asked.

The question of belonging is a complicated one for my Mizo friends too, as it is for me.

Lal Thanhawla, five-time chief minister of Mizoram and a Congress stalwart, once narrated how he was mistaken as a foreigner at a party hosted by a bureaucrat. His reply to that gentleman's unfortunate question is of great significance. The bureaucrat asked Lal Thanhawla, 'Sir, which country are you from?' Taken aback, Thanhawla replied politely, 'I am an Indian.' Not quite satisfied with the answer, the bureaucrat replied, 'But you don't look like an Indian.' Fuming, Lal Thanhawla shot back, 'So, tell me what does an Indian look like?'

What, indeed, does an Indian look like?

Fashion and Politics: Understanding the Earliest Indigenous Women's Movement in Tripura

Hamari Jamatia

It's the 1980s. A 'housewife' with a sewing machine is a powerful entity. Between cooking and laundry, entertaining guests and supervising children's homework, she seizes moments of solitude to make something of the fabric purchased from months of savings. Under her watchful eyes and nimble fingers, the cloth transforms into blouses, tops and dupattas. These women brought a new word into their households: 'zari'. It referred to the slim embroidered strips of fabric that they bought in rolls from the market. These were sewn onto the arms of the blouses and the borders of the dupattas, which they later matched with the handmade rignai (traditional wrap-around skirt known as mekhla in Assam and gale in Nagaland). The dupatta was gracefully draped around the body like a half-saree when stepping out of homes. The zari came in a rainbow of colours and added bling to the outfits.

At political gatherings, where women participated in large numbers, this '80s' fashion caught up and spread to rural areas. Increasingly, women began to pair the rignai with the dupatta. Alongside slogans for indigenous resurgence, women shared notes on the latest designs and fabrics. The new outfits were a political statement. Tribal women who were earlier mocked as backward and uncivilized were seizing back control of their narratives by dressing as respectable women who stitched together the past and the future with their sewing machines.

Traditionally, tribal women used to pair the rignai with a risha, a long strip of woven cloth, a foot in width, that was used to cover the upper body. It left the neck, shoulders and abdomen exposed and showed off the jewellery—layered coin necklace, broad armband and metal waistband—that glittered and jangled as they moved. As modern colonial conceptions about womanhood made inroads in rural Tripura, women began to change their sartorial choices by covering up in public. During my grandmother's time, it meant donning a cotton collared shirt while visiting the village market where the traders were mostly non-tribals. As soon as she returned from the trip, she would remove the shirt and wrap a risha instead.

In my mother's generation, the cotton shirts of my grandmother were replaced by cotton blouses and matching dupattas. As tribal families began to migrate to Tripura's capital city, Agartala, women began mimicking the ways of the urban space that believed that respectable women must cover up. Hindu tribal women additionally started wearing sindoor, bindi and bangles known as shakha pola (typically worn by married women in Bengal) and started replacing the traditional heavy jewellery with slim gold or silver chains. On the one hand, they saw migrants coming into Tripura as outsiders; on the other, tribal women were imbricating the cuisine, jewellery and womanhood of the former. Simultaneously, many non-tribal families found new favourites in pork, fermented fish and rice wine.

Recalling those days in the '80s, my mother says that the indigenous women's movement of the time brought back dignity to their culture by amalgamating the local rignai with the modern blouse. 'Before we moved to the city and began wearing it to markets and rallies, the urban population looked down upon us. Tribal women, to appear respectable, would wear saris in Agartala. I remember that when I used to go to the markets wearing rignai, the crowd used to stare at me. The women's movement changed that perception.' Tribal women had found a middle path as the Bengali 'bhadralok' culture found its new domain on their bodies. Additionally, the spread of Christianity among tribals created a simultaneous movement for asserting indigenous identity. Christian women not only ditched the saree but also the sindoor and bangles.

I grew up in the early '90s, watching two indigenous women leaders navigate between fashion, kitchen and public life. The first was my mother Pabitra Rani Jamatia and the second was Kripa Rani Debbarma. They, along with a dozen other executive members, operated the Tripura Sundari Nari Bahini (TSNB)—the first tribal women's organization in Tripura that served as both a platform for women's rights and as a feeder for the larger regional party, Tripura Upajati Juba Samity (TUJS). My father, Nagendra Jamatia, was a leader of the TUJS and became an elected member of the Tripura legislative assembly, while my mother was the general secretary of TSNB. Her duties involved formulating meetings, writing press releases, travelling to remote villages and giving speeches at public rallies.

Kripa Rani Debbarma, my mother's senior, was the President of the organization and the first indigenous woman to contest in the general elections in 1983, although she didn't win the seat. I first met her in 1993 when my family shifted to her government residential quarters at Melar Math in Agartala. The quarter was allotted to her husband Harinath Debbarma who was at the time the chief executive member of the Tripura Tribal Areas Autonomous District Council (TTAADC). Yong chwla (older uncle) and Yong Bwrwi (older aunt), as I used to call them, let us use two of the rooms as we didn't have enough money to rent a house of our own. We lived with them for six months.

I was around eight years old at the time and I watched the two women working closely to organize political rallies and conventions. Their political talks made little sense to a young, impressionable girl.

Instead, what fascinated me the most was their obsession with the loom and sewing machine. Whenever my mother and Yong Bwrwi sat down together in the living room, they each held in their hands a ball of cotton yarn and a roll of golden thread. They would intertwine the two so that it could be used to embroider the rignai. They helped each other set up the individual looms where they spent hours weaving the fabric. In those days, there were frequent power cuts in the evenings and plenty of mosquitoes indoors after dusk. Throughout the long hours of 'load shedding', as power cuts were called, the two women would continuously weave.

I believe that they found themselves in a situation where their position as leaders put pressure on them to lead by example. One of the earliest movements that they had fought and won had been to allow girls to wear the rignai to schools and colleges. Earlier, the dress code for girls and women had been the cotton saree. The indigenous movement demanded that tribal women be given the option to wear rignai and dupatta, instead, to keep traditions alive. When the government agreed to the demands, suddenly, there were hundreds of young girls in need of navy blue rignais as a counterpart of the blue cotton saree uniform. As there were no shops for readymade rignais in those days, the mothers of school- and college-going girls had to weave them at home.

Her duties as the primary caregiver to two children didn't allow my mother to enter active politics. Yet, she was a prominent face in the fight for women's rights. In today's world, it may appear paradoxical that a woman fought for gender rights while shunning political leadership, yet we have to understand events based on the social context of the times. In the '70s and '80s, women did not generally contest elections despite every rally and jansabha seeing them participate in massive numbers carrying the mantle of Tripuri identity.

I grew up accompanying my mother to meetings and rallies. Just like at our home, other indigenous homes always had a rolled-up loom waiting for the lady of the house to return and finish the weaving. Though the fabric for the blouse and dupatta came from the market, each woman wove their own rignai on the loom at home. An unspoken competition entered the space as women began to create heavily embroidered patterns that they would later compare at meetings. Before that, the various tribal communities were distinguishable by the colours and patterns of their rignais. Not anymore. The women of Agartala chose a wide variety of colours, and the availability of gold and silver thread made way for more and more elaborate designs.

The legend of Tripura Sundari

Thirty years later I met Yong Kripa Rani Debbarma again while researching for this essay. I had spent most of my adult life out of town and had missed out on witnessing their leadership beyond the 1990s. In her seventies now, she has become frail and has developed a minor hunchback. 'People say the hunchback is a result of years of weaving rignai,' she joked as soon as she saw me. Weaving requires sitting on the floor for hours with one end of the loom tied to the lap. The process requires patience, tidiness and an eye for detail. The arms and hands have to be in constant motion. It takes nearly fifteen days to finish making an intricately embroidered rignai. Yong Kripa was one of the best weavers of her time. As I spoke to her about her journey into activism, it was clear that she still enjoyed the memories of her younger days. She spoke at length about why she joined activism, about her major achievements, and why the TSNB disintegrated.

Tripura's women's movement cannot be understood without the context of its creation. In the early 1900s, Tripura used to be a tribal kingdom with a tribal-majority population. However, the social and political developments of the time such as Indian Independence and Partition in 1947, the Indo–Pakistan War of 1965 and the Bangladesh Liberation War of 1971 led to a large-scale migration of non-tribal Bengalis into the state. According to a report in *The Hindu*, 'Census data shows the population of Tripura's nineteen scheduled tribes dropped from 63.77 per cent in 1881 to 31.78 per cent in 2011. This is attributed to the migration of 6.10 lakh Bengalis—the figure almost equal to the state's total population in 1951—from East Pakistan (now Bangladesh) between 1947 and 1971.'[1] Tribals see this demographic change as a historical injustice caused by a lack of leadership that should have foreseen the situation and prevented it.

By the time the TUJS was formed in 1967, tribals had already become a minority. The TUJS immediately wanted a clear demarcation between 'our people' and 'others', and decided to launch a movement demanding protections under the Fifth Schedule of the Constitution, which later on changed to the demand for the Sixth Schedule. The initial leaders were indigenous young men and women who had studied at schools and colleges and had begun to understand the threat of the demographic shift on their language, economy, land and resources. The tribals were far too illiterate, dispersed and agrarian to stand a chance at gaining admittance to the different pockets of governance. In comparison, the immigrants were more educated and were historically more exposed to trade and national politics, which gave them easy access to administration, police, politics and trade. In such a situation, the early indigenous leaders felt that there was a pressing need to safeguard their identity and culture. They felt that tribal lands must be protected and, therefore, a landmass must be earmarked where land cannot be sold and bought by the migrants. Thus, the TUJS's first demands were related to the implementation of the Fifth Schedule, which would keep the land with tribals. Soon afterwards, the women's wing of TUJS was created. It was deemed necessary that political empowerment must go hand in hand with social change. The main ideas were to promote education among tribal families and to highlight the dangers of drinking in excess, a habit that was prevalent in rural areas.

It was a summer month in 1974, when women gathered at the Tulsi Bati School in Agartala to set up the organization. 'Hundreds of women had come to attend the programme. It was agreed that the time was ripe for women's participation in the overall fight for indigenous rights,' recalls my mother. Accordingly, the name 'Tripura Sundari' was chosen to represent the movement. There is a general perception that the name was derived from the deity that resides at the Matarbari temple in Udaipur, a famous Shakti Peetha. My mother, however, informs me that the name can be attributed to the legend of a former queen of a similar name, who is said to have protected the lands during an emergency. According to the story, a big army was on its way to attack and invade Tripura. Such was the terror of the impending attack that the king fled to save himself. At this juncture, the queen took charge of the administration and decided to lead the Tripuri Army, which eventually defeated its opponents.

TSNB derived its identity from the allegory about how women can be powerful instruments of strength and resilience. They believed that women needed to lead social change since it was they who were in charge of managing the domestic world. This management entailed encouraging families to send their daughters to school, promoting traditional wear, organizing vocational training workshops and raising awareness about the cons of drinking alcohol. Hundreds of women joined the organization formally and informally. It was assumed that the supporters of TUJS, the political wing, were automatically aligned with the women's wing and vice versa.

The rise of TSNB brought to the fore the question of insider–outsider in the state. It was clear that migration would continue and there would be struggles over land and jobs in the years to come. The objective, therefore, was to prepare tribals for the uncertainty and to earmark a portion of land that would be under the sole control of the indigenous people.

The first leaders of TSNB were Pabitra Bakti Jamatia, Bikram Rani Jamatia and my mother Pabitra Rani Jamatia. They were all wives of male politicians and had the privilege of living in Agartala, where they were exposed to local politics. They were literate, outspoken and filled with the fervour of aiding the transition of the tribal society. My mother liked to read and write, so naturally she became the writer of the group. She claims that she used to handwrite all the press releases of the time.

Yong Kripa didn't join the movement, initially. When asked the reason for it, she said, 'I was a young mother with two little sons. My father, of whom I was very scared, forbade me from entering politics as I would end up neglecting the children. I, therefore, chose not to attend the first meeting, although your mother had asked me to.' She couldn't stay away for long. One night, she dreamt of a woman holding a baby in her arms. 'The woman was beautiful, young and was decked in jewellery from head to toe. She stood on the podium of a local landmark called Kaman Chowmuni. Busy traffic was moving all around her. This woman moved her lips and said, "Where should I keep my child?"' Yong Kripa woke up from the dream feeling extremely disturbed. She shared it with her father, who told her, 'You dreamt of an autonomous tribal district for our younger generation to grow up in.' He then allowed her to join the TSNB and she soon became its President.

Soon, my mother and Yong Kripa started working as a team. The two women grew in fame through their involvement in garua meetings, local village-level meetings. They would walk to far-flung villages and organize talks about education, sobriety and the need to safeguard tribal rights. In the '70s, a majority of the tribal population supported the Marxist ideology. The two frail women would visit Communist Party of India (Marxist)-dominated villages to spread awareness about the need for the implementation of the provisions of the Constitution's Sixth Schedule in Tripura. Their political pitch had been prepared: the tribals were insiders who needed to protect themselves from outsiders. To do so, there was an immediate need for the tribal populace to embrace education, promote local culture and support the implementation of the Sixth Schedule.

Yong Kripa Rani was the star orator. According to my mother, she spoke with a lot of grace and conviction, which left the listeners amazed. One time, the two women had to visit a remote village called Tulasikok in the Khowai District to create awareness about the Sixth Schedule. They held a meeting at the village square where a few hundred men had gathered. These men were members of the CPI(M) and were hostile towards the TUJS. Recalling the event, Yong Kripa remembers that the men wore red caps and carried sticks in their hands. 'I leaned towards your mother and whispered in her ear, "We're dead today." I asked her to give the opening speech and told her I would follow next.' My mother acquiesced and opened the meeting. Later, she made way for Yong Kripa to take the mic. Yong Kripa recounts, 'I stood among the men and spoke about tribal unity and survival. I asked them, "Where do you want your children to migrate to if we cannot safeguard our land?" I think it touched a raw nerve because after my speech the gathering agreed to support our demands.' She also added that an old man walked up to her afterwards and touched her feet to pay his respects.

After more than a decade of indigenous movements, the Tripura Tribal Areas Autonomous District Council (TTAADC) came into being on 18 January 1982. The total area of the TTAADC is 7,132.56 square kilometres, which covers about 68 per cent of the total area (10,491 square kilometres) of the state. According to Yong Kripa, this was the biggest achievement of the TSNB as an organization. The women's movement could mobilize ordinary people to unite and create a legacy for future generations. In 1983, she contested the vidhan sabha elections from Simna constituency but lost. She says, 'The seat was traditionally a CPI(M) seat. I contested knowing fully well that I won't win it. But I still managed to get twice the votes that TUJS had got in the previous elections.'

Women's leadership in 1980

Over the years tribals and non-tribals have found a way to coexist with only occasional bursts of communal tensions. There are periods, such as the state assembly elections, when things escalate and both sides avoid venturing into each other's territories for fear of violence. On ordinary days though, we are just average men and women going to our offices, wrapping up our work and making a quick stop at neighbourhood markets en route to our homes. Yet, I do sense that we carry a certain unease in our minds. We can never be sure of when we might be in the wrong place at the wrong time. A scuffle over fruit prices, a rumour of rape or a disagreement over parking can create a spark that could immediately flare up into communal violence. The fear is so widespread that one of my aunts chastised me for returning to Tripura and settling down here. She told me that staying in any metro city would have been safer.

People like my sixty-year-old aunt have been traumatized by something known as '*Aashi saal ni danga*', meaning the riot of 1980— shorthand for the Mandai massacre and its aftermath. It is a topic that is never spoken about in mixed crowds but which breathes and lives among us like a shadow. While growing up, my brother and I were constantly reminded of how dangerously close our relatives had come to dying. If my mother returned from the market without sweets, she would make up a story about how a riot had broken out and she had to rush home. For years, we kids were easily pacified by the tale.

The riot had taken place between the indigenous people and the immigrants in June 1980. It had started on 8 June in Mandai village, where it was reported that 200 non-tribals were slaughtered by tribal mobs.[2] It was a culmination of the resentment over identity and livelihood. According to a report in *The Indian Express*, the riot took 308 human lives and injured 268 in a single day.[3] The planning and execution of the riot were put on the shoulders of the TUJS, as it happened in the aftermath of a strike called by it. In the mainstream media, which had no tribal representation at the time, the riot was presented as an attack by the tribals on the immigrants. Behind the headlines, however, were untold stories of tribal villages being burnt and many indigenous people being murdered as they fled their homes. Indeed, according to the former leaders of the now-defunct TUJS, in the days following the riot, many indigenous men were picked up by the police and either tortured or murdered in custody. Their argument is simple: in 1980, the majority of people in the state institutions—the elected government, the police and the civil administration—were non-tribals. When numbers were so skewed on one side, how could the weaker side plan and execute mass murder? In every riot, it is the stronger population that exploits the weaker one to establish their prowess. Yet, the narratives surrounding the incidents of 1980 didn't question this skewed power dynamic, nor did they involve themselves in ground reporting from far-flung tribal areas where the indigenous people had fled their homes. 'Violence took place on both sides but only we were shown as the perpetrators,' is a common lament among tribals of the older generation.

My father, an MLA at the time, was among those who were arrested in the immediate aftermath. My mother, who lived in the village with her in-laws, had coincidentally come to visit him at the MLA quarters in Agartala just before the riots. When the news of the killings spread, the small population of tribal leaders huddled together, fearing an attack at any moment. In those days, Agartala had a miniscule tribal population. The mob didn't turn up, but the police did and picked up all the men, thereby separating them from their wives and relatives.

My mother was sent to a refugee camp in the capital. Her memories are of the loneliness she felt in the camp despite the place brimming with people. 'The police brought in people from nearby towns who had all been affected by the riots. There were thousands of people sheltered in a school. I was separated from my family for the first time and didn't know if they were alive or dead. I was all alone,' she recalls.

She also remembers that for her first meal, they were served what is locally nicknamed 'frog rice', which is not what it sounds like. Frog rice were rice grains that were so big that they jumped from the plate when poured on it. It is no longer cultivated. 'I wept when I got the rice. It was my first meal after two days. I was young, hungry and habituated to eating rice three times a day,' she said, with the irony of being a rice farmer's daughter. She stayed at the camp for one month as there was nowhere to go. My father was in jail, she received news that her in-laws' home had been burnt and there was no communication with her own parents who lived in a different part of the state.

As the men were either locked away, hiding in the forests or in some cases murdered, the women had to become more proactive in the political field. Pabitra Bakti, one of the founding members of TSNB, called for a women's movement to resolve the situation. By word of mouth, a message was sent out to women to gather at a village called Killa, where they would start an indefinite strike demanding the release of the men. 'There were hundreds of men, including my husband, languishing in jail for two months without a trial. I thought to myself that if these many people are somehow killed, is there any point if my life is the only one that is spared?' In those days, it had become very unsafe to travel during the day, so they would travel on foot at night. In August, about 200 people, mostly women, made it to Killa where they sat on the relay hunger strike at the panchayat office. According to Pabitra Bakti, the CRPF chief stationed at the place was sympathetic towards the group of people and arranged water for them.

Yong Kripa was also present at the strike. She walked for several days to reach the venue on foot. She left a relative in charge of looking after her children before leaving her home. 'My husband was missing at the time. Last I had heard, he and a few other people had fled to Bangladesh to hide. They wouldn't be able to return home till police atrocities were curbed. Hence, I joined my maare (female best friend) Pabitra Bakti at Killa,' she remembers. The hunger strike went on for thirty days in which time more people joined the demand for the release of the men. Towards the end of the strike, when no resolution was made, the group decided to go to Delhi for a solution. 'We felt that the only way forward was to meet Indira Gandhi and acquaint her with the ground reality,' my mother recalls.

So it came about that in October 1980, the two women—Pabitra Bakti and my mother Pabitra Rani, along with two male companions, travelled to Delhi with a memorandum demanding the unconditional release of all indigenous men languishing in police custody. The men had been behind bars for more than four months by then. The two women spoke no Hindi or English but were united in their quest for justice.

On reaching Delhi, they were given accommodation at the official bungalow of the erstwhile king of Tripura, Maharaja Kirit Bikram Kishore Manikya. They stayed there for twelve days waiting for an appointment to see Prime Minister Indira Gandhi but they did not get one. Seeing their plight, a well-wisher shifted them to a Congress youth hostel whose name neither my mother nor Pabitra Bakti can recall. After they shifted there and the PM's office was informed, things changed immediately. Within three days, my mother and Pabitra Bakti found themselves in the office of Indira Gandhi face-to-face with the PM herself. 'She had lost her younger son Sanjay Gandhi four months ago, so she must have been grieving internally but she didn't show it. She was very kind towards us,' my mother says. Since the two women didn't know how to speak in Hindi, they grabbed the PM's palm and wept. 'It was only after we submitted the memorandum that the Centre understood the situation on the ground. Till then all media reports, including those published by international media houses, were presenting the riot as a large-scale violence on the migrant population. After meeting us, they were amazed by how little of the information about us made it to them,' my mother adds.

By the time the two women returned home, all the men had been released from police custody. 'Your father was all smiles when he saw me,' my mother remembers.

Despite gaining popularity in the 1980s, the TSNB dwindled in later years. The TUJS split into multiple regional parties in the '90s due to internal disagreements and TSNB soon followed suit. My mother tried to salvage the momentum of activism by forming an NGO called Hills Women Society, but it couldn't continue for long. The old team members had dispersed and she also lost a close aide to a disease.

Yong Kripa says she is unable to understand why indigenous women are no longer interested in forming strong regional women's organizations like the TSNB. 'Today's women are so educated and intelligent, if they wanted to, they could do so much more than we ever did,' she sighs.

Tripura: A Roadmap for Ethnic Reconciliation

Subir Bhaumik

India's Northeast, once the sprawling eastern frontier of Britain's South Asian empire and now a distinct constituent region of the post-colonial Indian Republic, sits on one extreme of what James Scott describes as the 'Zomia highlands of Southeast Asia'. These lands at elevations above 300 metres stretch from the Central Highlands of Vietnam to Northeast India, encompassing parts of Vietnam, Cambodia, Laos, Thailand and Myanmar, as well as four provinces of China and nearly the whole of India's Northeast. Zomia's more than 100 million residents are minority peoples 'of truly bewildering ethnic and linguistic variety' with a distinct social organization, geographical location, subsistence practices and culture, which have led them to take on states for preserving their freedoms. States want to integrate Zomia peoples and territory to increase their landholdings, resources and people subject to taxation—in other words, to raise revenue. Scott argues that these minority groups are '... using their culture, farming practices, egalitarian political structures, prophet-led rebellions, and even their lack of writing systems to put distance between themselves and the states that wished to engulf them.' Tribes today do not live outside history, according to Scott, but have 'as much history as they require' and deliberately practice 'state avoidance'.[1]

Zbigniew Kazimierz Brzeziński, once US national security advisor and scholar, described this long stretch of indigenous ethnicities from Northeast India to central Vietnam as Asia's 'arc of instability'.[2] The US used some of these battling ethnicities, like the Lahus and the Hmongs, to combat the Vietnamese and the Laotian Communists in the battle for the dominance of Indo-China. Many of these indigenous groups sided with Western imperial rulers against local nationalist movements they saw as majoritarian; some stood aloof from these movements and sought autonomy and institutionalized mechanisms from both the colonial rulers and those leading post-colonial nation-states to protect their unique ways of life. After decolonization, many of these ethnicities have violently challenged the majoritarian post-colonial nation-states in South and Southeast Asia. Often, they have also opposed population flows from more populous communities—sometimes encouraged by the power-holder groups running the nation-states because any large-scale demographic changes tend to lead to much loss of land and livelihoods.

Sometimes, the majoritarian nation-state has used demographic change to control tribal movements for greater autonomy or independence. Bangladesh's military regimes in the 1980s and '90s organized the mass transfer of land-hungry Bengali peasants to the Chittagong Hill Tracts to marginalize the ethnic tribespeople and neutralize their armed insurgency. The peasants were useful as voters in any democratic exercise to undermine tribal preponderance and also provided a physical shield against tribal insurgency.

But in Northeast India, the post-colonial state has been held responsible for the failure to check the flow of both Bengali Hindus fleeing religious persecution in East Pakistan and Bengali Muslims desperate to escape poverty and deprivation and seeking land for livelihood. The ethnic conflict between Bengali settlers and indigenous tribes in Tripura should be seen in this larger regional context and not in isolation. Any effort to find a way out of this conflict should focus on land, much as the problem begins with land—or the loss of it. Indigenous tribals who have lost land to Bengalis, either due to government rehabilitation schemes or due to unequal economic competition, need to be provided alternate lands for the pursuit of livelihoods they are comfortable with.

Since many tribal farmers have managed to succeed as rubber planters under the Left Front's push for such plantations in marginal forest areas, where they were given land rights from the 1970s to the 1990s, the way forward to address tribal angst seems to lie in finding for them adequate lands appropriate for high-value commercial agriculture (not necessarily rubber, with its long gestation period and adverse ecological impact) and then giving them ownership. In primordial agrarian societies, land is not merely an economic livelihood resource, but its possession is often the symbol of the collective.

It may not be easy for any government in Tripura to restore alienated tribal lands from Bengali peasants who now own it. Such efforts by the Left government in 1979–80 led to violent clashes in Teliamura that finally erupted into state-wide riots, leading to hundreds of deaths. It may be worthwhile to explore the possibilities of reclaiming large tracts of fertile land (possibly 45 square kilometres) that may be possible if the 15 megawatts Gumti hydel project is decommissioned. The project produces barely half of its installed capacity but submerges a huge tract of once-fertile land, which, if reclaimed, can be gainfully used to rehabilitate a large part of Tripura's landless tribal peasantry. The symbolic value of the possible re-empowerment of indigenous tribespeople may be strong enough to kick-start a process of ethnic reconciliation in Tripura. But more on that later.

The end of the monarchy

The 1947 Partition left the princely state of Tripura with no choice but to join one of the two post-colonial South Asian nation-states:

India or Pakistan. After much palace intrigue and political activity, the Regent Maharani Kanchanprava Devi, who was running the state on behalf of the minor king, Kirit Bikram Manikya, decided to exercise the Instrument of Accession to join India. Just before Partition, she had gotten wind of a brewing conspiracy to merge Tripura with East Pakistan. An Islamic party, the Anjuman-e-Islamia, led by a rich contractor named Abdul Barik, alias Gedu Miah, had managed to win the support of some leading palace nobles like Durjoy Kishore Dev Barman a.k.a. Durjoy Karta for his plans to merge Tripura with East Pakistan. He had strong support from the Muslim League, which had been bolstered by its effortless takeover of the Chittagong Hill Tracts, despite strong local resistance. But the Regent Maharani Devi moved swiftly to sign the Instrument of Accession that made Tripura a part of the Indian Union on 15 October 1949.

Tripura's merger with the Indian Union opened the floodgates of Bengali migration from East Pakistan that forever changed the demography of the erstwhile princely state, leading to a fierce ethnic conflict that has ravaged the tiny state for more than three decades. Peace has now returned to Tripura after a uniquely successful counterinsurgency campaign in the early part of the twenty-first century. But I will argue that unless social justice on ethnic lines is reinforced by economic development, in which the tribals are stakeholders rather than silent rejects, and their land and livelihoods are restored, tribal insurgency and violence may resurface in the tiny state. Tripura is now a red rag to those who seek to protect the rights of indigenous peoples in India's troubled Northeast. Powerful nativist movements in neighbouring Assam and Meghalaya and elsewhere in the region hold up Tripura's example of demographic transformation to justify their campaign against migration from neighbouring countries. That, in turn, intensifies the nativist-settler conflicts and unsettles the volatile region. So, only if Tripura takes the lead in the restoration of tribal lands and rights and in undoing the marginalization of the indigenous peoples by some innovative sociopolitical engineering, its success in economic development and in providing relatively corruption-free governance will help check the festering ethnic rancour that often explodes into anomic violence.

Twipra, as the indigenous tribespeople of the state call it, means 'land beside water'. In Tripura's days of yore, some of its kings controlled large tracts of eastern Bengal. Maharaja Bijoy Manikya is said to have 'taken a bath in several rivers of Bengal'. So, Tripura's 'Bengal connection' is no post-Partition phenomenon. When the Manikya kings controlled Comilla and parts of Chittagong, Noakhali and Dhaka divisions of contemporary Bangladesh, they ruled over tens of thousands of Bengali subjects. In 1280 CE, following the submission of Ratna Fa to Mughisuddin Tughril, the Tripura kings first invited many Bengalis of different castes to settle in their kingdom.

After the advent of British power, the Tripura kings continued to earn much of the royal revenues from the fertile Chakla–Roshanabad tracts of the Comilla region of eastern Bengal, but their status in that area was that of a tax-paying subject of the British Crown. In Hill Tipperah (whose boundaries are coterminous with that of the present state of Tripura), the Manikya kings were sovereign rulers. For a lot of Bengalis from Comilla who paid taxes to the Maharaja, Tripura was their natural homeland and their move into the hill state from East Bengal (East Pakistan) after Partition was like moving from one part of the royal domain to another part of it.

Further, it was not just for the love of Bengali culture and language or to be able to utilize its potential as the lingua franca between several tribes speaking different dialects that the Manikya kings encouraged Bengali migration into the hill state. Bengalis were also used to organize and maintain the structure of a modern administration and the hardy peasantry of eastern Bengal were issued jungle-avadi leases to reclaim large tracts of the undulating Tripura terrain for wet rice settled agriculture that boosted royal revenues.

This Bengali migration started gathering momentum from the beginning of the twentieth century. The Manikya rulers encouraged selective migration, though Maharaja Bir Bikram did create a Tribal Reserve to protect the land rights of the tribals. Hence, on the eve of Partition, the indigenous tribes of Tripura were not as decisive a majority as the tribespeople of the neighbouring Chittagong Hill Tracts, where Bengali speakers were less than 2 per cent of the population in 1947. In Hill Tipperah, since the end of the nineteenth century, Bengalis accounted for around 40 per cent of the population and the tribespeople were barely ahead as a majority. However, the Partition speeded up the process of demographic change and reduced them to a minority within two decades after 1947.

Demographic transformation

The large-scale demographic change led to severe alienation of tribal lands—starting with the organized rehabilitation of Bengali peasants in not merely flatlands adjoining urban centres but also in hill areas. The tribals particularly resented the loss of flatlands in the foothills where they had moved to settled agriculture by giving up the slash-and-burn jhum cultivation practices of their ancestors. Loss of these fertile lands forced many tribals back to the high hills where their only option was the migratory jhum cultivation, whose yields had started going down due to drop in the 'jhum cycle'. With less land available due to refugee resettlement, the tribal cultivator was compelled to return to the same jhum pasture sooner than before, leading to a drop in productivity. Hence, jhum yields almost similar to those in settled farms in the 1930s had dropped to less than half in three decades. The crises of loss of land and livelihood was further compounded by the loss of political power.

The end of princely rule and the introduction of Indian-style ballot-box democracy left the tribespeople, as they lost out on numbers, facing the threat of imminent marginalization in their share of political power. Forty years after the end of the monarchy, Tripura got its first, and only, tribal chief minister in Dasarath Deb (born Dasarath Debbarma and popularly known as 'Raja Dasarath' in the hills), when the ailing hero of the state's first armed insurrection took over the top job for four years after the Left Front returned to power in 1993. For the tribals, not having their own man at the top and enough of them to run the government added to their insecurity. Their marginalization made Tripura the bogey boy for other states in the Northeast that live in the dread of their indigenous populations being outnumbered and marginalized by East Bengali and Nepali migrants.

The example of rapid demographic change, with which Tripura has come to be associated, finds a parallel in Sikkim, where the Bhutia-Lepchas have been outnumbered by the Nepali-speakers in the last century and the end of royal power has denied them any significant political clout in a post-Chogyal scenario. The fear of a Tripura repeat in their own homelands has inspired powerful nativist movements in neighbouring Assam and Meghalaya. When the CPI(M)-led Left Front first came to power in 1978, the founder of the Tripura communist movement, Biren Dutta, pleaded with the CPI(M) state committee and the party's top leadership to install Dasarath Deb as the chief minister.

But the party's Politburo observer Promode Dasgupta pushed Nripen Chakrabarty to the top job, on the grounds that he was a more experienced administrator and the state was a Bengali majority state. This, in Dutta's opinion, was the 'one big mistake by our party in Tripura'.[3] He argued that had the CPI(M) made Dasarath Deb the chief minister in 1978, it would have gone a long way to assuage tribal apprehensions and would have reinforced their faith in the communist movement. 'Tribal extremism would never have taken off had Deb been made the chief minister and we would have been able to spread the communist movement to other tribal-dominated states of the North-East. But we missed that great chance by foisting Nripen Chakrabarty who was then described by tribal extremists as the refugee chief minister.'[4]

Until the communists came to power in 1978, successive Congress governments had shown hardly any concern for tribal sensitivities. They allowed thousands of Bengali refugees into core tribal areas earmarked by King Bir Bikram Manikya Bahadur as a Tribal Reserve. The tribespeople had good reasons to feel that they were being reduced to 'foreigners in their own land'. In 1943, King Bir Bikram had earmarked 5050 square kilometres as Tribal Reserve; but in 1948, the Regent Maharani's Dewan A.B. Chatterji (vide order no. 325 dated 10th Aswin, 1358 Tripura Era or 1948 CE) threw open 777 square kilometres of that reserve for refugee settlement. Later, more of these areas were opened up for refugee settlement. The pauperization of the tribals can also be discerned in the growing number of tribal agricultural labourers in the three decades since the Partition. In 1951, cultivators constituted close to 63 per cent of the total tribal workforce, while only 9 per cent were in the category of agricultural labourers. By 1981, only 43 per cent of the tribal workforce were cultivators and 24 per cent were agricultural labourers.

But it would be wrong to assume that tribals alone became landless paupers, with their lands taken over by Bengali settlers who grew at their expense—a stereotype that tribal extremist groups seek to create. While it is true that tribals today account for 41 per cent of the agricultural landless labourers in Tripura, the rest are non-tribals, almost wholly Bengalis. The percentage of landless agricultural labourers in Tripura's rural workforce is largely in keeping with the population ratio of the two communities in the state.

While the Bengalis who arrived were accustomed to sharp class differences in their erstwhile homeland, East Bengal, the tribespeople of Tripura were not. At an individual level, the indigenous people lost lands mostly to Bengalis, rich or poor. Studies done by the Law Research Institute in Guwahati in certain areas of Tripura show the huge land loss suffered by the tribespeople at the hands of the Bengali settlers. The study analysed the land transfer pattern in seven 'non-Scheduled' and an equal number of 'Scheduled' areas in south and west Tripura. In the former, 60 per cent of the land transfers were from tribals to non-tribals. In the latter, the position was worse, with 68 per cent of the total land transfers made from tribals to non-tribals.

Of the villages under study, the heaviest tribal-to-non-tribal transfer took place at Hawaibari on the Assam–Agartala Road.

The refugee vote gave the Congress control over the state assembly in the 1970s after Tripura emerged as a full-fledged state following the reorganization of the Northeast after the 1971 war with Pakistan, which led to the emergence of Bangladesh. But they lost the state to the CPI(M)-led Left Front in 1978, which ruled Tripura for ten years. The Congress returned to power for five years only to be voted out again in 1993. The Left ran the state for twenty-five years until it lost the assembly polls in 2018 to the BJP. Like the Congress in 1988, the BJP was helped by a tribal party in 2018. The alliance helped them win most of the twenty seats reserved for scheduled tribes in the sixty-member state assembly and paved the way for a surprise win. So though tribals are now just over 30 per cent of Tripura's population, any party or coalition winning their support secures an edge in the electoral contest.

Tribal insurgency

Under the Left Front's rule, Tripura witnessed two violent bouts of tribal insurgency. The Tribal National Volunteers (TNV) formed in 1978—the same year the Left first came to power in Tripura—pitched for Tripura's independence, unleashing a series of brutal attacks against Bengali villages, killing men, women and children at random. Occasionally, they attacked policemen to loot weapons but more to enforce their writ over large tracts of hill forest land through area domination. The violence was aimed at driving out Bengalis from areas under the newly formed Tripura Tribal Areas Autonomous District Council, which many tribal leaders see as the territorial nucleus of a future separate tribal state.

The fiercest phase of TNV violence was in the run up to the 1988 Tripura state assembly polls when 117 Bengalis were killed in a month. But after the Left Front, blamed by the Congress for failing to protect Bengalis against insurgent violence, lost the elections, the TNV signed an agreement with the Congress-led government of India. The agreement gave tribals three more reserved seats in the state assembly—a total of twenty in a sixty-member house—but little else. The TNV guerrillas who surrendered were promised rehabilitation.

The second bout of tribal insurgency was witnessed after the Left returned to power in 1993. TNV fighters unhappy with the rehabilitation formed the Tripura Resurrection Army, which later broke up and paved the way for a new and deadly group: the National Liberation Front of Tripura (NLFT). One-time left-wing tribesmen formed the All Tripura Tribal Force, some of whose fighters surrendered but the rest remained behind to form the All Tripura Tiger Force (ATTF).

The NLFT and the ATTF unleashed not only violent attacks on Bengali villages but resorted to large-scale abductions of Bengalis—not just businesspersons and professionals but also small traders and farmers. The rampant abductions became a feature of the second spell of tribal insurgency in Tripura. It helped the insurgents raise much in funds for financing their campaign but also ended up criminalizing the movements.

The state's new chief minister, Manik Sarkar, who had taken over from the ailing Dasarath Deb, initially tried to start parleys to bring the rebel groups to the table. But when that did not happen and rebels stepped up their violent campaign, Sarkar resorted to tough policing, authorizing his police chiefs, first B.L. Vohra and then G.M. Srivastava, to take stern action. Vohra initiated a Punjab-style police response to insurgency modelled on the lines of K.P.S Gill; while Srivastava, a protégé of Gill during his Assam tenure, even used surrendered militants to strike at rebel bases inside Bangladesh. Both Vohra and Srivastava went after extremist collaborators, regardless of their political affiliations, to choke the funds and supply chain of the underground groups. The results were immediate, as some statistics from 2003–05 will attest.

The number of extremist incidents fell from 380 in 2003 to 210 in 2004. Civilian fatalities decreased from 205 to 70 and Security Forces

(SF) fatalities from 216 to 105. Terrorist fatalities rose marginally from 61 in 2003 to 63 in 2004. The year 2005 marked a further drop in rebel violence. The January–July period in 2004 saw 31 civilian, 17 SF and 47 terrorist fatalities (total fatalities: 95); the same period in 2005 had 12 civilian, 6 SF personnel and 12 terrorist fatalities (total fatalities: 30).

More crucially, as many as 573 militants surrendered in those two years (2003: 251; 2004: 322). The year 2004 saw the surrender of 72 cadres of the Montu Koloi–Kamini Debbarma faction of the NLFT on 6 May. On 25 December 2004, 138 cadres of the NLFT's Nayanbashi faction subsequently surrendered. The casualties inflicted on the insurgent groups as well as their failure to replenish them through recruitment led to a significant decline in rebel numbers.

In the early 2000s, Tripura had emerged as the 'abduction centre' of the Northeast, accounting for nearly half of all abductions for ransom in the region. But rebel abductions also started to drop as police action intensified—from 542 abductions in 2000, it dropped to 177 in 2001, 159 in 2002, 216 in 2003, to 105 in 2004. By 2012, abductions by rebels were in double figures and nearly non-existent.

Roadmap for reconciliation

Though tribal insurgency in Tripura is now well under control, the movement for a separate tribal state has gained momentum. The growing popularity of The Indigenous Progressive Regional Alliance (TIPRA Motha), which pitches for the creation of 'Greater Tipraland', was evident when it swept the 2021 polls to the Tripura Tribal Areas Autonomous District Council, winning eighteen of the twenty-eight seats. The Tipra Motha is led by royal scion Pradyot Kishore Debbarma. But while the Tipra Motha is not very clear in delineating its 'Greater Tipraland' demand, the creation of a new tribal-dominated state carved out of the present state of Tripura may not be easy and viable. It may also exacerbate ethnic conflict on a scale not witnessed before. So it may be more desirable to initiate a process of ethnic reconciliation by addressing the land and livelihood issues faced by the tribal peasantry. It is in this context that the Tripura government and all political parties need to look at the possible decommissioning of the Gumti hydel project, which will make possible reclamation of a lot of fertile lands for redistribution to the landless tribal peasantry for livelihood.

The project has not only disturbed the fragile ecology of the Raima valley in the south district of Tripura but also left a permanent sense of loss in the tribal psyche. All tribal organizations, including the Communist-backed Gana Mukti Parishad, fiercely protested the commissioning of the Gumti hydel project in the 1970s. But the Congress government in the state crushed the protests. It was determined to augment Tripura's deficit power supply, but it ended up augmenting the catchment area of tribal unrest by dispossessing thousands of them of their only economic resource and collective symbol, their land.

A thirty-metre-high gravity dam, the Dumbur dam, was constructed across the Gumti river about 3.5 km upstream of Tirthamukh in south Tripura district for generating 8.60 megawatts of power from an installed capacity of 15 megawatts. The dam submerged a valley area of 46.34 square kilometres. This was one of the most fertile valley regions in an otherwise hilly state, where arable flatlands suitable for wet rice cultivation are a mere 28 per cent of its total land area. Official records suggest 2,558 tribal families were ousted from the Gumti project area—but these were families who could produce land deeds and were officially owners of the land they possessed. Unofficial estimates varied between 8,000 to 10,000 families or about 60,000–70,000 tribes people who were displaced by the project.

In the tribal societies of the Northeast, ownership of land is rarely personal and the system of recording land deeds against individual names is a recent phenomenon. So, most of those ousted by the

Dumbur dam and the lake it created failed to get any rehabilitation grant and were forced to settle in the hills around the project, returning to practising jhum cultivation. The Left government later announced that all Dumbur oustees, wherever they are, will be covered under the Kutir Jyoti programme. A list of 500 Dumbur oustee families were supplied to the power department. The department has given connections to 114 families who do not have power connections under the Kutir Jyoti Programme. But what these families need more than free electricity is arable land and resources from which to earn their livelihood. The dam destroyed the once-surplus tribal peasant economy of the state.

Tripura's leading economist Malabika Dasgupta has shown in her study on the Gumti hydel project that its 'attempts either to protect the environment to the exclusion of considerations for the well-being of the people or to improve their level of well-being without consideration for the environmental impact of such policies [and] can neither protect the environment nor improve the standard of living of the people.'[5] The Gumti, Tripura's principal river, is formed by the confluence of two small rivers, Raima and Sarma—the former flowing out of the Longtharai range, the latter originating from the Atharamura range. Before the dam, the Gumti flowed southwards through a gorge in the Atharamura range beyond the confluence point of Raima and Sarma. It spilled over a series of rapids, which were locally known as the Dumbur falls at the point of Tirthamukh (literally, Pilgrim's Point), a place considered holy by the tribals and also the Bengali settlers who would bathe in the river during the Poush Sankranti every winter. Beyond Tirthamukh, the Gumti flows westwards up to Malbassa village and then changes direction again, cutting through the Deotamura range. After crossing the Deotamura, it flows for another 60 kilometres before it enters Bangladesh. After flowing for about 80 kilometres through eastern Bangladesh, it joins the Meghna river that flows into the Bay of Bengal.

The upper catchment of the Gumti comprises eleven gaon sabhas—nearly sixty villages in all—in the Gandacherra block of Tripura's Dhalai district. The upper reaches of the catchment area are steep and hilly, located on the east of the river, but as it flows towards Tirthamukh, it is flanked by small flat-topped hills locally called tillas, with many lungas or lowlands between them. And as it comes down to Tirthamukh, the Gumti valley waters huge flatlands all the way along its course into Bangladesh. Before the commissioning of the hydel project, the upper catchment supported a small population of tribals.

The small Bengali population practised wet rice cultivation around Boloungbassa and Raima and some were into trading, while the tribals, originally almost all slash-and-burn cultivators called jhumias, had begun to settle down to wet rice cultivation too, having learnt it from the Bengali farmers. The kings of Tripura had settled some Bengali farmers even in such remote areas to encourage tribals to pick up wet rice cultivation and abandon jhum, which is ecologically damaging. Before the dam, the hills around the present project area were sparsely populated and the area was almost wholly under dense forest cover supporting wildlife.

The *Tripura Gazette* of 1975 talked of sighting 'large herds of Indian elephants in the Raima–Sarma region along with some tigers and bears in the dense forests.' The vegetation was rich and so were the flora and fauna. But after the hydel project was commissioned, not only did almost half of the tribal families displaced by the dam move into the hills in the river's upper catchment area, but the roads built to first transport construction material and then to support the hydel project opened up the rich forests of the area to illegal loggers.

It is my contention that the present ethnic conflict that pits the Bengali settlers against the indigenous tribespeople in Tripura has much to do with the large-scale land alienation of tribals because land is seen not only as the prime economic resource in a rather backward pre-capitalist agrarian society like Tripura but also as the symbol of ethnic preponderance; the psychological alienation of the tribespeople was further aggravated by the Gumti hydel project, which, in one stroke, contributed the most to the ongoing process of land alienation; the project has caused huge damage not only to the ecology of the Raima–Sarma valley but also to ethnic relations in the state; that the project is now a white elephant and can be decommissioned to make way for large-scale land reclamation that can be used to resettle landless tribespeople in a major gesture of undoing injustice.

Why the dam must go

The Gumti hydel project must be decommissioned for several reasons.

The project is now not producing more than 8 megawatts of power from an installed capacity of 15 megawatts even in the peak season when the reservoir is full during monsoon. Experts say the siltation levels will continue to increase and unless the reservoir can be dredged, there will be no rise in output. The power output from this project will progressively diminish. With huge natural gas reserves now discovered in Tripura and major gas thermal power projects already in operation (including one with the capacity to generate 726 megawatts against the state's current peak demand of roughly 320 megawatts), it is a waste of funds to invest in the Gumti hydel project. Tripura also plans to install 500 megawatts of renewable power, mainly solar, by 2030. If the state can produce several times more electricity than it now uses, there is a strong case for decommissioning the dam that will free a huge area for other pressing causes. An ideal power strategy for Tripura would be to produce around 1,000–1,500 megawatts of electricity, feed half of that into the north eastern grid, use 300–400 megawatts within the state keeping in mind the rising demand, and sell the balance to Bangladesh. In the long run, as Bangladesh augments its own power capacity, the surplus Tripura power could be used locally in the event of major industrialization or fed into the regional grid for neighbouring perpetually power deficit states like Mizoram which lacks the gas reserves of Tripura. Since more than 45 square kilometres can be reclaimed from underwater if the Gumti hydel project is decommissioned, a huge fertile tract of flatland would be opened up for farming and resettlement of the landless tribal peasantry of the state. The fertility of this land is likely to have increased after so many years underwater.

Before the dam, this area's fertility was a talking point in the state. After so many years underwater, this is likely to be very fertile. Tripura is a food deficit state and turning this area into a modern agrarian zone will solve the state's food problem forever. Needless to say, the entire tribal landless population of the state, estimated at between 25,000 to 27,000 families, can be gainfully resettled in the Gumti area after the entire land in and around the reservoir area is reclaimed. Each family can be given prime agricultural land. The problem of tribal land alienation can be tackled in one go. The resolution of conflict needs both symbols and substance, and this gesture could provide both. Never before has a development project been dismantled to preserve the interests of the indigenous people. Since this project is proving to be a bit of a white elephant, it is not very difficult to justify its decommissioning in view of its potential to solve the problem of tribal landlessness in one stroke.

If the entire or almost the entire tribal landless population can be gainfully resettled in the Gumti project area, it will free the hilly forest regions from human pressure. Since most of these landless tribals practice jhum cultivation, which is dangerous for the ecology of the hills and the forests, it is essential to settle this entire population in wet plains like the Gumti area. The hills cannot take the high pressure of human settlements that the plains can. So from an ecological viewpoint, the resettlement of the landless tribals of Tripura in the Gumti project area will be welcome. The state's forest cover, now receding, will improve and degraded forests may be turned into gainful plantations by large-scale private investments. The area likely to be reclaimed should be used only for resettling the tribal landless, a compact area in keeping with Maharaja Bir Bikram's tribal reserve concept. This decommissioning proposal should be implemented before ethnic polarization between Bengali settlers and indigenous tribespeople snowballs beyond control.

More than 2,000 dams (mostly small dams like Gumti) have been removed since 1912 in the US alone. Half of those demolitions happened in the last decade.[6] The trend is picking up elsewhere in the West as well. Tripura's present government must consider doing away with the Gumti hydel project too, and as soon as possible. A 2003 study by four American experts has this to say about dam decommissioning:

> In contrast to their larger counterparts, smaller dams are typically older, no longer serve their original purpose, have deteriorated and many (though not all) have reservoirs filled with sediment. Although they store only small volumes of water and sediment, they may impose other ecological impediments on rivers including blocking migration routes and impounding unique habitats. Removal of these structures is often a cost-effective alternative to repair and maintenance.[7]

This policy prescription that is considered relevant in the US will also make much sense to Tripura because the Gumti dam is nearly fifty years old; has outlived its utility because its reservoir is filled with sediments and huge pools of weeds; it can hardly produce any electricity, especially in the dry season when rainfall is not sufficient; many of its reservoir patches are already cultivated by tribal peasants. In the summer of 2012, towns like Udaipur and Sonamura located along the downstream stretch of the Gumti river experienced a drinking water crisis and the lift irrigation projects dependent on Gumti also suffered. An argument has now been made that restoring the normal flow of the Gumti river (that is only possible by decommissioning the Gumti dam) is essential to save the irrigation projects and drinking water projects downstream. If the normal flow is not restored, it will seriously affect agriculture in the Udaipur–Sonamura stretch of the Gumti river.

Becoming Northeast Indian:
The Garo Encounter

Ramona Sangma

The politics of identity and a consciousness of being from the margins is not a recent phenomenon in the Northeast. The geographical isolation arising out of rough and inaccessible terrain, lack of communication, and a general unawareness of the region have contributed to the sense of alienation pervading the minds of the natives of these hills. This alienation has manifested in many ways—a few positively and a good many, negatively. Preoccupations about questions of ethnicity, identity and a sense of belonging and loss have been reflected in the many writings on and from the Northeast. But there have been as many writings on the experience from the perspective of the 'outsider' as well. All are, upon reflection, two authentic experiences and expressions of the same story.

Among the many tribes that dot the entire region are the Garos. Other than the Garo Hills region of Meghalaya, they inhabit small pockets in Assam, Nagaland, Tripura and the plains of Bangladesh. The Garos had a number of sub-tribes as well, with their own variants of the Garo language, but time and proximity between the sub-tribes have rendered these differences obsolete. Only the Atongs and Rugas have been able to maintain a respectable semblance of their own identity, mostly due to the use of their own dialect in areas where they are a majority.

Encounters between Garos and 'others' had begun long before events began to be recorded by British officers and American missionaries in the eighteenth and nineteenth centuries. There were interactions between the tribe and the outside world much before the tribe was introduced to that world by colonial rulers and missionaries as ferocious headhunters. Trading and barter of goods between traders from the plains and the inhabitants of the hills had been established by the Mughal period, but it was not without incidents of kidnapping for ransom or killing at the slightest provocation by the tribesmen. These fierce tendencies were more marked in the Garos of the remote and interior hills, who long remained a nuisance to the British, even as those occupying the more accessible areas adjoining the surrounding plains became far more docile. By the mid-nineteenth century, the British had had enough, and expeditions to subdue the Garo hills were put in motion. By 1873, Tura was established as the headquarters of the Garo Hills District of Assam, and by 1875, the first American Baptist missionaries had arrived and set up camp at Tura.

A Garo Jungle Book written in 1919 by William Carey, often used as a referral guide by scholars on the history and culture of the tribe, gives an unflattering description of the Garos in terms of their physical appearance and their savagery. The title itself alludes to savagery and barbarism,[1] which by all means would have made an impression on American readers back home, eager to hear tales of alien cultures far removed from Western thoughts and ideals. In the book, he recounts the earliest encounter recorded and reported by a British officer, John Eliot in 1789, and published in a volume of 'Asiatic Researches'. Carey refutes Eliot's claims of having met a Garo of the hills and contends that he possibly encountered a Garo along the borders of the hills. He contended that the portrait of the Garo man in the report looked nothing like the Garos he was acquainted with. He looked more like a 'Hindu' person, or a person of mixed blood. While Carey may not have been wrong, and indeed, Eliot could not have ventured deep into the hills without being attacked, he had succumbed to the White man's penchant for painting all natives with the same brush.

There is no Garo stereotype in terms of physical features or otherwise. All Garos don't have small slit eyes. There are as many naturally wide-eyed Garos as there are with single-fold eyelid eyes. Garo noses come in all shapes and sizes. There are tall Garos and short ones. Looks seem to depend more on family than on tribe.

However, the colour of a Garo according to Carey's account is black. There is no description of the variants or shades of black in the book. While the lack of details may be dismissed as an oversight, it certainly does not account for the various shades of fair, medium and dark amongst even those considered the 'purest' Garos with no known history of mixed blood.

In the preface to the 1966 edition of this book by James M. Wood, mention is made of the fact that 'by and large the greater number of Garos do not read English'. To assume as late as 1966, that few 'read English' was similar to assuming that the community had gone no further than when they, the British, had left. But presumptions about the Garos, nay, the entire Northeast, are neither surprising nor unexpected. In the 1980s, a traveller from Garo Hills was asked abroad if she had ever tasted cake. The question came from a lady whose family had a history of connections with Garo Hills during the colonial period. *A Garo Jungle Book* presumably was her education on the Garos. William Carey is certainly appreciated for his early documentation of Garo history and culture. However, like all writings of the era, it is not devoid of White colonialist prejudices that prevailed even amongst the most well-intentioned of chroniclers.

Colonial writings had often been written for the consumption of voracious readers back home who were piqued with curiosity about natives in far-off exotic lands—the more shocking the narrative, the bigger the appreciation for the intrepid writer. The mundane and the ordinary would appear tepid, sans heroism and admiration for the sacrifices made. Considering the circumstances of history and their involvement in the quest for civilizing the uncivilized, the British may be forgiven for their transgressions in stereotyping people unfamiliar to themselves, and for adding a quantum of intrigue in their literature on the natives. On the other hand, the meticulousness of British officers in maintaining records of minute details of their activities, and the activities of natives, is admirable. To a community that relied on orality and word of mouth, these writings, however flawed, are an insight into the mind of the early Garos.

An introduction as a Garo often entails a curiosity about the matrilineal system that our society follows. No discussion on culture is complete without a discussion of the system. Reactions are often varied—some show genuine curiosity, a few snigger, most feminists laud the system and a good number of those belonging to the majoritarian patriarchy find it unimaginable. The intricacies of matriliny practised by the Garos since ancient times are certainly difficult to explain over an hour's sitting, or worse, over a questionnaire with pointed questions that pertain to a single aspect of the practice, to which we are sometimes subjected.

To the uninitiated, matriliny is not the exact opposite of patriarchy. If it were, it would be far simpler. A simple reversal of roles between a man and a woman within the home would suffice as an explanation for the system. Our ancestors thought otherwise, not without reason, and added a good number of conditions for the Garo version of matriliny. Here, it may be added, that like patriarchal societies, there are varied versions of matriliny practised by each society. The crux of the Garo matriliny system lies in the inheritance of property by the daughter rather than the son. It is only natural then, that lineage would follow suit. A Garo child thus writes the mother's family name, unlike a child of patriarchy.

So, the husband switches to the wife's surname as well? This question inevitably follows, not without a tinge of laughter. The answer, more often than not, wipes the condescending smile off the questioner's face. No, he retains his surname and we are addressed in the 'normal' way, much as every married couple is in the known universe.

And the men inherit nothing? Our ancestors were neither cruel nor callous and 'inheritance' in ancient times were homes in hamlets and agricultural land. Land was owned by the community, not individuals, and every household was apportioned a piece of community land for farming. Like the Native Americans believed, homes were neither locked nor bolted, for as the saying goes, nobody stole because nobody owned.

The men went to battle—for we were a quarrelsome tribe, as noted by the British. Their survival was uncertain, and villages would be populated by the elderly, the womenfolk and children. Oral stories narrate how we were once a patriarchal society, till a grand conference was held by the elders of the community, where after many deliberations, it was decided that daughters would inherit property and take care of aged parents.

This narrative is often met with disappointment, especially by curious young millennial listeners. One, because of the drabness and practicality of the reasons cited for switching from patriarchy to matriliny. Two, because 'inheritance' in modern parlance is associated with wealth and vast swathes of profitable property. Three, because there is no romanticism, nor a fantastic, supernatural myth associated with matriliny.

In matriliny, the couple's residency is matrilocal, wherein the man moves into the wife's home, permanently if she inherits property and responsibility, or temporarily if his wife is absolved of duties towards the parents. For an outsider, especially a 'mainlander', this arrangement is unimaginable. It symbolizes the curtailing of the power of the man within the family, it implies power to the woman and an inability to silence her. Here again, the ancestors played a trick. It was, after all, the men who decided the switch from patriarchy to matriliny. And the probable reason would be that in the eventuality of losing a son in battle, the fear of which was real, they would be left at the mercy of the daughter-in-law. They would, perhaps, rather spend the remaining years of their lives in the hands of their own child, a daughter, who had better chances of survival than the sons. The trick was then to ensure men were assured of power within the family. The designated head of the household in a Garo family thus became the man, which, incidentally, is another disappointment to those who assume the women wear the pants.

Ironically, a Hollywood celebrity moving into a woman's home evokes no debate on who wears the pants. On the other hand, a tradition followed by a society in a nook of Northeast India garners questions of power and assumptions based on ill-informed and misinterpreted information. The internet abounds with articles on Garos and their customary practices by scholars and visitors who often spend not more than a day touring villages, conversing with Garo friends, having a drink of the traditional bitchi (rice beer) and then using sparse information to write about practices that are considered unique and quaint.

There are times when questions conjure up scenes from old Chinese martial arts comedies—where a matriarch wields insane power over members of her mob, where the men bow in deference as she walks by, and anyone looking at her in the eye receives a blow and a lash of her tongue. This power imagined by enthusiastic visitors is highly unlikely and rather far-fetched, for the role of a woman in a Garo household is like any other woman elsewhere in the world. She remains a nurturer, a partner to her husband, a nurse to aged parents and a queen in her kitchen.

The curious visitor is unconvinced. Where is his authority, living as he is, under the roof of his wife? Does she dominate? Do men suffer from domestic abuse at the hands of the woman? Can she beat him up? To the last question—the make of a man is no different in any part of the world. It is impossible, and the predicament is the same for all women. They would if they could. If for no other reason than simple exasperation!

The males in the family wield all authority. The brothers and uncles, husbands and sons. The woman traditionally plays the role of caretaker and custodian of family property, and decisions are made on her behalf. An intricate web of checks and balances ensures that collective decisions are made; no single individual wields absolute power. Had there been possibilities of such encounters in the distant past, perhaps the Garos could claim they taught the Greeks a thing or two about democracy.

By now, our guest is confused and flustered. What appeared to be an uncomplicated 'tribal' way of life turns into an elaborate, interconnected mass, like a riddle of tangled wires that lay hidden behind neat drawers beneath our modern-day electrical gadgets. Robbins Burling, an eminent American anthropologist, did realize the complexities of the workings of our society. He lived in a Garo village, participating in the daily lives of villagers and witnessing occasions of joy and tragedy. Yet, it took him a decade to untangle the wires and make sense of how society functioned and survived.

The Garo Hills have had a fair share of tourists in search of a spectacle. There have been visitors, especially before social media became a vital part of our lives, who wanted to visit remote villages to see 'naked people'. Barely a decade ago, one such request was received and evoked amusement at the man's ignorance rather than anger at what might have been perceived as an insult. Needless to say, it is far easier to see naked people on the internet than in remote villages of the Northeast.

The trend of seeking authenticity, and the popularity of cultural tourism in undiscovered lands untouched by modernism, in recent times, have brought a good number of tourists to the region. However, a Garo is yet to learn the art of making a livelihood out of tourism. In the scheme of things that turn the world around, to an ordinary Garo, his guest is king. A tourist is a guest, and so is everybody else outside of his home and village. They are to be treated with respect, offered the best hospitality, and sent off with a full stomach with memories to match. Nobody charges money from a guest welcomed to the home and village. Here, convention, tradition and morality are intertwined in the treatment of a guest.

'The Host'

I will tell you, sister
What happened last night—
At dusk came Babu and a man,
A friend from a faraway land.

Imagine my shock, imagine my shame,
When I realized
That in my home,
That all I had
Was a roll of tamaku,[2]
And pieces of gue.[3]

I saw the look in husband's eyes,
He whispered to my ear—
'Go to the neighbours, borrow a chicken,
Yam from Sarangpa,
Salt from Masin.
You know they owe me some.'

I know they owe him nothing, sister,
But what could I do?
You know how a man says things

To save face,
Even to his wife.

All went well—
We bid goodbye.
You can imagine my relief,
My duty as host fulfilled.

My chickens are growing, sister,
The seedlings are sprouting,
A time will come
When Sarangpa will need some,
When Masin will come.

~

The primary reason why the British found it necessary to subdue the Garos inhabiting the hills was because of the frequent and bloody attacks on the lower hills. Carey describes how bands of armed tribesmen would appear suddenly and swiftly attack, and disappear just as swiftly, leaving bloody and gory scenes of violence behind. When trading commenced between the hill Garos and tradesmen, there were instances of kidnapping amidst fears of traders not keeping their word. These suspicions laid a strong foundation for a turbulent relationship between the Garos and traders from the plains, which, in time, extended beyond trading—leading to distrust and animosity between communities. Over time, with more frequent interactions out of necessity, and gradual intermingling with various communities, both reconciled to the presence of the other. But cultural differences persisted, especially in methods of dealing with differences that inadvertently came about. The general assumption is while a tribal quickly loses patience and resorts to physical action, a non-tribal resorts to trickery and wiles.

The plains at the foothills of Garo Hills bordering Assam and Bangladesh had interactions earlier with communities other than those in the hills. As a result, with earlier access to education and exposure to different cultures, the outlook of those living in the plains, in closer proximity to other communities, was more accommodating. In fact, a certain degree of adaptation and assimilation became inevitable. A fine example would be how in a few places, Garos have adopted and are practicing patriarchy.

Despite dependency on each other, especially in matters of commerce, and the fact that no community can exist in isolation, differences in codes of behaviour, attitude and a general difference in worldviews have led to sporadic clashes in the past. Fortunately, barring a few unpleasant incidents, better sense has prevailed and civil society from both sides has often intervened to maintain communal peace, especially in sensitive border areas.

The equation between major and minor communities in this region is no different from the rest of the country. Tribal communities, however, are significantly more insecure due to the size of their population and geographical territory. The fear of influx is real, of being overpowered by more 'advanced' groups, of exploitation of resources and a dilution of their cultures. These insecurities manifest themselves in many forms— at times, in belligerence or in demands for legislation to protect land and resources.

Land, to the Garo, is central. Its customs, traditions, culture and old religion are based on nature and its bounteousness. It is the fulcrum on which every aspect of the Garo way of life revolves. Loss of land is akin to a loss of identity and possession of it is a matter of pride, akin to wealth and prosperity, irrespective of how fertile or productive the land may be. Rivers, streams, hills, caves and forests are vital to their survival, and threats of dispossession often lead to disharmony. So, when an interracial marriage leads to a non-Garo man having authority over land, especially if his wife is a nokma, or village chief, suspicions are aroused because the attachment to the land is often overpowered by commercial and monetary considerations.

By and large, women are far more agreeable to interracial unions and this becomes a bone of contention between the sexes. Women feel restricted and men consider it a dereliction of duty towards the community. Herein lies the incompatibility between matriliny and ingrained patriarchy, elements of which remain and are often misinterpreted. Matriliny ensures a certain security for women and children. Homelessness on the dissolution of marriage is rare for both the man and the woman, for a man's parental home remains open for the family members as long as it exists. Certain social securities are ensured for both, and it has worked in society's favour since time immemorial.

An honest look into allegations of racial bigotry reveals certain truths about experiences on both sides. Every insider is an outsider somewhere else. Instances of racial assertions are a reality in every nook and corner of the world. The world has become a global village, where every community struggles for a distinct identity, for the preservation of their ethnicity amidst fears of being overwhelmed by larger, more powerful global cultures. In this scenario, being a victim of prejudices has become an ordinary affair.

A person of Northeast origin is distinctively different in looks and demeanour compared to people from the rest of India and he/she is all the more conspicuous outside of the Northeast. Much as we, as a country like to harp on the unity in diversity jargon, the reality is quite something else. There are as many derogatory names Northeasterners have been subjected to, the most common being 'Chinky'; as there are allegations of name-calling in the region against outsiders. Disdain for students under the 'reserved' category is an equally common phenomenon, as are comments on food habits, which are often a result of ignorance. These prejudices have neither helped in bridging the gap, nor have they mitigated feelings of alienation.

During the student agitation against implementation of the Mandal Commission, students from the Northeast, too, were at the receiving end. Students who were admitted under the reserved category were made to feel undeserving of being part of prestigious institutions, with the attitude that they had an unfair advantage over harder-working students or that they were allotted seats on a platter. Funnily enough, nobody cared to explain nor clarify the spirit and purpose of reservations or the constitutional safeguards provided to disadvantaged fellow Indians. It was as if there were multiple Indias—the smaller Indias being insignificant and of no value.

Similar attitudes prevail at the state level in Meghalaya. Lack of opportunities, dependence on the government and intense and aggressive competition for survival have led to demands for a relook at the quantum of reservation for communities. The debate does not end here though. Further down, within the communities themselves, there are allegations of nepotism and the 'creamy layer' using these safeguards to corner undue advantage.

The Northeast experience has undergone a drastic change in the metros over the decades. Students are no longer dependent on the Northeast Railways, which was for long the fastest mode of travel to reach Guwahati and head home. Dependence on postal money orders is a thing of the past; and social media has helped in disseminating better information about the region.

Information on social media, however, is not always accurate. As Garos, we often have to reiterate that we are an unglamorous, unexotic and ordinary people. We no longer practice many ancient traditions, we have adapted to the changing world, and a good many of our people have also become citizens of the world. But social media influencers who occasionally pop in and out of the region prefer to portray us otherwise. Ordinariness neither sells, nor does it garner one million views on YouTube or 10,000 likes on Instagram. So, followers are made to believe we live farther than we do, in the farthest reaches of the remotest corner, wearing the skimpiest of clothes and practicing the most bizarre and ancient of traditions.

Modern-day Garos are highly obliging—their battle-savvy days being a thing of the past. Hence, when a young and popular influencer requests, for example, the staging of an ancient tradition of groom kidnapping, she is instantly gratified. A young woman sets her eyes on a young man and decides he is the one. She informs her father, who in turn gathers the males in the family. They hatch a plan and waylay the unsuspecting young man. The man is kidnapped and brought to the home against his wishes. Intoxicated and badgered relentlessly, he finally agrees to the match and the couple is married instantly.

The narrative is that it is an ongoing practice and is as uncomplicated as depicted. True to expectations, the video collects thousands of views. The influencer has cleverly managed a coup. The British, back during their Raj, had intervened in this practice a number of times, rescuing the reluctant grooms, till they realized the young men required no rescuing. Men were expected to resist matches, they were expected not to give in easily. The harder to persuade, the more the resistance, the higher the respect. The kidnapping is merely symbolic, and all resistance is a pretense. In all probability, the young couple were already in agreement before family members were told.

Social media influencers, however, would hardly include such details in their content, their priority being impact rather than authenticity. The reality is, a Garo wedding is rarely as dramatic and is as ordinary as any other. Marriage ceremonies are hosted by the bride, and in modern times, concessions are made for special circumstances or interracial unions. A successful wedding is one where all guests are fed well without glitches till the last hour. Groom kidnapping was left behind long ago, as a practice that no longer has any relevance to modern living.

The ways of life of the Garo people have changed now, and so have the concerns. The preoccupations of the past are no longer the preoccupations of today. Environmental concerns have taken precedence in recent times. There is a resurgence of pride in one's own culture, and attempts at the revival of dialects no longer in use. These may be interpreted as the positive impacts of education and awareness or as expressions of insecurity over fears of a gradual loss of identity.

It is, in fact, a combination of both. The concerns for environment are genuine—and often, the ones with concern are at odds with those who depend on its exploitation for their livelihood. The plantation of cash crops has not come without a price. It has led to a radical loss of indigenous flora, and along the way, loss of a way of life associated with it, for, Garos by nature, associate culture with natural surroundings. The replacement of traditional architecture with more permanent concrete structures, practical as they are, is also partly a result of depleted forests and difficulty in foraging thatch and bamboo from the forests. The entire region, crisscrossed by water bodies, where the scarcity of water was unknown, is now faced with the constant threat of rains playing havoc with ever-dwindling rivers and streams. Slash-and-burn cultivation practiced by the ancestors is no longer sustainable. It entailed abandoning land after a season of farming for nature to recoup and regenerate. With a growing population, this practice has only deepened the environmental crisis, for land is farmed incessantly season after season at present. Organic vegetables being in vogue, and seasonal offerings from jhum fields better suited to the Garo palate, the high prices of these items are no deterrent to lovers of traditional cuisine. The farmers, thus, find no reason to shift to other less damaging methods.

The question of identity also rears its head regularly. Arguments and counterarguments on who is a Garo do the rounds occasionally. There have been demands to deprive of certain rights those perceived as non-practitioners of Garo culture, particularly those who waver from the matrilineal system. At times, customary rights to property and lineage of the woman have been also questioned, with murmurs to begin a movement to alter them. But Garo customary laws have never been inflexible. Although ancestral property as per tradition is inherited by the daughter, decisions on acquired wealth and property are left to the wisdom of the parents. Identity, however, promises to be an issue that will keep recurring in the future.

The importance given to indigenous people in recent times, by bodies like UNESCO, has also filtered down to this corner of the world. A resurgent vigour in preserving land and culture is palpable among the educated and the youth. The concept of sustainable development, with minimum damage to the environment and agreeable to traditional modes of living, has become a keyword of hope. Yet, there are detractors for whom economic and commercial success take precedence over culture and environment. A conciliatory balance between the two appears to be nowhere in sight. Society, in the past, has overcome similar turbulences, and it is only to be expected that it will overcome this crisis as well.

Northeast India has shown grit and endurance in the face of obstacles it has had to endure. Its sense of nationality has always been as fragile as the 'chicken neck' that connects it to the rest of India. Its history and terrain have both been a boon and a bane.

Like the rest of the region, Garos too, have survived militancy, regional differences and social upheavals. Their experience has been no different from the rest of the region, and much of it has been the consequences of history. There can be no easy answers to what the future holds. Adaptability and reason have held people in good stead over the centuries of their existence. The pace at which society has moved in the past two decades, the evolving mindset of the young, their growing confidence, and the fact that we no longer live in isolation, provide a beacon of hope for the future.

Am I the Insider or Outsider or Both?

Patricia Mukhim

The insider–outsider debate has occupied centre stage in Meghalaya's politics since the state was created in 1972. Before that, while the struggle for a separate state was going on, people were enthused to join the movement because the Assam government led by Bimala Prasad Chaliha had presented a bill to make Assamese the sole official language of Assam on 10 October 1960. The first to protest against that bill was Ranendra Mohan Das, a Bengali and the then MLA from Karimganj North assembly constituency in Assam. His contention (and one can agree wholeheartedly with his argument) was that the bill sought to impose the language spoken by one-third of the population on the remaining two-thirds, a large chunk of which were tribals. Despite protests, on 24 October 1960, the bill was passed in the Assam legislative assembly.

The support of the majority of Assam's MLAs for language chauvinism was undoubtedly intended to appease a certain vote bank—that of the local Assamese majority—but it was also an attempt to send out a message to the Bengali population and, indeed, all the other non-Assamese people that Assam was for the Assamese first—and others had better learn to live with that reality. Naturally, this created political unrest in the linguistically diverse state of which the people of what is now Meghalaya were also a part. Facing blowback in the Bengali-majority Barak valley areas of Assam, the Assam government of the time agreed to include Bengali as an additional official language but found itself in a cleft as there were counter-protests from Assamese-speaking groups opposed to the inclusion, who started a language movement that led to violence and bloodshed in Assam. The Khasi and Garo people were onlookers to all this. Their leaders felt that if they continued to be under the rule of a largely non-tribal government, they would not be in a position to conserve their cultures and traditions despite the existence of the District Council (an autonomous institution created under the Sixth Schedule of the Constitution), which was poorly funded even then, or to be in policymaking and decision-making positions for the welfare of the indigenous tribes. Those were the first stirrings of what then went on to become a non-violent statehood demand movement.

As a child, I recall being taken by my mother for these language protests in Shillong where people shouted slogans of, 'We want Hill State; no Hill State no rest', followed by 'We oppose Assamese'. The Hill State movement that followed led to the creation of Meghalaya in 1972. A few leaders emerged from the movement: people like Captain Williamson Sangma from the Garo Hills and Hoover Hynniewta, H.S. Lyngdoh, B.B. Lyngdoh and S.D.D. Nichols Roy from the Khasi Hills. Many others played their roles in the movement although their names were hidden from fame. They are remembered only by their family members who saw the sacrifices they made. Some of them are alive even today but were not invited to the 50th Statehood Day celebrations of Meghalaya in January 2022.

The Khasi-Jaintia and Garo people who formed the majority of the population of Meghalaya succeeded in convincing then Prime Minister Indira Gandhi to grant them their demand for a separate state. Alas! The demand for a separate state was not based on a vision document. Despite trying my best to get hold of any documents to show what the people then invested their energies and passions in and what it was that the leaders sold them at the time, I could not get any. On 21 January 1972, the Indira Gandhi government at the Centre granted full statehood to Meghalaya. Following that declaration, Statehood Day was celebrated by the leaders of the Hill State movement at one of the best hotels in town then—a legacy of the British—Hotel Pinewood. But beyond that, there was no apparent attempt to think out a roadmap for development or to chart out the trajectory in which the state was going to take off.

Meghalaya is a state blessed with rich natural resources of coal, limestone and uranium. A state with the right kind of economic vision would have first sorted out this aspect. Resources exported out in their raw form add little to the state economy and fail to create employment. Limestone is the raw material for cement and coal for thermal power. But both minerals have long been exported to Bangladesh. Lafarge, the French cement manufacturing company with its base at Nongtrai in Shella, has been mining limestone from Meghalaya to feed its cement company in Chatak, Bangladesh, by way of conveyor belts. Coal, too, was exported to Bangladesh until 2014 when the National Green Tribunal (NGT) banned the dangerous and inhuman rat-hole mining of coal, where young boys are sent down the mines to dig horizontally at the coal seams and put them in carts which are then brought up to the mine surface and loaded in trucks. There have been several instances when mines have collapsed and buried people underneath, but such stories were kept hidden by the mine owners. Since most of the labourers are migrants from Nepal, Assam and Bangladesh, no questions are asked by their poor relatives. They die and get buried under the earth. It was only in 2012 that news reports of mining accidents surfaced in the Garo Hills and the NGT took a closer look at an incident in which thirty coal miners were trapped in a mine and fifteen died. In 2014 the NGT came up with a blanket ban on rat-hole coal mining.

Interestingly, despite the ban, coal continued to be illegally mined and illegally transported and it would be difficult to believe that this could have happened without the connivance of the state authorities. It could not have continued otherwise. The government of Meghalaya took the issue to the Supreme Court seeking that coal mining be allowed as it deprived the state of resources amounting to Rs 600 crore annually. The apex court heard the case and also weighed in the arguments placed by the amicus curiae representing civil society voices from Meghalaya who said that rat-hole mining should not be allowed. The apex court then ruled in 2019 that only scientific coal mining would be allowed.

Meanwhile, in December 2018 another tragic mining accident happened in a place called Ksan in East Jaintia Hills where fifteen people were buried alive. Only one person escaped to tell the story. Due to a petition filed in the Supreme Court by an activist lawyer, Aditya Prasad, the entire state machinery got to work to bring in navy divers and life-saving equipment using Indian Air Force helicopters, but despite much effort only body parts could be retrieved. Finally, the search was abandoned after nearly two months. This saga of coal mining accidents continued but was sought to be hushed up. And since there is such a thing as compassion fatigue, civil society activists who had moved on to other issues did not pursue the other mining accidents so relentlessly. Besides, it had become dangerous for activists to venture into the subject of illegal coal mining after what happened to two local women activists, Agnes Kharshiing and Amita Sangma, in November 2018. They were beaten up mercilessly and left for dead in a forest in East Jaintia Hills for trying to follow the illegal coal mining trail. By sheer providence, a police official found Sangma and later Kharshiing, who had suffered severe head injuries. It has taken her several months in hospital to regain her health.

The lack of vision and apathy towards a well-thought-out development plan is evident from the fact that a cement company created by the then Assam government—Mawmluh Cherra Cements Ltd (MCCL) established in May 1955—which was producing high-quality cement, was allowed to decline until now when it has ceased to function to its optimal efficiency and has to go down the path of a public-private partnership. This is when the private cement companies in the Jaintia Hills such as Star Cement and Topcem cement, among others, are doing brisk business and expanding their areas of operation. But these private companies have learnt to survive in a climate where rent-seeking is part of the system. They pay off pressure groups and anyone who is a threat to their existence and we hear very little about their contribution to corporate social responsibility.

Value addition to the natural resources of Meghalaya happens on a very small scale in the turmeric-producing sector. Lakadong turmeric, which is known to have a curcumin content of 7.9, the highest in the world, grows in Meghalaya. It is only now being branded but its production is still not up to scale. And that's the problem with states like Meghalaya. They need to produce low-volume, high-value products. However, all this needs planning not at the level of the state secretariat but with the people, the growers, the producers and those who package these products. The grower cannot also be the marketing person. But this has been the lot of all farmer-producers here. And a glut in the market as happens from time to time to the banana farmers of Garo Hills, can completely impoverish the farmers.

Yet, these are issues that are not discussed because they don't translate into electoral successes—or so we are made to believe.

The reason why we as a tribal state don't like to put down anything in black and white, could possibly be because we were oral tradition tribes and never had a script until a Welsh missionary, Thomas Jones, gave us the Roman script in 1841. In the Khasi language (spoken by the Khasi-Jaintia people of Meghalaya) there is a saying, '*Shi kyntien, ka hok*', meaning that each word is truth. Once a word is spoken, it cannot be taken back. Perhaps this is the reason why the oral is given primacy over the written.

That brings me to an interesting aspect of this oral tradition. When the Khasi, Jaintia and Garo leaders decided to fight for statehood, they did so under the banner of the All Party Hill Leaders'

Conference (APHLC). This political party was formed in 1960 and was recognized by the Election Commission in 1962. It fought elections in 1969 and in 1972, after Meghalaya was formed. But in November 1976, Late Captain Williamson Sangma, Meghalaya's first chief minister, and a few delegates of the APHLC met at Mendipathar, where they unilaterally decided to merge with the Congress Party and to give a decent burial to the APHLC. They claimed that this was not because of an internal decision but external pressure. Captain Sangma's team then approached the Election Commission to recognize the merger and to derecognize the APHLC as a political party. The Election Commission granted their request. A few leading members of the APHLC, then comprising D.D. Pugh, B.B. Lyngdoh (who was also a lawyer) and P.R. Kyndiah, who later became a union minister and governor of Mizoram, were completely against the idea of the merger and approached the Supreme Court. In a detailed order, the Supreme Court ruled in favour of those who sought to retain the Party and the rose symbol of the APHLC. But the court's remarks were equally interesting: 'APHLC has been recognized as a political party in the State of Meghalaya since 1962. The party has no written Constitution. It is, however, not disputed that the APHLC is a democratically run party. In normal working in a democratic organization, the rule of majority must prevail.'

It is not known how the Supreme Court then, even without a vision statement of the APHLC and without its aims and objectives clearly being spelt out, ruled thus: 'APHLC is a regional party but with high ideals of working out the salvation of the area as proud partners in a larger scheme of advancement of the whole nation without at the same time losing their identity, culture, customs. When a party like this has to disappear from the political scene as a distinct party it is a very grave and serious decision to take.' Finally, the Supreme Court ruled in favour of those who still wanted to retain the APHLC.

My point here is that people are willing to be led by oral commitments even today and don't seek anything in writing. The manifesto is never read. It is word of mouth that continues to prevail, which is why it is so easy to whip up emotions rather than to argue with logic and reasoning. And it is precisely that which has made populist rhetoric more credible than reality. This is the modus operandi used by political aspirants and pressure groups since 1972.

From 1972 to 1977, the leaders who got us statehood never actually got their act together. First, the border between Assam and Meghalaya was not agreed upon as per the North-Eastern Areas (Reorganization) Act, 1971. This issue remains unresolved except for a memorandum of understanding signed on 29 March 2022 between the chief ministers of Assam and Meghalaya to resolve about 50 per cent of the areas under dispute. Settling the border conundrum should have been a priority, but fifty years down the line this matter continues to be a sore point with occasional clashes and violence. Assam has settled Nepali people along the borders, knowing they are intransigent when it comes to ceding space. The Khasi and Garo settlers have retreated from the borders for fear of the intermittent backlash and because Meghalaya does not have police outposts in the borders of West Khasi Hills, Ri Bhoi District or West Garo Hills, whereas Assam has strong Border Police outposts.

There has been little growth worth talking about. Under the Assam government, the educational institutions set up by the missionaries and private individuals, including the government-run Pine Mount school, were educational hubs that people from across the region flocked to because of their excellent standards. Those standards have fallen drastically under the Meghalaya government. Now Meghalaya fares very poorly in terms of education and health, no matter which agency measures these outcomes. Poverty is high at 37 per cent and landlessness has shot up to 76 per cent of the rural populace (Socio-Economic and Caste Census of 2011). Roughly 56 per cent of women in the age group of 19–45 years, which are the childbearing years, are anaemic (National Family Health Survey-5). The nutritional status of children is poor, leading to stunting and wasting. This data is in the public domain as it comes from the National Family Health Survey (NFHS) and the NITI Aayog. Maternal and infant mortality in Meghalaya is only above Bihar at the bottom of the list. The human development indices of Meghalaya, which of course no politician wants to read and take action on, are all terrible. So there's no question of development. Since 1993, the MLA Local Development Scheme, which is today worth Rs 2 crore a year (meaning 10 crores over five years) has been around. But most MLAs use the money at the fag end of their term to entice voters. This money meant to augment water supply, create community assets, etc., is used as largesse. There was an MLA who gave Rs 7,000 per person in a non-farming area, saying it was to purchase cow dung for fertilizing their farms. Some MLAs distribute plastic tables and chairs to the local traditional institutions and some household items to the poor in the constituency. Some political scientists call this practice 'patronage democracy'.

Whichever way we look at Meghalaya, there has been no development except for the Shillong–Guwahati highway and the Shillong–Tura via West Khasi Hills highway that was taken up by the National Highways Authority of India. But even they were able to complete the highway only at great cost, with their JCB bulldozers occasionally being set aflame for not appeasing local groups.

With this sort of development lacunae, there is nothing much that politicians can showcase to the public. In five decades, Meghalaya does not have a single state-owned medical or engineering college or even an agriculture college. The latter was offered to Meghalaya, but as always it was spurned on the plea that 'outsiders' would come in. Then there's also the issue of land acquisition, which has always been the stumbling block to development. Unlike other states, land here belongs to communities, clans and individuals. Over time though, community land has gone into the hands of a tribal elite that now does contract farming and also gets a better price whenever the government needs to acquire land. There's a well-oiled system where people close to the government and even those in government find out which new roads are coming up and where. Accordingly, they quickly acquire land along those areas and when the time comes for the government to acquire land, they sell it at several times the price. In Meghalaya, the cost of land acquisition is far higher than the cost of building a road or infrastructure.

The irony of ironies is that a student's body has been able to hold the state to ransom for over forty years by not allowing the railways to come in. Again, the alibi is that railways would create an influx since most of the labourers would be brought from outside. This also means that the job of porters, etc., is below the dignity of the locals. The only railway line connecting Guwahati to Meghalaya is at Mendipathar in the Garo Hills, where resistance to development plans is almost nil. The unspoken reason for the resistance to railways is the strong truckers' lobby, which has a hold over pressure groups and politicians. No government in Meghalaya has dared to take the pressure groups head-on on this issue for fear of an electoral backlash. In recent times though, some of the local indigenous business persons have wondered why the government does not consider their views while taking a call on whether or not to have the railways up to at least Byrnihat near Guwahati, if not further.

In Meghalaya, projects are never completed on time. Practically, all of them suffer from time and cost overruns but no one is ever penalized. The Central government, as the chief financier, never bothers to audit, evaluate and monitor these projects. A hotel project called the Crowborough Hotel in the heart of the city and bang opposite the old Legislative Assembly building was started sometime in 1988 and completed in 2022, after it had been taken over by the Taj Hotels. Projects are delayed for several reasons, but this hotel project went through litigation where the state government was always on the back foot. Each time someone bid to complete the hotel, the job went undone.

~

Whenever elections arrive there is a general disaffection about the lack of development; but that hardly translates into a language that the common man understands. Hence, emotions are cleverly channeled into something that most Meghalayans have experienced since 1979. The outsider is blamed for taking away jobs, businesses and even land. True, much of the land in the heart of Shillong, in Police Bazar and the British-designated European Ward—an area of about ten square kilometres—is partly owned by the non-tribal business people from the Marwari, Sindhi and Bengali communities. The Bengalis who came to the hills of Assam in British times were brought in by the colonial rulers when they entered these hills after their victory over the Burmese in the Battle of Yandabo in 1826. Those Bengalis came in as clerks from the then Bengal province comprising the present West Bengal and East Bengal, which later became East Pakistan and is now Bangladesh. The offspring of those Bengali clerks became our teachers, doctors, lawyers and bankers and served the state well. But they were also seen as fierce competitors because they were considered 'brainy'. It was not difficult to raise the bogey of hatred against them. Hence, 1979 happened and there was an ethnic cleansing where Bengalis were targeted. There was violence and communal clashes which forced many Bengali families to flee Shillong. The next target of attack were the Nepalese in 1987, but even Biharis and other non-tribals were not spared. Cowsheds were burnt and people were burnt alive.

Whenever I have narrated this part of our history to the rest of the world I have been castigated as someone who has no love or loyalty for her people. The reason it is easy to label me is because my father who never really lived with us and who I knew very little about was an Assamese Muslim. That slur continues to this day when one points out this bitter truth of how non-tribals suffered for no fault of theirs except that they competed to also get a share of the development pie as citizens of the state, having been born and brought up here.

This ethnic tension carried on until about 1994, after which a militant outfit, the Hynniewtrep National Liberation Council (HNLC), was born in the Khasi-Jaintia part of Meghalaya. The Garos had their own outfit called the Garo National Liberation Army (GNLA). The HNLC targeted non-tribal businessmen, who were extorted, and if they did not pay, they were shot in broad daylight. For all the ethnic violence that took place in the state since 1979, not a single person was convicted for the crimes. The rule of law was a grave casualty. No one has so far been convicted for the many killings and kidnappings done by the HNLC, which included police officials. When business persons who were extorted would go to the home minister, then (I would not like to mention the name of this gentleman) he would tell them to negotiate with the militants. It was at that time that the non-governmental organization Shillong, We Care came up and took the bull by the horns.

Shillong, We Care, which I humbly led, comprised a band of brave people who dared to come up and take responsibility for the future of the state. This group comprised doctors, teachers, college students and other concerned individuals. It provided a platform for people to speak up in an atmosphere that had become pregnant with fear and where life came to a standstill after dusk. Members of Shillong, We Care would walk along the Laitumkhrah area and request shop owners to keep their shops open just to create a climate of sanity and normalcy, but they would refuse saying it was pointless to keep their shops open if there were no customers. This carried on for several years. Shillong, We Care requested the police department to put up writings on the wall that said, 'If you are extorted, call 100', across the city. It was just to give a message to the militants that we were not going to take things lying down.

From 1998 until 2015, the HNLC would call a bandh every 26th of January and 15th of August, the Republic Day and Independence Day respectively, and things would come to a complete standstill on those two days. Shillong, We Care decided to break this bandh and walk to Polo Ground where the official function was held. Other politicians who started defying the bandh calls were late T.H. Rangad, MLA of

Laban, and late R.G. Lyngdoh, MLA of Laitumkhrah. They got people from their constituencies to walk with them carrying the Indian flag. This small band of people believed in not being tamed to stay home and cower with fear at the diktat of gun-toting militants. R.G. Lyngdoh as the state home minister in 2000–01 was singularly responsible for being tough against militants by asking those who wished to come overground to do so, while putting pressure on those who decided to remain underground. He cut off their sources of funding by filing FIRs against all those who were suspected to be paying protection money (extortion) to the HNLC. That included most of the shop owners in Police Bazar and Laitumkhrah and also businesspersons. These people were caught between the devil and the deep sea. They all had to seek anticipatory bail and now had an excuse not to pay the HNLC. When the militant group's funding dwindled and they were being hunted by the police, their activities slowed down. Currently, they are reduced to a dozen or so and are in talks with the government. But between 1994 to 2000, they inflicted a body blow to the business and economy of Meghalaya, with quite a few businessmen moving out of the state. Many no longer felt safe to remain in the state or to put up resistance, when the indigenous population itself was silent against militancy, barring a small group—Shillong, We Care.

It is one of the sad commentaries on Meghalaya that there are very few organizations within the once cosmopolitan city of Shillong that are inclusive and provide a non-threatening space for people to voice out their concerns. It is also a fact that the non-tribal population have lived in fear and have not been able to assert their rights as citizens of a free country in Meghalaya. Those who had been forced to move out since the 1979 violence and later carry with them a scar that is difficult to obliterate. They question: 'What did we do to deserve this?' They argue: 'Our parents and grandparents have lived and served the people of Meghalaya without counting the cost. So many students have passed school and college thanks to non-tribal teachers who never treated their students with partiality or favouritism. So why target us?'

These are questions articulated outside of Meghalaya. The atmosphere is still not congenial to pose these questions in Shillong because that might be quickly misunderstood as an attempt of the minorities to claim their spaces in a state that 'belongs' to the indigenous people who fought for it so that they have the ultimate right to rule over it. Interestingly, there were seven open constituencies in Meghalaya in 1972: Mawprem, Laban, Laitumkhrah, Malki, and Shillong Cantonment, all in Shillong, and Phulbari and Mahendraganj in Garo Hills for non-tribal representatives to contest, as these had a sizeable chunk of the non-tribal population. Later, however, these constituencies were delimited in a manner where the non-tribal population is no longer a majority anywhere. So now, other than Phulbari, which has a sizeable Muslim population and still elects a Muslim, non-tribal MLA, all fifty-nine other constituencies are represented by local tribals.

The insidious hate campaign against so-called outsiders and now the demand for the Inner Line Permit (ILP), which could hamper Meghalaya's economy, is being pursued vigorously. The clamour for the ILP rises to a crescendo as we approach the elections and, like waves, settle down once the elections are over. Elections are when the knives are sharpened and differences get accentuated. Pressure groups for the 'Jaitbynriew', people of one ethnic root, with a proprietary claim on 'defending their people's rights' will get busy pushing those claims and raising the electoral pitch. Issues such as the lack of healthcare, educational facilities and the appalling human development indices, which repeatedly show Meghalaya as scoring poorly in maternal health and being one of the states in this country with very high maternal and infant mortality, and the wasting and stunting of children, will be conveniently forgotten. These are times when the patriotic pitch will also rise to ear-assaulting decibels.

Political aspirants from constituencies with a big chunk of non-tribal population go with the promise of protecting them. But no one asks, 'protection from what?' In the five-year course of their tenure, these

MLAs hardly ever publicly speak up for the minorities. They know that doing so has a political cost. The last politician who did that was a veteran and Meghalaya's chief minister in 1979. That man was B.B. Lyngdoh. After him, all others have trodden the path of appeasement politics.

It is no wonder that Shillong is remembered with mixed feelings by those whose families suffered the brunt of the 1979 ethnic cleansing. In 2018, another issue came to the fore—the 'Sweepers' Line' issue. This is a locality inhabited by a population of Mazhabi Sikhs, who were brought to Shillong by the British at a time when sanitary latrines were unknown and dry latrine waste had to be manually disposed of into rivers every single day. The locals would not do that job. These Mazhabi Sikhs were granted a living space by the Syiem (chieftain) of Mylliem in an arrangement with the British rulers. These people have lived and worked in Meghalaya for over a century. Their living space in a 2.5-acre plot next to one of Meghalaya's busiest markets—the Iewduh—had become a sore point. Their population has increased manifold and although the housing was meant only for municipal workers, over the years their adult children and grandchildren who were not employed by the Shillong Municipal Board also found shelter there. This overcrowding was bound to have serious repercussions and health consequences for the space's occupants. The habitation has now turned into a slum and houses the odd troublemaker. It shows the lack of foresight of successive governments in Meghalaya that they never thought of taking a count of the municipal workers and relocating them to a healthier place and asking the other adult dependants to find their own space. Those working for governments, in any case, have to vacate their living quarters upon retirement. The same yardstick should have been used here.

But in the absence of any such strategy, things were left to ferment until an open clash grew out of an argument between a local tribal driver and a young Mazhabi Sikh lady who wanted to bring water from a nearby tap but found a public transport bus obstructing her way because the driver had taken a short break, possibly for tea. His helpers and handyman were on the bus and got into an altercation with the girl. Later, a clash ensued between the driver, his two helpers and the Sikh men who had come to the rescue of the young woman. An FIR was filed by the Sikhs at the local police station but the matter was amicably resolved. But it did not end there. Things took a communal turn because a section of indigenous people took the whole matter as an affront. That was when trouble ensued, parts of Shillong came under curfew, and the internet was shut down.

Now, the government of Meghalaya has worked out a plan to resettle the Mazhabi Sikhs in a housing colony elsewhere. However, the Harijan Panchayat Committee has, in turn, demanded 200 square metres for every family and Rs 20 lakh as construction cost. There are 342 Sikh families numbering to about 2,000 individuals in the present settlement. The Meghalaya government has not given any commitment to that demand and the matter now lies in a sort of limbo but will likely resurface as an important election agenda for all those contesting from Mawkhar North constituency, which is where the area is located and whose inhabitants form a substantial vote bank.

And that's how Meghalaya stumbles from one election to the next, with tall promises made and most forgotten by the first year. This is a state of unequal citizens. If 'othering' means excluding people from the development trajectory that they have a right to, then there are about 90 per cent that make up this 'other'. They struggle to make a living and make ends meet. They are the unfortunate section that are forgotten once elections are done and dusted. They have no voice, and a large chunk of them are women who are single-handedly running a home because they have been abandoned by their partners/husbands. They fall out of the policymaking agenda of the government. In a village called Kharang, nearly all those looking after cattle and sheep are children below the age of fourteen. They dropped out of school because their parents are unable to support them. Mothers still often give birth to seven or more children, as 'family planning' or 'spacing' are alien words for them. Illiteracy and superstition both add to the burden that women carry. These are the forgotten 'others' that we hardly focus on even as journalists. Perhaps, the only time they have a 'voice' and agency is during elections, but then they get paid some cash by candidates to vote and are happy and ready to suffer the consequences for the next five years. Questioning is not something they are taught to do. Women who even dare to talk about politics must remember that they are 'the hens that crow' and, therefore, a bad omen. That's Khasi society's way of shutting up women and putting them in their place. They are a huge constituency and form the bulk of voters but can hardly ever dream of contesting. The sixty-member Meghalaya legislative assembly has never had more than four women at a time, sometimes even less. The women who are elected are either wives or daughters of politicians. Such is the plight of women in a much-romanticized matrilineal society.

When we get down to brass tacks, therefore, many in the present state of Meghalaya suffer 'othering' in different ways, but mostly in having their voices muted. When will this section find its voice? Or will they ever find a voice in the cacophony of contesting voices?

Shillong Girl

Vatsala Tibrewalla

When I am asked where I am from, I unequivocally answer, Shillong. It is a prompt and proud response. More often than not I get a follow-up question or a quizzical glance. 'My family is ethnically from Rajasthan, I am Marwari but I grew up in Shillong,' I always have to clarify. I do not look or sound like I am from Shillong, but I feel that I belong to the city and the city belongs to me. I often wonder if this feeling is enough, and when I do, a familiar knot within me starts to tighten.

My father proudly retains an old letterhead of the first business firm that was set up by his ancestors in Shillong. It reads: 'Established 1881', indicating that my father's great-grandfather migrated to Shillong from Shekhawati in Rajasthan in the 1880s or earlier. Over 100 years later, I was born as a fifth-generation Marwari in Shillong in 1988. My early years were spent in our ancestral home, bang in the middle of the bustling commercial centre of the town, Police Bazar. As was the norm in the community, the gaddi, or 'the seat of business', was situated on the ground floor of the household and the family resided on the first floor. Our immediate neighbours were all Marwaris.

Most of these families migrated to Shillong in the late 1800s. The migration was linked to the establishment of Assam as a separate province of British India in 1874, with Shillong as its capital. The Marwaris have historically been a migratory community whose movements are driven by market opportunities. After the decline of Mughal authority, significant Marwari population shifts happened to British commercial hubs Mumbai and Calcutta in the 1800s. Similarly, as word spread about Shillong emerging as a new administrative centre in the east, Marwari traders sensed business prospects. Fuelled by their spirit of enterprise, they began to trickle into the city. Most families began with government supplies as their primary business. Over time, they branched out into ventures such as automobiles, textiles, sawmills, cinema halls—anything and everything that the new town needed. My family, for instance, started out by supplying food grain, animal fodder and firewood to the government in the 1880s. They branched out to operating movie theatres in the 1960s, wholesale trading of automotive and electrical parts in the 1970s, retail trade of textiles in the 1980s, and hotels and restaurants in the 1990s.

By the time I was born in 1988, India had long been an independent country and Meghalaya had been carved out from Assam as a separate state in 1972, with Shillong as its capital. The late 1980s and early 1990s were a particularly disturbed time in the city's history. An organized and often violent movement against dkhars, meaning 'outsider' in the Khasi and Jaintia languages and used only for non-tribals, was underway. Most of my early childhood memories are restricted to life at home or school with a distinct and all-pervasive recollection of the trouble. To me, a four-year-old child in 1992, trouble meant a city-wide curfew, which, in turn, meant extended school holidays. I barely left the Marwari cocoon of Police Bazar as a young girl, except to go to school. I studied at a Catholic convent in Shillong, and at the tender age of six I was acutely aware of my cultural and religious identity—I was a non-tribal, non-Catholic girl. Tribals consisted mainly of Khasis, a few Jaintias and Garos from other parts of Meghalaya, and some Mizos and Nagas from neighbouring states. Within the non-tribal bucket were mostly Bengalis and a few Marwaris—collectively everyone from states outside of Northeast India. The Assamese and Nepalis were considered to be somewhere in between the tribals and non-tribals.

The school I went to endeavoured to create a non-segregated environment and we were prohibited from speaking anything but English. Ethno-religious differences, however, were very stark as the communities we each came from coexisted in the city but operated within their own silos. The first layer of distinction was based on race, as non-tribals or dkhars were clearly distinguishable by their typically South Asian facial features. The second layer of difference was based on ethnicity—tribals from other states and other regions of Meghalaya were different from the Khasis. Finally, among the Khasis, the majority in the school were Catholics, and based on its ethos of educating Catholic girls, the institution sometimes highlighted this aspect of students' identities. This led to a narrative that was partially based on facts but led to stereotyping: non-Catholic girls didn't study catechisms and weren't called to take sacrament during mass; Bengali girls were known to oil their hair and smell fishy; and Marwari girls showed up with remnants of mehendi on their hands after Diwali. Non-tribal girls, who collectively comprised less than 15 per cent of the class, were generally assumed to be academically inclined and non-sporty. While ostensibly not too much was said, students and teachers alike were aware of the differences. There were invisible lines that separated us and unsaid rules that pushed us to stay in our buckets. We made friends not based on shared interests but on shared identity. Our parents encouraged this and, in some cases, enforced this. Needless to say, most of my school friends in those early years were non-tribals.

For a young malleable child who was just starting to develop her sense of identity, carrying the label of being different was a heavy burden to bear. It was frightening and confusing. It led to an inherent reticence in my personality as I constantly tried to exercise a sense of caution around my tribal classmates and teachers. It was a behaviour I had internalized from my parents' generation, who had been forced to do so while adapting to living through the troubles.

In addition to carrying around the label of being dkhar, I also (literally) stood out. I was distinctly taller than most kids my age—both girls and boys. As a child, already grappling with being called an outsider, this amplified my discomfort as I was not only 'Marwari' but the 'really tall Marwari girl'. I remember walking through the streets of Police Bazar and being looked at with amazement. Passersby would gape at me, laugh and casually remark '*jrong bha*', really tall, to my face. They did that assuming I didn't comprehend the language based on my racial appearance. In reality, I had grown up in Shillong and studied Khasi as a subject! At school, teachers furrowed their eyebrows and sympathetically asked who in my family was so tall, almost questioning what had led to my 'condition'. I grew up with a mild hunch and a severe inferiority complex, even though I did well academically. At the age of sixteen, I left Shillong to join a boarding school in Dehradun. Teachers and students there enthusiastically asked if I played basketball or was an athlete while complimenting my height. I remember thinking back to my early school years in Shillong, where basketball was a sport almost exclusively played by Khasi girls. There were no try-outs, nor any encouragement to experiment; just an inherent selection bias that led to a self-fulfilling prophecy.

A lot of time has passed since my formative years in Shillong, but even now more than three decades later, I feel irrevocably fraught with a nagging feeling of being different—not a good kind of 'different', rather an uncomfortable 'different'. I internalized a cause-and-effect relationship between differentness and discomfort as a child. This feeling sits at the core of the entangled knot, which I have been carrying within me my whole life.

When I visit Shillong now and read the newspapers, I reflect on the usage of the more politically correct term 'non-tribal' (as opposed to dkhar, which has pejorative connotations) and it still feels like a problematic label to me. Why is it then so widely and unabashedly used in Shillong—colloquially, in publications and even government documents?

~

I wonder what previous generations of Marwaris experienced while growing up in Shillong before the trouble began. Did they feel uncomfortably different too?

Curious to find out more about this, I meet with octogenarian Shankar Lall Goenka, a prominent figure in the Marwari community who grew up in Shillong in the pre-Independence years. Goenka's grandfather and great-grandfather first arrived in Shillong in 1872 from Churu in Rajasthan. The family set up a base in Shillong, beginning a grocery supplies business, and went on to establish themselves as highly successful businesspeople and philanthropists. Born in 1935, Goenka, like his predecessors, has spent his whole life building businesses and supporting communities in Shillong. When I ask him about his early years, he speaks fondly of his time in school and college when differences between communities were restricted to small cultural nuances. With a soft manner and twinkling eyes, he tells me that he never felt different from his Khasi peers as a young boy in school and college. He talks fondly of how grand the Diwali celebrations of the Marwari community were in those days and how throngs of Khasis from villages would come into town and participate in the celebrations. He also mentions that areas like the gritty Khasi neighbourhood of Mawlai were so safe back in the day that he and his friends would walk back through the neighbourhood even in the wee hours of the night.

His revelations surprise me pleasantly. The Shillong he grew up in sounds much nicer than the version I am familiar with. Bandhs and shutdowns during Durga Puja and Diwali (important non-tribal festivals) were common when I was growing up in Shillong. Further, being non-tribal and walking through Mawlai was an absolute no-no. In fact, Mawlai still evokes a certain amount of trepidation in non-tribal circles. For as long as I can remember, whenever my family drove back to Shillong from Guwahati, the question of whether to take the route through the interior streets of Mawlai was raised. My father usually said it was all right to go through as long as we kept our heads down and didn't stop. Other friends and family systematically avoid that route into town to date. What happened in Mawlai, I ask Goenka. He sighs and explains that what started with small incidents of stone-pelting had morphed into more serious incidents and the neighbourhood came to be associated with systematic attacks on non-tribals during the peak of the trouble.

When was the first time he felt like an outsider, I ask him. He says it was in 1972, the year of Meghalaya's statehood, exactly a hundred years after his grandfather originally arrived. That year he lost a bid for a government tender even though his rates were the most competitive because they preferred someone local. The hill state movement of the preceding years and its culmination in Meghalaya being carved out of Assam as a separate tribal-dominated state was pivotal. The tribal identity had extended beyond cultural considerations in these hills and been triumphantly asserted politically. As a result, non-tribal communities were made acutely aware that they were not local to the area. He recalls that one of the first violent flare-ups against non-tribals happened in 1979. That's when things felt a bit out of control.

On the face of it, outfits such as the Khasi Students Union appeared to be at the forefront of this organized movement against dkhars. They led rallies and spread propaganda that swayed the sentiments of the masses, but it seems the political machinery was actively working in the background. Looking back at the legislative environment in the 1970s and '80s after Meghalaya was granted statehood, this is apparent. It seems that the violence and societal ostracization had deeper and more systemic roots. In the years leading up to the trouble, first in 1979 (when it was inspired by the movement in neighbouring Assam to evict 'Bongals' or outsiders) followed by flare-ups in 1987 and 1992, there was already a shift in the business and administrative environment. In 1971, the Meghalaya Transfer of Land (Regulation) Act was passed, which deprived non-tribals of the right to buy and sell property. Any non-tribals who wished to engage in commercial activities had to acquire a trading licence from the Khasi Hills Autonomous District Council (KHADC) which, along with the licence fee, meant dealing with layers of red tape. Tribal businesses were exempt from this prerequisite. Further, 80 per cent of the government jobs were reserved for the Khasis, Jaintias and Garos and 5 per cent for other scheduled tribes and scheduled castes, leaving just 15 per cent as the general category that was open to both tribals and non-tribals.

These laws and regulations heavily constrained the ability of non-tribals to secure employment or engage in commercial activity. Moreover, the community was now being physically confined to a few pockets within the city. This was unprecedented, especially for the generation of non-tribals who by then were naturalized citizens of Shillong, and had known no other home in their lifetimes. It was as though the administration had begun to actively restrict livelihood opportunities for them and their future generations. This set the tone for the violent movement that followed in the next decade. The late 1970s saw the emergence of student groups (self-proclaimed NGOs) that championed the tribal cause and demanded stricter enforcement of the new regulations. What began as rallies and demonstrations led by NGOs to mobilize sentiment turned into a savage ethnic cleansing movement.

Considering the diminishing employment opportunities and the targeted violence that followed, masses of Bengalis and Nepalis began to flee (or were made to flee) Shillong. There were a few Marwari families that moved away to Guwahati and Kolkata; however, the community largely chose to remain in Shillong. I ask Goenka if he or anyone in his extended family ever thought of moving and making a life elsewhere. He gently shrugs and says that his roots were already too deep in Shillong and moving was never an option. He adds that Marwari businessmen were entrenched in the local economy and, besides, Shillong was home.

In my quest for answers, I speak to my own father, a fourth-generation Marwari resident of Shillong. Born in 1956, he, too, has spent his whole life building businesses in Shillong.

From what he tells me about his formative years in school in the 1970s, it appears that differences had already become apparent by then. His college friends' circle consisted mainly of Marwaris, and he was not encouraged by his elders to develop friendships outside of the community. He says he had no Khasi friends as that was the cultural norm at the time. With a half-smile, half-frown, he tells me that the infamous (famous, for some) Bull Lyngdoh was his classmate in school. Lyngdoh went on to become the President of the Khasi Students Union between 1984 and 1990 and led the often violent anti-outsider movement that targeted non-tribals. My father adds that Lyngdoh was very meek and humble in school and that he could hardly believe what he read about him in the newspapers. I ask him if he ever felt worried about his future in Shillong and if he considered leaving. He says the only time the thought occurred to him was after he lost his friend Surendra to the trouble.

I now begin to put into context that the same trouble that had meant school holidays to me as a four-year-old was an existential crisis for my father and mother, who as young parents had begun to worry about the future of our family in Shillong. My brother and I were largely shielded from their anxiety and didn't know what was going on in the city, but bits and pieces of news made their way to us even then. Even our parents could not hold back their reactions in certain instances.

I remember my mother receiving a phone call one day and using a phrase I had never heard before. At first, she confirmed multiple times if it was really Surendra, her friend Sangeeta's husband, the caller was talking about. She then looked very pale and kept saying in Hindi, '*Yeh toh anarth ho gaya.*' As a child, I immediately picked up that something serious was going on. More phone calls came in and were made. My brother and I managed to piece together that something bad had happened to our friends' (Golu and Chimpu's) father.

As I write this, I am unable to find a precise contextual translation for the word 'anarth', which literally means disaster. I bring in my mother and we try to come up with an English word that accurately describes what she had meant that day. We go through words such as unimaginable, unbelievable, unfair, unnatural, tragic. In the end, we give up as she sighs and says, 'What happened to Surendra was profoundly wrong.'

All those years ago, I neither knew the literal nor the contextual meaning of the word but even as a child without being directly told, I was acutely aware that the worst possible thing had happened. I remember my heart sinking with fear. Chimpu and I grew up together, never speaking about his father's passing away. As my mother and I revisit our painful memories of that incident, I start to wonder how those who were directly impacted by the violence have been dealing with theirs. I visit Sangeeta Tigrania and her younger son Chimpu, who still live in Shillong and have continued to remain close family friends. I am unable to get myself to ask questions but they are eager to talk. Sangeeta tells me that her husband was returning from a business trip in Guwahati on 6 October 1992 when his car was ambushed by a mob in Mawlai and he was burnt alive. She talks about how her brother-in-law who had been called to identify Surendra at the morgue had returned shell-shocked that night, unable to describe what he had seen until the next morning. When the corpse arrived home she had been warned not to look under the sheet and for years after that, she wondered if that mound of burnt flesh underneath had really been her husband. She looks at Chimpu and tells me that he was only four years old then and was only aware that his father had gone to Guwahati and never returned. A couple of months later, after a trip to Guwahati with his uncle, he came home and asked her which Guwahati his Papa had gone to. 'I looked everywhere, but I couldn't find him, Ma,' he had tearfully lamented.

Exactly thirty years later I sit in Sangeeta's house and sift through carefully preserved newspapers from that ill-fated week. I take in the macabre reality of my childhood in Shillong in black and white. News of road blockades, violence and killings dominate the front pages of *The Shillong Times* leading up to 8 October 1992 and beyond. Surendra Goel's story is one of the most brutal along with that of Gouri Dey, a Bengali woman who was gang-raped and killed in Malki. Several other victims remain nameless—a teenage college student, a gardener, a baker and a whole family of eleven.

Chimpu has recently moved back from Australia to Shillong. I ask him if the culprits were ever found and punished. He shrugs and says the government appointed an enquiry commission but no offenders were identified. Besides, the family was terrified to pursue any legal action. As Chimpu packs the newspapers and a copy of the B.N. Sarma commission report for me in a folder, I ask him why he gave up his cushy job in Melbourne and came back to Shillong. He says, 'My grandfather passed away a few years back and my uncle and aunty have their own life now. I didn't want my mother to be by herself and, besides, our roots are still deep here and this is the only home we know.'

Three decades later, the cruel murder of Surendra still lingers in their lives. Despite having lost a precious family member to violence based on racial identity, they continue to believe they belong to Shillong. It is the same feeling that I have when I think about where I am from—a deeply intrinsic sense of attachment to the city despite all the labels that insinuate that I am an outsider. Assertions about whether one truly belongs to a place are most often based purely on ethnicity. The significance, however, of physically having lived somewhere for an extended period is grossly underrated. The sense of belonging only grows through the generations, as one does not identify with any other place apart from where they were born and raised. Our forefathers at least had physical memories of their original homeland and perhaps were attached to it. A hundred and thirty years later, Chimpu and I know of no other home apart from Shillong.

The quantifiable impact of the trouble was to life and property but a deeper psychological injury pierced through my parents' generation as they lost spouses, siblings and friends to ethnic cleansing. They were targeted because of how they looked and where their ancestors had come from. The trauma was passed on to our generation. The overarching narrative in an average dkhar's mind was and continues to be that as a community we are unwanted and unsafe in Meghalaya.

After the vicious pogrom of 1992, the trouble transformed into a less barbaric version. Curfews and bandhs continued to disrupt the normal functioning of businesses and impact daily lives till about 1995. The late 1990s were dominated by the rise of armed militant organizations, which meant several instances of rampant extortion and kidnappings targeting non-tribals. In 1998, our next-door neighbour from Police Bazar, Gautam, whom my brother and I carpooled with sometimes, was kidnapped on the way to school. Fortunately, he returned home physically unscathed albeit with a great degree of emotional trauma that remains with him and his family to this day. After that incident, I remember a frenzy at home. Overnight, my parents decided to pack off my brother to a boarding school in Bengaluru. Several other Marwari children were sent away too. Others like me who remained in Shillong were sent to school with guards accompanying them. My brother recalls his first year at boarding school with a shudder. He understood why my parents had sent him away, but that didn't make it easier for him to adapt to this massive change as a fourteen-year-old.

The new millennium started with cautious optimism but there was still more to come. I recall a beautiful spring-summer Sunday family picnic by the Umiam Lake in May 2002. My closest girlfriends and I were there with our parents. We had wandered away from the adults as we tried to hunt down touch-me-nots and my friend Kanika's father, Deepak uncle, came looking for us. He'd beamed and said, 'I've found my beautiful girls!' We'd driven back with our hearts full and that lovely feeling had carried on to Monday. At the end of the school day, I felt something was off when I got a message from my mother telling me to go to her friend's place. She said she would pick me up from there. Confused, I waited for her to fetch me. When she finally arrived an hour later, I realized she had been crying. She embraced me and softly told me that Deepak uncle and his brother, Vijay, had been shot! Were they going to make it, I'd asked. She looked to the ground, unable to meet my eyes, and said they were both gone. 'But he was with us just yesterday, Ma!' I had exclaimed before breaking down.

Brothers Vijay and Deepak Chandhoke, non-tribal contractors, were shot dead in cold blood soon after they won a tender to construct a large hospital. Their family believes that was a result of a tribal competitor's wrath against non-tribals securing an important contract. It was almost as if each time the community started to feel safe in our own hometown, we were reminded that fear and loss were always around the corner. After the heart-wrenching loss of their fathers, their teenage children were hurriedly moved to schools outside of Shillong in the middle of a term. Every incident like this had secondary repercussions apart from the primary scathing loss of a family member. The wider implications were always similar—uprooting of children from their hometown, shutting down of businesses, which often led to job losses (even among tribals), and years of lingering trauma and fear for entire families.

Despite the lingering shadow under which I grew up, I am very grateful to have some happy memories of my years as a schoolgirl in Shillong in the mid-2000s. I evolved from a four-year-old sheltered Marwari girl from Police Bazar and slowly started to make friends based on how I felt about people as individuals rather than representatives of racial identities or what my parents thought of them. As trouble eased and incidents became less frequent, the visceral fear that my parents' generation had developed towards tribals started to gradually dilute among my counterparts. I integrated with like-minded tribal classmates and we began to understand each other's cultures better.

Having a more diverse group of friends helped me open up my mind and I began to appreciate that not all tribals were discriminatory and violent. Over time, I also realized that even though our cultural beliefs were varied, our families were more similar than different—everyone had arguments with their siblings and we were all taught what was right and wrong by our parents.

Discriminatory attitudes, however, continued to remain deeply ingrained in our systems. I remember my Mizo friends teaching me the word 'vai' (the equivalent of dkhar in Mizo) and how they used it as a term to describe typical attributes of non-tribals (colloquially, 'That colour is so vai'). As a teenager who was trying to fit in, I embraced the usage of this term myself. The understanding between us friends was that I wasn't dkhar or vai like an average person on the street was. As adolescents breaking barriers, we laughed a lot every time I used the word, not realizing we, too, were perpetuating stereotypes of our own. I felt a misplaced sense of 'cool' as I laughed at my own people—I had gained acceptance.

After 2004, I moved away from Shillong to New Delhi, then to London, and eventually to Singapore. Interestingly, I continued to witness prejudices against migrant communities in every city and country I chose to live in. I experienced being on the other side of the tribal/non-tribal equation while studying at Delhi University, where students native to the Northeast regularly faced racism and ostracization by 'mainland' Indians. The more I moved around, the more I realized how this issue went beyond the non-tribals of Shillong. I felt helpless when the feeling of being uncomfortably different continued to haunt me even after I managed to completely 'escape' Shillong and India. The torment of discrimination against outsiders was also palpable in other countries I had chosen to live in. A majority of the population in the United Kingdom voted for Brexit in 2016 and Singapore imposed draconian measures on foreign residents and workers during the Covid-19 pandemic. It has taken me a while but I have come to realize that the story of the Marwaris of Shillong is not unique by any measure. Every human civilization and nation-state has multiple instances of organized discrimination against non-indigenous migrants or minorities.

As I write this essay in 2022, most of the world has finally emerged from the dark shadows of the Covid-19 pandemic that engulfed us for two years. I live and work in Singapore and am a 'global citizen' of a world where we clarify pronouns and people of colour have systematically been inserted into major television shows and advertisements. The human race has never endeavoured to be as explicitly inclusive as it is now. In this new and woke version of the world, I, too, have made progress by increasing my self-awareness and overcoming deep-rooted biases. Yet, the feeling of being uncomfortably different still manages to catch me off guard every once in a while.

My intention in writing this piece is not to point fingers or blame anyone for what happened in Shillong with the non-tribals. Neither have I touched upon the cultural nuances of Marwaris that make them a closed and conservative community, often not willing to integrate culturally. Hence, I do not seek to have the final word or pass judgement on the issue. I am well and fully aware that all of this is beyond the scope of my writing. I have merely attempted, through my life and experiences, to document yet another tragic story of an immigrant community that has been bearing the brunt of discriminatory attitudes. Further, this is a desperate lamentation about how deep these wounds run in families who continue to experience intergenerational trauma for years after being exposed to violence.

The last fifteen years have passed relatively peacefully in Shillong. The state of Meghalaya has finally begun to achieve its potential as a tourism destination blessed with nature's bounty. Shillong has started to be associated with clear-water rivers and beautiful hilly gorges rather than painted as a place fraught with communal disturbances. This has been a blessing, a virtuous circle for the most part as there is now a real incentive to maintain peace. Unfortunately, the dkhar/non-tribal/

outsider narrative is still widely present in society and it continues to manifest itself leading to occasional flare-ups from time to time. Recent agitations have centred around issues such as the NRC, the CAA, the Inner Line Permit and the issue of unemployment. It is almost always the same story—there is a public rally or demonstration followed by random acts of violence, which lead to shutdowns and curfews till tensions subside. The only saving grace is that these occurrences have been less frequent and fewer lives have been lost in recent years.

It is a cold and grey October afternoon in Shillong as I write this. I am ready to leave home to interview a Marwari senior citizen when I am firmly stopped by my mother. She says she just received a frantic call from a family friend saying there is trouble brewing in Police Bazar. Upon enquiring further, my mother's friend nonchalantly tells us that the flare-up was due to a rally over unemployment and was organized by one of the so-called NGOs. She adds that when this sort of thing happens it is common for people on the street, usually dkhars, to be randomly assaulted. Maybe some cars will be burnt too. Impatient to complete my interview and used to such flare-ups, I insist that things will be all right and coax my mother to let me go. As I leave the front door, I decide to quickly double-check with another cousin who lives and works in Police Bazar. He confirms that the police came around and asked shops to shut down, and warns that I better steer clear of the area. He sternly adds that for now, things may seem to have settled down, but when something goes awry, it happens in moments. That can be the difference between life and death. Stunned, I return indoors. The familiar knot within me returns too.

A Doubtful Existence

Abhishek Saha

My eighty-year-old paternal grandmother, a Partition refugee, is out of Assam's NRC. As communal and gendered violence raged during the division of the British Indian Empire into India and Pakistan in 1947, especially on the western frontier of Punjab, millions were forced to move in search of a haven. In 1949, faced with an uncertain future in the Muslim-majority East Pakistan and the looming threat of violence, her family migrated from Mymensingh to Assam. Today, whenever Thakuma[1] looks back at her life, the word 'deshbhag'—division of the country—becomes an important yardstick. If I ask her, say, about her teenage years or her marriage or some of her relatives, Thakuma often relies on phrases like '*deshbhag er aage ...*' or '*deshbhag er pore ...*'— before or after Partition—to explain the specifics of her stories and emphasize the everlasting effect that Cyril Radcliffe's lines had on her and millions of others.

The preparation of the NRC was an unprecedented exercise of asking 3.3 crore residents of Assam to prove their Indian citizenship, based on lineage, through documents and oral testimonies. The process, monitored by the Supreme Court, asked the state's residents to prove that they or their ancestors were residing in Assam (or India, and not the territory that is today Bangladesh) before the cut-off date of 25 March 1971. The anthropologist Nayanika Mathur has called the Assam NRC 'a first in the history of modern nation-states anywhere in the world'. The exercise cost the government exchequer Rs 1,600 crore. When it was finally published in August 2019, the NRC ended up stripping over 19 lakh people—including 7 lakh Muslims and 5 lakh Bengali Hindus, as per Assam government estimates—of their Indian citizenship.[2]

Technically, the current NRC is an update of the one prepared in 1951 in Assam. But the old one was significantly different from the one put out in 2019, both in the method by which it was prepared and in its purpose. The 1951 NRC was based on that year's Census, which was Independent India's first. It was prepared by transcribing and collating the information collected during the Census in Assam from census slips and was completed in just twenty days, between 9 February to 28 February 1951. It was not foreseen that this would become a citizenship record.

In the 1951 NRC, Thakuma's name appeared alongside those of her siblings. Subsequently, the electoral roll of 1965 denotes her as a twenty-four-year-old resident. Yet, in 1997, amidst speculations of many 'foreigners' hoodwinking their way into electoral rolls of Assam and widespread demands for the revision of the same, Thakuma was one among lakhs to be marked 'Doubtful Voter' or D-voter by local election officials across the state—even as all other eligible voters in our family remained bona fide Indians. Why did it happen? I haven't found a satisfactory answer till date. My father and others in the family struggled to ascribe a particular reason for Thakuma being denoted as a doubtful voter. My Right to Information query to the Election Commission in 2019 yielded a response from district officials in Barpeta that there is no concrete information on why she was marked as 'Doubtful'.

Thakuma hasn't been able to cast her vote since that 'D' was put against her name on the voters' list. But such is the opacity and inefficiency of the system that in the last two-and-a-half decades, Thakuma has never been summoned by a Foreigners Tribunal (FT) to appear and prove her Indian citizenship—as is the expected process—thereby keeping her status in limbo. Moreover, because she is a D-voter, she has been automatically excluded from the NRC published in 2019. And such is the entangled mesh of Assam's citizenship determination exercises, that as someone who had objected against her exclusion in the draft NRC, Thakuma had to submit her biometrics to the state. Now, the biometric data is locked, effectively barring her from applying for an Aadhaar card till her citizenship status is cleared. Hence, today, she doesn't have a voter ID card or an Aadhaar card—both essential documents. She faces a rising wall of bureaucratic red tape in interactions with the government, as all services are increasingly linked to the Aadhaar system.

My grandmother's case is hardly unique. There are allegations by numerous Bengali Hindus, Bengali-origin Muslims ('Miya' Muslims) and Nepalis that people from their communities have been marked 'D' for no known reason. For instance, Durga Khatiwada, a Nepali writer and Sahitya Akademi award winner, was marked 'D' in the late 1990s, only to be declared an Indian by an FT in 2015. Shah Alam Bhuyan, an Assam police personnel, was marked 'D' in 1997 and later certified to be an Indian in 2017. A series of RTI queries filed by a Barpeta-based activist in 2019 led to the revelation that for at least thirty-six persons in that district who were marked 'D', the government had no answer as to why they were designated so.

Thakuma's father Rabindra Mohan moved with his family to Bhuragaon, a small village by the Brahmaputra in Morigaon district, in 1949. His in-laws had migrated to Bhuragaon a few years earlier. But soon, Rabindra Mohan felt the need to move out of the aegis of his brothers-in-law and establish his own business. He decided to move to Barpeta Road, a town in western Assam's Barpeta district, where a considerable Bengali refugee population was already living. In 1956, at the age of fourteen, Thakuma was married to Narayan Chandra Saha. My Thakurda, a young trader of jute and mustard then, was around eleven years older than his wife. His family, also refugees, had migrated to Barpeta from Mymensingh in late 1951.

My father was the second of the couple's four children. Thakurda's business was not thriving, and Baba's upbringing was humble. But he managed to get a chance to study medicine in Guwahati, where he met my mother. Ma had grown up in Dhubri, where my maternal grandfather was a stenographer at a prominent matchstick factory. My maternal grandparents trace their origins to Mymensingh and Pabna in East Bengal.

As the son of two established doctors, I had a comparatively privileged upbringing in Guwahati. I studied till the tenth class at Don Bosco, the city's most prestigious Catholic school for boys then, and completed high school at Cotton College, an iconic colonial-era institution. Most of my school friends were Assamese and my parents' professional circles were multi-ethnic. With two of my uncles marrying into Assamese families, our extended family was culturally diverse. Yet, in retrospect, I think that hints of identity contestations were always underlying the comfort of the apparent progressivism of my boyhood days. At our school, students had to take up compulsory Assamese and Hindi classes till class seven, and then choose either of the languages for the next three years. The school did not offer my mother tongue Bengali as an option. However, learning Assamese in school helped me in training myself to read and write Bengali, since the scripts of the two languages are nearly identical. Thereafter, exploring my own linguistic and cultural roots became a personal journey—thanks to my parents' relentless efforts, which included making me and my sister watch Satyajit Ray's films and listen to Rabindranath Tagore's songs.

In Don Bosco, I spoke Assamese with friends—and once, sometime in middle school, even paid a 'fine' of Rs 10 as a punishment for, as my class teacher put it, 'not speaking in English in class'. I opted for Hindi as a subject from class eight. An important reason behind that was that Hindi might be more helpful whenever one moved out of Assam for higher education, which a lot of students from the state did. In my board examinations, I did well in Hindi—only to realize, within the first few days of engineering college in Ranchi, that my spoken Hindi was flawed. I was rebuked by my north Indian classmates for not rolling my tongue to pronounce the 'd', say, in 'gadi (car)' and, instead, uttering 'gari', with an 'r', like in Bengali. Over the next four years, I overcame the initial bumps in pronunciation and my Hindi improved. Using Hindi as the predominant medium of communication while living in Ranchi, Delhi and Kashmir, refined my command of the language. Today, I often break into Hindi even in the middle of a conversation in Bengali.

My insouciant acceptance of linguistic fluidity notwithstanding, for many in Assam, language is a core part of identity. It is something from which a sense of belonging has been drawn historically. Bengali migrants—both Hindus and Muslims, who came for predominantly different reasons—posing demographic, political and cultural threats to indigenous communities has been a long-standing concern in the Assamese consciousness, originating way back in the colonial period. The issue dictates political discourse in Assam. In the face of the continued influx of migrants and refugees, the socio-political push for the recognition, safeguarding and use of the Assamese language and culture has continued for a long time now. It has led to protests and violence on several occasions.

When Assam became a part of British India following the Anglo-Burmese War of 1826, the British colonial rulers established their system of administration in their new territories, which they annexed to the Bengal Presidency that also included Bihar, present-day Jharkhand and Odisha. The official language of lower courts and revenue administration in the British areas of Assam—which until 1838 did not include Upper Assam—was changed to what were then the official languages of Bengal province, Bengali, Hindustani and Oriya. This was finally changed to Assamese in 1873 due to sustained opposition that was initially led by two American Baptist missionaries, Nathan Brown and Miles Bronson.

In the 1960s and the '70s, Assam saw widespread riots over language issues. During the six-year-long Assam Movement (1979–85), the primary demand put forward by the leaders of the agitation was the detection, disenfranchisement and deportation of all 'illegal foreigners' from the state. The movement was marked by ethno-communal rioting, including incidents such as the massacre of thousands of Muslims in Nellie in 1983; widespread protests and a crackdown by the state; the killing of over 850 anti-government protestors who are remembered as martyrs of the Assam Movement; political instability and economic blockades.

Although historically both Hindu and Muslim Bengali migrants and migrant-origin residents have been in the crosshairs of Assamese ethno-nationalist politics for being 'outsiders', there has been a gradual shift in the narrative of majoritarianism with the recent triumph of Hindu nationalism led by the Bharatiya Janata Party (BJP) in the state and the Centre. Now, it is increasingly the Bengali-origin Muslims of Assam, the Miya Muslims, who find their identity, citizenship and religion threatened, while Bengali Hindus have benefitted from the BJP's political imagination. The BJP's rhetoric in Assam has constantly vilified the Miya community, calling the community a threat to indigenous Assamese identity and culture.

In 2019, the BJP implemented the CAA, which made it easier for undocumented migrants belonging to six non-Islamic religions— Hindus, Sikhs, Buddhists, Jains, Parsis and Christians from Afghanistan, Bangladesh and Pakistan to apply for Indian citizenship. Although the amendment's purported aim is to easily grant Indian citizenship to those who have faced religious persecution in the three neighbouring Muslim-majority countries, the Narendra Modi-led government did explore the possibility of combining the CAA with a pan-India

NRC. The proposal of the NRC–CAA combination triggered debates as to whether the duo could be used by the state to snatch away the citizenship of Muslims. The Central government held off on the implementation of both, following massive protests and violence in the country. Meanwhile, in Assam, the CAA deepened the existing Assamese–Bengali fault lines. Protests erupted in Assam arguing that the CAA would lead to the inundation of indigenous peoples and cultures by Hindu migrants from Bangladesh. The ideological premise of the anti-CAA protests in Assam was different from the pan-India one—here, the protests opposed the acceptance of the Bengali Hindu 'Bangladeshi' through the CAA and not the exclusion of Muslims or destruction of formulations of Indian secularism.

The BJP-led Assam government had positioned the CAA as a panacea for Bengali Hindus excluded from the NRC. It could be argued by the proponents of the CAA that a Bengali like Thakuma will benefit from it. But as a 1949 migrant, my grandmother, and lakhs of others like her, are completely eligible to be Indian citizens in Assam without the mercies of the CAA. The problem is that citizenship determination mechanisms in Assam have not been fair and just toward people like her. Many Hindu Bengalis, a vast majority of them claiming to be pre-1971 migrants to Assam, continue to face citizenship issues. However, the CAA has not been much help to them. The CAA Rules, which were notified just before the national elections in 2024, revealed that applications made under the new law would have to meet strict documentary requirements, including documents from the countries (Afghanistan, Bangladesh or Pakistan) people have come from. For most Assam residents stuck in the citizenship determination exercises, such a provision would pose an insurmountable obstacle. Until April 2024, only one person had applied for citizenship under CAA in Assam.[3]

I had no idea about my grandmother's citizenship predicament when I moved to Guwahati in 2018 as *The Indian Express*'s Northeast correspondent. After being away for around a decade, the new job provided a homecoming opportunity. I was twenty-eight and had spent the previous three years reporting on Kashmir for the *Hindustan Times*.

That summer, as I was settling in and trying to get acquainted with my hometown all over again, I could not help observing that Guwahati had changed remarkably. A plethora of high-rise residential and commercial buildings peppered the cityscape; arty cafés and rooftop bars lined major streets; small hatchbacks gave way to muscular SUVs even as all important roads remained perpetually chock-a-block with traffic. Some things, however, remained unchanged. Age-old narratives of identity politics had resurfaced with the final draft of the NRC soon to be published and unrest against the Citizenship (Amendment) Bill was beginning to ferment.

On my first day at work, while I was busy preparing a list of preliminary contacts to touch base with in Assam, Raj Kamal Jha, the newspaper's chief editor, called. Speaking in a mix of English and Bengali, Jha said that the preparation of the NRC—coupled with the initial anti-CAA protests that were just beginning to gather steam— was the most important story to chase in the region at that moment. He asked me to draw flow charts of the laws and rules governing citizenship in India and the making of the NRC and paste them on the wall next to my desk. On his advice, I started reading up on Assam's citizenship issues and talking to government officials, lawyers and activists to understand the NRC better—and Venn diagram-like figures slowly started taking shape in my notebook. For me, these diagrams, with terms like 'Citizenship Act', 'Section 6A', 'Rule 4A', 'Legacy Data', 'NRC Seva Kendra', 'FTs' and 'Detention Centres' sprawled across circles and arrows were the first indicators of how complex the citizenship determination mechanisms in Assam were.

As I began work, I was faced with a professional conundrum. I had imagined that covering the citizenship crisis in Assam would be a dispassionate journey. Editors and newsrooms expect daily news reporters like me to get the story, fetch quotes from 'both sides' and write the report, without getting emotionally attached to the characters or their stories. I had done that quite successfully in Kashmir, amidst a raging violent conflict. But as I began understanding the citizenship crisis unfolding here and became aware of my grandmother's predicament, I became increasingly conscious of my positionality. I belonged to a family at the receiving end of the citizenship determination exercises I was reporting on. I asked myself whether I would be capable of being an 'objective' reporter. Or would my stories run the risk of being unnecessarily critical of the state's processes? How does knowing that your grandmother is excluded from the NRC affect your journalistic understanding of others out of the list? Would I be able to remain the dispassionate journalist or inadvertently become the angry grandson?

I never wrote about my grandmother's case for the newspaper. With each report that I filed on the NRC exclusions, on people declared as 'foreigners' by the FTs and on 'foreigners' lodged in detention centres, I learnt a bit more about how lives were shattered by these processes— and yet, at home, my grandmother was equally tormented. Therefore, while writing my book, I tried to investigate Thakuma's story alongside covering the citizenship woes of scores of others. I interviewed my relatives, filed RTIs and chased decades-old archival news reports and magazine articles on citizenship issues. At the end of it, I realized that enquiring into Thakuma's citizenship question as a journalist helped me investigate the citizenship processes in Assam to a much greater depth than I would have probably done had I not acknowledged my positionality. I feel covering the NRC story as a journalist as well as as a grandson of refugees, and trying to understand Assam's citizenship determination exercises from the perspective of a member of a family that has borne the brunt of such processes, has helped me become more empathetic to the stories of thousands of people battling statelessness in Assam. It gave me a ringside view of the crisis and made me a better storyteller. It made my book *No Land's People* bluntly honest.[4]

~

The reason behind Thakuma's NRC exclusion, her being a D-voter, is only one element in the tangled citizenship determination mechanisms ongoing in Assam. It's one of the many pieces of a jigsaw puzzle—one of the circles in the Venn diagrams that I had drawn. The marking of people as 'Doubtful' in the electoral rolls was only one of the multiple simultaneous, and sometimes conflicting, methods through which marginalized people risked being stateless in Assam.

The NRC was not the first citizenship determination process to be put in place in Assam. It intersected with an already existing, parallel mechanism of citizenship determination in the state: the Foreigners Tribunal, a quasi-judicial body unique to Assam. Both systems asked people to prove that they or their ancestors were residing in Assam or some part of India (and not Bangladesh) on or before 24 March 1971. The difference between the two, however, was that while the FTs looked into the citizenship of those suspected by the state, the NRC asked every resident of the state to prove their citizenship.

FTs were first established in Assam in the mid-1960s; today, there are a hundred in the state. They adjudicate on two types of cases: those against people on whom a 'reference' has been made by the Border wing of the Assam Police, a division established in the early 1960s to keep an eye on suspected undocumented migrants in Assam; and those against D-voters. The latter are not allowed to cast their votes until the FTs clear their status—but many people received notices from FTs after years of being marked as D. Many others, like Thakuma, haven't yet been summoned by an FT and simply remain suspended in D-voter limbo. As per the latest available government data, 1,43,466 persons have been declared as 'foreigners' by the FTs during their decades of existence, while 1,21,598 have been declared Indians.

Though the two processes might seem to clash with each other, they also form a loop. To fit into the existing processes, the NRC was so designed that a person declared to be a 'foreigner' by an FT cannot be included in the NRC, even if her documents pass the NRC's scrutiny independently. Neither can a person whose case is 'pending' in an FT, or a D-voter like Thakuma, be included in the NRC until her status is cleared by an FT. Moreover, someone who has drawn a 'legacy' from such persons has to be excluded from the NRC. As a result, the NRC was exclusionary for families in which children born in India might have drawn a 'legacy' from their 'foreigner' or D-voter parent. Such a regime can divide families—for instance, if a child draws a 'legacy' from, say, the father who is a 'foreigner' or has a case pending at an FT, then she will be excluded. But, say, the child's mother drew her 'legacy' from her citizen parents, then she would be included. What completes this loop is that the 19 lakh people rejected from the NRC will now have to appeal to the FTs for their inclusion. Hence, apart from adjudicating the cases of D-voters and those suspected by Border Police, Assam's FTs will now opine on people excluded from the NRC as well.

The functioning of the FTs has been severely criticized by multiple quarters. Higher courts, legal experts, academics, journalists and human rights groups have questioned whether the political establishment arm-twists the FTs by incentivizing the declaration of more people as 'foreigners'. The Gauhati High Court has asked the Assam government to review orders passed by the state's FTs, after noting an affidavit by the state administration that in almost 85 per cent cases, those who were declared suspected illegal immigrants were finally found to be Indian citizens.[5]

The High Court and the home and political department of the government of Assam together run the FTs. The court, which monitors the functioning of the FTs, also interviews candidates for selection as FT members. But the members are appointed and their salaries are paid by the state government. Investigative reports by media houses like *The New York Times*, Vice News, *The Indian Express* and Scroll.

in and rights groups like Amnesty International have shone a light on how in recent years the BJP-led Assam government has pushed the FTs to exclude a higher number of people, mainly Muslims, as 'foreigners'.[6]

FTs, till recently, did not adhere to the judicial principle of 'res judicata', and thereby often tried the same person to be a 'foreigner' even if they have been already declared to be an Indian by another FT. Moreover, FTs can pass ex parte, 'by or for one party', orders because Section 9 of the Foreigners Act says the onus of proving that one is not a foreigner is on the alleged foreigner. The suspect individual must prove that they are Indian—if they are absconding and don't appear before the FT to do this, the FT member can pass an order in their absence. As per government data, between 1985 and 28 February 2019, FTs in Assam declared 63,959 persons 'foreigners' in ex parte proceedings, without hearing their side of the case. On comparing this figure with the 1,29,009 persons declared 'foreigners' by FTs up to October 2019, the staggering proportion of ex parte decisions—close to 50 per cent— becomes clear.

Once a person is declared to be a 'foreigner' by an FT, they are liable to be arrested and put in one of the six 'detention centres' in Assam, although they might appeal in higher courts to establish their Indian citizenship. As of July 2021, sixty-one 'declared foreigners' and 120 'convicted foreigners' were incarcerated in detention centres—the number coming down drastically after two Supreme Court orders granted conditional bail to detainees who had spent two or three years in the centres. A vast majority of 'declared foreigners' do appeal to higher courts to prove that they are Indians. Persons declared 'foreigners' by FTs are generally not accepted by Bangladesh as its citizens, leaving them stateless. On the NRC, Bangladesh has maintained that it is India's internal matter and of no consequence to them.

People declared 'foreigners' in Assam live in a twilight zone: India doesn't recognize them as citizens, and Bangladesh will not accept them. Deporting Bangladeshi citizens who are convicted of judicial crimes in India like overstaying their visa—bureaucratically called 'convicted foreigners' in Assam—can be done easily, but the repartition of 'declared foreigners' is diplomatically untenable. The prospect of deportation is abysmal; according to data from the Ministry of Home Affairs, of the 1,29,009 persons 'declared foreigners' till October 2019, only six were deported: four to Bangladesh and two to Afghanistan. The rest continue to live here in India, sans essential rights and often in hiding from law enforcement or, if out on bail from a detention centre, then appearing before the local police routinely to mark their presence at a given address. Somewhat similar is the situation of the people excluded from the NRC. Their lives have been suspended as several processes of the state have erratically started demanding the NRC despite the Central government repeatedly stating that mere exclusion does not make a resident a 'foreigner', and that only the FTs can decide who is a 'foreigner'. However, the appeals process at the FTs remains stalled even after four years of the NRC publication. Moreover, key players, including the NRC state coordinator's office, have challenged the 'finality' of the NRC published in 2019. As the nineteen lakh excluded people endlessly wait to file their appeals, the fate of their Indian citizenship stands uncertain.

One Sunday morning in August 2022, I drove from Guwahati with my parents to Barpeta Road to meet Thakuma. I was home after completing a master's programme at Oxford University and had to visit her. Thakuma's declining years have been reduced to a basic life at our family house. Her health has deteriorated with age and her eyesight is almost completely lost. The usually three-hour-long drive took longer that day, thanks to torrential rains all the way.

I was seeing Thakuma after over a year. She hugged me and asked about my life abroad. She pestered me to get married soon as all grandmothers do. As the family conversations went on over steaming cups of tea that rainy afternoon, my father and my uncle touched upon the D-voter problem. They discussed how, without a Voter ID or an Aadhaar, their mother was bereft of an identity document. They pointed out that if she wants to travel by air, she can't. If she wants to open an account with a bank that asks for KYC information, she can't.

From her face, it seemed that Thakuma could not care less about the prospect of an air ticket or bank account at her age. 'I never knew that this D-voter issue would persist for so long,' she said grimly. 'This tag will probably not leave me till I die.'

Thakuma being marked a D-voter despite appearing in the 1951 NRC and 1965 electoral roll and the state not knowing precisely why she was marked as such reflect the systemic flaws plaguing the citizenship determination exercises in Assam. Such omissions are plentiful—the processes suffer from anomalies that often end up unjustly denying people of their citizenship rights and dignity.

In the course of my reporting in Assam, I met people whose citizenship has been suspected because of minor mismatches in the spellings of their names or that of their ancestors; because they couldn't get proper legal advice in time; because they weren't able to appear at the FT on the given date; because their multiple documents were considered unacceptable by the state; because their poverty and illiteracy rendered them incapable of going through the rigmarole of Kafkaesque mechanisms. I met children excluded from the NRC whose parents were in. A primary school kid excluded from the NRC told me how he was jeered at by his classmates and told that he would now be sent to Bangladesh. I met relatives of multiple persons who had killed themselves fearing that they would lose their Indian citizenship because of the unfairness inherent in the mechanisms. I interviewed serving and retired defence personnel whose citizenship was under investigation and they and their families were out of the NRC. Mohammad Sanaullah, a retired serviceman, described to me how tears had rolled down his cheeks when he was sent to a detention centre for being a 'foreigner' after having served as an Indian Army soldier in Kashmir and Manipur. He is out on bail now and his case is pending at the Gauhati High

Court. 'I asked myself what sin have I committed that after serving my motherland for three decades, including at the LoC in Kupwara, I am being detained like a foreigner,' he recounted.

Like Sanaullah's words, some other comments, too, still ring in my ears. Monirul Islam, a grocery store owner in a village in central Assam who lost his uncle in an accident on the way to a NRC hearing, broke down when I asked him about the political murmurs about the BJP wanting to get the mammoth exercise redone. He asked me, 'How many times do we have to prove our Indian citizenship? Isn't it better you kill us all rather than this non-stop harassment?' I remember meeting Maizan Nessa, a housewife in Goroimari, who had sold her nose ring for Rs 900 that morning to pay for travel to Golaghat, around 400 km away, to attend a last-minute NRC hearing. She had asked me if I knew what the future held for her family and I could offer no consolation. But the silver lining, however faint, was that people in such dire circumstances also exuded hope and resilience. There was a desperation to belong. Everyone whom I spoke to, whose citizenship was doubted by the state, was willing to give whatever it took, to leave no stone unturned, to prove that they were Indians, not Bangladeshis.

A reductive understanding of Assam's insider–outsider issue—such as over-dependence on the bureaucratic capacity to make a list that will segregate 'citizens' and 'non-citizens' like a magic wand—fails to appreciate the reality of the situation. In a country where there is illiteracy and poverty, identity documents that have to be decades old to prove legacy from before 1971 may often suffer from inconsistencies that could make it extremely difficult for people wanting to use them as evidence to prove citizenship. Documents are washed away in devastating annual floods amid the erosion of the sandbars on the Brahmaputra river. In the NRC's documentary regime that relies on heteronormative family structures, producing satisfactory documents has often been an uphill task for women and transgender persons.

The NRC was conceptualized and ideologically supported as an essential technology-driven tool to check undocumented migration into Assam from Bangladesh. All it did was create a complex and often confusing web of bureaucratic, legal and administrative procedures that further marginalized weaker sections of society and produced conditions of precarious citizenship and statelessness. The preparation of the NRC, a mammoth exercise inspired by an ethno-nationalist demand to detect 'foreigners', and the functioning of the FTs compel us to ask whether such processes can at all effectively determine citizenship, especially in a society affected by poverty, illiteracy and divisive socio-political narratives. An analysis of such processes begs us to ask whether the state can weaponize documents, the flaws and inconsistencies in them, or their absence to make the citizenship of people, especially those belonging to ethnic and religious minority groups, precarious.

The rains had stopped and the sunset was bright orange. We packed up and prepared to leave. We had to reach Guwahati before nightfall. As I started the car's ignition and slowly pressed the gas, Thakuma's frail frame, draped in the white saree and waving goodbye, faded away in the rear-view mirror.

Gaping at the Gaze

Sangeeta Barooah Pisharoty

There is so much that a gaze can hold.

It is not a mere raising of the eyes and dropping them. Between seeing and looking away lies a judgement, isn't it?

If a gaze can be beholden and ardent, it can also be disapproving and discriminatory. Think about it; is it not also an apparatus to filter 'us' from 'them'? A screen to separate what is acceptable by a majority; what is a standard parameter, or not? What doesn't fit can then be gazed at with suspicion, isn't it?

It was a suspicious gaze that was frequently placed on me—no, not me alone, on several from my ilk. I mean those who come all the way— from the hills, the vales, the brooksides—from the northeastern corner of the country to work/study/see a 'mainstream' city.

Beyond our hills and dales—I grew up thinking—live people who are not from my country. They don't belong here. They are foreigners. Only when the suspicious gaze rested on me in the country's first city, Delhi, back in the 1990s, did the veil lift for me, telling me that distance needn't always make the heart grow fonder. Distance can discriminate, can marginalize people. Distance can be unknowing. Beyond a distance, it may matter little if you are within the margins of the country or just beyond the international borders. The majoritarian gaze may sieve and compartmentalize you all the same—us and them. A mere gaze can thus create the other. A foreigner.

The tongue that you speak, the size of your eyes, how high are the cheekbones, the texture of your hair—the gaze scrutinizes them all; brackets them as acceptable or untrustworthy; aids in blossoming the categories of 'us' and 'them'.

The us-and-them gaze came into play when I looked to rent a house in south Delhi several summers ago, while hunting for a job, too, in the city; even while just walking on its streets. The bluntness of the message the collective gaze conveyed to me was difficult to ignore: You clearly don't belong here. Where are you from anyway? Thailand? Burma? Malaysia? China?

At the airport check-in desks, ticket counters at historical sites, meandering through the markets, while hailing an auto rickshaw, that gaze tailed me everywhere. Push the door into any provision shop—could be in swanky South Extension or downmarket Janakpuri, Sheikh Sarai or Lado Sarai, Khan or INA Market—I had to be prepared to receive two types of gazes. One that said no, we don't stock things that you may like to eat (therefore, leave); or the other that smelled business and switched on to English to ask, looking for Thai noodles? Green curry paste? Pickled vegetables? Fresh bok choy? Basa? Eel?

No words need to be spoken here. Their gaze can just descend on your eyes, rather on the size of the eyes, and lo! You are slotted. Foreigner!

Being a recipient of a 'foreigner' gaze in your own country day in and day out can be exasperating. At times, it can draw out a laugh in you, too, for the ignorance about the country among its denizens. But when the truth eventually dawns that the distrust can also have violent magnitudes, that laugh abruptly dies on your face.

It is no laughing matter when your name is Nido Tania in a mainstream city; when they sneer at you; push and shove; try and test your imperturbability. The standard advisory to Nido and his ilk should then be: Better drop your gaze and shuffle away. How about lifting the very eyes for which I am being reckoned as the other and defying their gaze? Nah, never; it can be life-taking. Nido lost his life in Delhi's Lajpat Nagar for lifting his discriminated eyes to challenge that majoritarian gaze.

Between 2020–22, many from my ilk learnt the hard way that when there is a Covid-19-pandemic-like circumstance, it is advisable to stay away from a public place in a mainstream city. Lest you attract a cluster of majoritarian gazes that is outright accusatory. The gaze can rain so many questions on you: Can't speak Hindi, eh? Are you Chinese? What do you not eat, eh? Spreading disease among us? Bloody foreigners.

Oh, that word! Foreigners!

Growing up in Assam in the 1980s, that F-word meant 'Bangladeshi' for us. A stranger's gaze on the street was enough to slot someone into that bracket. In a lungi, eh? Too many children? When did you cross over to Assam? The suspicious gaze showered so many such questions on the lungi-clad kind.

The standard safety advice to the ones from that ilk would also be then: Just drop your gaze and shuffle away. Lift the eyes to meet the judgemental gaze and question? Nah, the local factor can be highly injurious to the body and mind. If caught with that slightly different tongue in your mouth, even a kangaroo court by the roadside can decide your nationality. Doubtful voter … encroacher … termite. Bloody foreigner!

Call! Call the Border Police at once; hand them over; issue a notice to appear at a Foreigners Tribunal.

But I was born here; voted in the elections; buried my parents here— they may resist. The majoritarian gaze at the tribunal has, however, decided it anyway. Order, order, here is a foreigner. Push! Push them into the detention centre. Beware! We have made a high-tech holding centre for your kind by now, the gaze can convey to them. Foreigner!

But I am Hindu, not a Muslim, some among them may still resist. By now, is it not established that only Muslims are to be counted as

Bangladeshis in Assam? Hindus are Bengalis, don't you know, they may argue. But the majoritarian gaze is steadfast. So what? You are still not us, you are the other! The illegal foreigner.

Hindu or Muslim, am I not one of your kind? Can you not gaze at me as a human being, several among them may still pipe up. They may try and reason, am I not in the land of Bhupen Hazarika? Can I also not intermingle and assimilate and be you, there may be pleas in their gaze. So many came by the banks of the Brahmaputra and merged with the land. Can I also not? Remember what Bhupen-da sang? *Milibo lage, milabo lage? Manuhe manuhor ba-be?* Man must stand with man, isn't it? A demon can't be human, didn't he say? And if tomorrow a demon indeed becomes human, will you not be ashamed, O man?

Well, it is just a song for us; not a passport for illegal Bangladeshis to settle down in Assam and become Assamese. Embracing the gamusa can't be your talisman. You are a foreigner. A foreigner is a foreigner. Forever.

But I have the papers to prove I am not a foreigner.

Fake.

Or, well, I don't have papers to prove all the decades that my family lived here.

We knew it!

A pandemonium may occur. But we are nineteen million now; a sea of humanity without all of the right papers! After the update of the NRC, our ilk is nobody's people; fallen into the crease between two nations created by Partition. Are you now not happy at our despair?

Nah, I am still in fear of you, the gaze conveys. You are just too many. You may gaze at us as a majority but don't you know how we gaze at ourselves? How will you comprehend the fear of a small community in a large country where your voice is powerful so long as you have the numbers electorally? We are not yet as many in our own land, you see. Our 'jati, mati, bheti', the language and land, culture and cultivation, our very identity, all can slip out of our hands if we drop the gaze fixed on you. Just one census report can diminish us to a minority in our motherland. We will collapse into the crease too. Don't we know that you create large families to occupy our land? Even the government can see through it now. That's why we need a powerful leader, you see. That's why our banners are still up: Go back. Go back! Foreigner, go back!

Growing up as part of a mainstream, however minuscule it may be, has its advantages though. The food you eat, the language you speak, the dress you wear, the cultural rituals you follow … they rim around you so tightly that you end up almost believing that the world is only yours. What counts is only 'us'. How accepted you feel then! The taste of it is so intoxicating that it can act like anaesthesia; can easily numb your sensitivity towards the other. It helps you slot them in a watertight compartment almost to the level of dehumanizing them, and you don't mind doing it: O they can eat anything! They can live anywhere! Can work for hours together! Oh, they are so dirty! Can't be trusted at all! Uncivilized! Rapists! Robbers! Termites!

My landlord in Delhi's Green Park was rather upfront about his distrusting gaze towards the other: Rent must come on the first day of the month and no cooking anything smelly.

You mean I can't cook meat or fry fish? Not that exactly, but don't you people eat things that stink?

Which food are you referring to?

He couldn't tell; only rested that gaze on me that said, take it or leave it. I am the majoritarian gaze, so I decide your fate. I lowered my gaze and shuffled away. For about a year, the lid on the bottle of bamboo shoots that my mother so dearly packed for me remained tightly fixed, lest I lose the roof over my head. If the aroma of your traditional food is part of your identity, then you can say, I agreed to forgo it to circumvent that majoritarian gaze in Delhi. A part of me wanted to discard what was dear to me just to be acceptable to them.

Being a part of the majoritarian gaze in Assam, I did know the taste of it. That collective gaze can be quite empowering, you see. It allows you to construct a world that need not recognize the existence of the other. Only the 'us' matters. You can lift your eyes and look away, leaving behind a judgement.

Oh, they have low morals! See how they dress up! No shame! Men or women, they just drink and play music! The web of 'they' created by the majoritarian gaze in a mainstream city has been all-pervading.

And let's not forget, the majoritarian gaze can discipline the other too. Even after years have elapsed, I can recall noticing that majoritarian numbness towards the other at a neighbour's in an Upper Assam town. It was a particularly cold December evening. The boy who worked at the yard was the other; an adivasi from the Tea tribe. The master caught him carrying to the bathroom half a bucket of hot water from the kitchen. On being asked why, he conveyed that it was meant for a footbath to counter the biting cold. All hell broke loose. Oh, but you people don't feel the cold like we do! So don't waste the hot water! The bucket was snatched away. Lowering his gaze, the boy walked into his room and didn't come out to have dinner. No one asked him why. The lights were shut soon. The other was tamed.

Winter night or summer day, the temperature of the majoritarian gaze is always high. So high and heady that it can dictate terms to anyone it seeks to control. If need be, it can get scathing: You are a married Assamese woman and no sindoor in the parting of the hair? Assamese girl and don't know how to wear mekhela sador? In the thick of Assam's anti-foreigner agitation, diktats were passed by men in trousers to the women in salwar kameez and jeans—wear only mekhela sador. The gaze of the other at the majority must recognize that mekhela sador is the identity of the community, not a crinkled sari that ends at the ankle. That's the outfit of a foreigner!

But why should only women be Assamese, your gaze may challenge theirs. Lest you forget, it's the patriarchal gaze, and it thrives.

These aside, have you ever noted the hegemonic gaze at the other? At times, it can get competitive.

No, no, we Assamese don't eat pork; we are fond of fish, even ilish, like you, a relative answered with a sense of finality to a Bengali visitor from Kolkata some springs ago. The guest, by then, had laid claim on her community as the country's primary fish-eating brigade and was gazing at the Assamese as predominantly pork eaters; essentially, consumers of a meat not quite considered 'clean' traditionally. An indignant Assamese fought back.

Flipping the times, I can only chuckle at such hegemonic gazes that compartmentalize us and them, and how. If for that Bengali guest, the operative part of asserting her food hegemony to the people living further east was by trying to establish how refined her community's taste is in the entire eastern sphere of India by loathing a particular kind of food, for my caste Hindu Assamese relative, it was to compete for a parallel space with hers, but only by claiming hegemony over a wide section of her community, essentially by denying the fact that pork is their primary meat and, therefore, Assamese eat pork too. Run the risk of placing a challenging gaze on her ilk, and there is every chance that a bunch of eyes would roll before asking in return: Are those pork-eating Assamese not really the other? Wasn't the guest enquiring only about us? Anyway, since when have they started to decide what the Assamese should eat?

The gaze may go on to question: Is the Assamese that we speak not the real one? The Lower Assam lingo exists, we agree, but it is not the real Assamese tongue! The yellow and green gamusa exists, we reckon, but that is not the real Assamese gamusa! Some may eat pork, but we Assamese are primarily fish-eaters. Oh, the headiness of the majoritarian gaze! It can be highly intoxicating.

Like the Assamese are 'only fish-eaters', the Nepalis of Assam have been stereotyped as milkmen, the Adivasis as only tea garden labourers; the Bengalis as downright cunning; the Miyas as land-hungry. The majoritarian gaze has catalogued one and all; in other words, has positioned the other as per the dominant gaze. So, not for nothing did I land up in my school year after year dressed as a Nepali milkmaid in the annual go-as-you-like-it competition. Though I thought I played the part terribly, year after year, I still succeeded in cornering a prize or two, and now I know why. My small slanting eyes and sharp nose fitted the majoritarian gaze of a Nepali woman so perfectly. That a

Nepali woman must only be a milkmaid was like my friend taking part in the competition as a teacher with a pair of thick black spectacles, the only defining feature of the role she played aside from holding a few textbooks. She picked a few prizes too. Such is the power of the stereotyping gaze!

It is no rocket science that the phenomenon—us and them—only draws lines between people; accentuates lack of knowledge and discriminates. What needs to be acknowledged, though, is that its long-term consequences can consume one and all, throwing up outright hatred and odium over which none may have any control. Not even the majority. Don't believe it? Then let me remind you of Bijoy Shankar Baniya, a photographer hired by Assam Police to document a drive in 2021 to raze the huts of the encroacher, the other. The decades-old hate-filled majoritarian gaze hanging in the air like a haze surrounded the young Assamese man, Bijoy, and stimulated him enough to jump on a dying man. To him, that dying man was the other and, therefore, had to be dehumanized at all costs. Throw him into a ditch where he no longer feels the loss of home like we do! Rather, show him his place. Oh, they can live anywhere! They are not us; they are robbers, land grabbers, don't you know? Rapists too! Termites certainly! So crush, crush the other with all your might! Bijoy jumped and jumped on the dying man as if swirling all those thoughts in his head to draw the power and validation from the majoritarian gaze for his cold-hearted act.

That September night, I looked at myself in the mirror, rather at my Assamese majoritarian eyes intently. Is there hatred for the other? Or compassion for the dying man, like a human would feel for another human? As Bhupen-da had said, *Manuhe manuhor ba-be …*

I gazed at myself for a long while but could spot only shame in my eyes. I lowered my gaze. For the first time, it emerged to me so clearly that a gaze can bring shame to an entire community. I looked away, leaving my judgement hanging in the mirror.

The Fence across My Courtyard

Rashmi Narzary

He stoked the fire and the specks that rose from it shone in his cloudy, cataract-filmed eyes. The many wrinkles on his face held more memories and stories in their folds than the mysterious night around him. When cajoled, he would sometimes share a few. 'They had a separate enamel mug set aside near the well. I remember,' he told her and closed his eyes for a brief while as if he didn't wish those old memories to come out before them. 'It was white with a black rim running around the mouth and with a dented handle. That mug … they didn't touch it. It was for those like us. I drank, washed it and kept it back, separately.' He was speaking of decades ago. But things haven't changed much today. Rather, the undercurrent rushes deeper and more furiously than the times he was speaking of. He was young then; he is old now. They call him Apha. Father.

Apha is a Bodo, his community being the earliest settlers of the Northeast Indian state of Assam. He belongs to the largest ethnolinguistic group in the state, which is a faction of the greater Bodo-Kachari family. Though they are spread across the northeastern belt of India, in Assam they are concentrated in the Bodoland Territorial Region comprising the five districts of Kokrajhar, Baksa, Udalguri, Chirang and Tamulpur, with a sprinkling in other districts as well. Till recent times, of course, there was only Kokrajhar district, with Gossaigaon as its subdivision. And so those two were the most affected and affecting places that Apha often talks of. A handful of Bodos have made their homes in the neighbouring countries of Nepal, Bhutan and Bangladesh as well.

But for now, Apha's stories meander around the Bodos of Assam. His forefathers have lived here in Assam, and he and his descendants live here too. Yet, he, his forefathers and his descendants are not Assamese. His language, costume and script are vastly different from those of the Assamese. Just like those of Assam's tribal inhabitants who belong to around fourteen recognized plains tribe communities and around fifteen recognized hill tribe communities, Apha, too, is made to feel like a lesser citizen within his home state. The pulse in his veins is that of an identity crisis. His food preferences, his tribal religious practices and his accent, when he makes sincere attempts to communicate in Assamese, are mocked. He feels a nagging sense of prejudice and deprivation, for reasons political, social and structural. What mainland India metes out to the Northeasterner, the greater Assamese society meted out to Apha. It is precisely here that his tales of angst begin, and it is that angst that led to dissent and rebellion among tribal communities of Assam.

Apha's is a story of being an outsider within the inside, a story of unbelonging in his own homeland, a tale of being peripheral at the periphery.

The flames in Apha's little fire in his courtyard leapt high, lighting his old, weather-beaten face and making him push back his khamplai*. That evening, he wanted to share some more of his memories. And she sat beside him, eagerly looking at his eyes.

---

*   Low wooden stool to sit on.

'It was many years ago when my cousin Lantha and his wife went to visit a relative in Majuli during the winter …'

'O wow!' she interrupted with excitement, 'The world's largest riverine island! Winters in Majuli are enchanting! I know Majuli to be a major seat of the inclusive, all-embracing Vaishnavite faith founded by Sankardeva between the fifteenth and sixteenth centuries in Assam. It brought a socio-religious revolution into Assam, often referred to as the Ekasarana Dharma, am I right, Apha? Now that's intriguing, really! Isn't the island dotted with Vaishnavite monasteries? The ones they call Xotro? From what I gather, it is a beautiful religion that has welcomed into its fold people of all ethnicities, religion, caste and creed. Sorry for interrupting, Apha, so did your relative visit one of the xotros?'

Apha looked up at her and smiled, 'He did, child, despite being dissuaded by his relative's neighbour, who was a Mishing belonging to Jengraimukh, on the same island. This young Mishing man had let Lantha know that they wouldn't be allowed into the xotro, they never were since he was a little boy. He said he would show him around all of Majuli, but would not be able to show him a xotro. Nevertheless, obstinate that Lantha was, he wouldn't let the man be at peace till he at last agreed, very reluctantly though. And so this young Mishing man … I forget the name … Okon Chayengia I think it was, well never mind that …'

She laughed, 'Never mind that, Apha, we assume he was Okon Chayengia.'

And Apha resumed, 'Okon Chayengia and Lantha cycled down all the way to the xotro, riding their cycles sometimes over the embankment that held back the mighty Brahmaputra from pouring into their villages, and sometimes across fields and sandbanks. Lantha was excited. Because like you, he, too, had heard that Sankardeva's religion embraced one and all.'

'And didn't it?' Curiosity made her eyes glisten in the light of the fire. Apha picked a few twigs from the bunch lying next to him and pushed these into the fire that was ebbing now, pulling his khamplai closer to the fire once more.

'It did. That's how it began and that's how it was supposed to be. But over time, when those who founded it were no longer around, this supposedly fair and indiscriminating religion came to be taken over as the legacy of the upper-caste Assamese. Then on, it no longer remained the accessible faith that welcomed all under its egalitarian wings. Those at the helm of affairs at the xotros began to shun tribals. They were no longer embraced into its folds, were not made wise nor enlightened, nor given refuge and not shown the difference between right and wrong. Understandably, Christian missionaries took the opportunity and reached out to the starving souls of the tribals in Assam, bringing education, healthcare and food to the deprived. And so it was that when Lantha arrived with Okon Chayengia at the xotro at Bongao, they were barred from entering. And right in front of Lantha, Okon was rebuked by a bhakat, a monk of the xotro, who happened to be much younger than Okon, because even after knowing that they were not allowed in, Okon Chayengia dared challenge the traditions of the xotro premises. Deeply humiliated and hurt, Lantha vented his anger on the cycle and kicked its wheel so hard that it got damaged beyond riding. So while returning, poor Lantha had to push it all the way back.'

Apha poked the fire hard and with vengeance with the stick in his hand. The fire signified the bitterness storming up within him all over again. 'The Mishings, who form a majority of Majuli's dwellers, too, are not allowed in there. Flowers from the altar were not put into their palms, you know, they were flung at them from afar.' She looked at the fire; she thought it was beginning to simmer within her too.

'And the Assamese?' she asked.

'They're allowed in, of course,' he replied. 'Years later, my son, too, wasn't allowed in,' he said after a long pause.

Apha's son had just been born when the Assamese Official Language Bill was passed in the state assembly on 24 October 1960. The bill had provided for two official languages: Assamese and, for an interim period, English, which would be replaced by Hindi. In a state where the population that spoke Assamese was 31 per cent in the 1931 Census and 56 per cent in the 1951 Census, how justified was that bill? Most of the tribals in Assam (the region then included what are now Meghalaya, Mizoram and Nagaland) belonged to the Indo-Mongoloid stock and spoke a language that belonged to the greater Tibeto-Burman family of languages. So, for all the Aphas, the Okon Chayengias and the Lanthas, the Karbis, Garos, Dimasas, Rabhas and all other tribes who neither understood nor spoke Assamese, how fair was the imposition of Assamese for all or any of the official purposes of the State of Assam?[1]

'Dissent that had only been running as an undercurrent all along now came out in the open as protests,' Apha started to recollect. 'That a language the people didn't know should be imposed for all official work did not go down well. We felt sidelined, outcast by Assam. Political forces at the Centre and the state worked towards their own advantage, tearing down the social fabric further and adding to the angst.' He adjusted the aronai* closer around his head, covering his ears. 'Nowadays you speak of the Northeasterner being nudged by India to the fringes of the nation with attempts to be held there in body and spirit, deprived of all possible advantageous situations. You say, most from the heartland do not know us, have not heard of us. Sadder still, they do not show an inclination to know us or hear of us. But child, sadder than even that is the fact that within the Northeast, within my own state, exists such a heartland which despite being in the fringe itself, has dominated us and imposed their supremacy over us. We have been simmering for long,' he said, looking at the fire and following with his eyes the sparks that rose from it to vanish into the night sky. Sparks that had risen every now and then but had no intensity to turn into a fire.

Not for long though.

---

*   Muffler used by Bodo men.

Matters got worse when in 1970, Gauhati University decided to introduce Assamese as the medium of instruction in all colleges affiliated to it and under its jurisdiction. A sense of apprehension regarding employment prospects, bordering on a threat, began to percolate among the non-Assamese tribals. Even if they were given employment, they wouldn't be able to work in an official language they did not know. The same apprehension was there among the students in colleges and universities. When such socio-economic insecurities crawled in, ethnic groups further alienated themselves from the greater Assamese society and huddled tighter among their own. So rather than being a binding, common language, which perhaps the imposition of Assamese was anticipated to be, it did just the opposite. It tore down Assam into fragments, in spirit and effect. The languages and dialects and thereby the identities and ethnicities of the numerous indigenous tribes of Assam lay trampled. However, the root cause of dissent owing to a sense of injustice, discrimination and deprivation among tribals in Assam, especially the Bodos, can be traced back to colonial times. Now though, with a renewed threat to their existence and also due to massive immigration, the seeds of establishing their own identity were sown in each tribe. To bow out without asserting themselves was not like them. And so a steady process of tribalization began in Assam.

The All Bodo Students' Union (ABSU) launched the Bodo movement in 1987, demanding a separate state to be called Bodoland. This was a consequence of the failure of the Plains Tribes Council of Assam (PTCA), which had, since its inception in 1967, demanded a separate union territory for the Bodos and other plains tribes, to be called Udayachal.

Political leaders sought out their mileage from the situation and over the years, while one set of tribal leaders took to mediation and talks with the powers in Assam and Delhi, to detach from a biased Assamese society, another faction took up armed revolution. The governments at the Centre and the state began to refer to them as insurgents, ultras and militants. Earlier, when for the very same reasons, seemingly misled Assamese youth formed the United Liberation Front of Assam (ULFA) in 1979 to embark on an armed rebellion in protest against the Centre's upper hand over Assam, they, too, were called insurgents and militants—never Assamese insurgents, Assamese ultras or Assamese militants. But when a handful of misled Bodo youth took up arms for similar reasons, they became Bodo insurgents, Bodo ultras and Bodo militants.

Due to the prefix Bodo that was constantly used by the media, by the public and even by the political leaders of Assam, it pounded into the masses the impression that Bodo was synonymous with insurgents, militants and ultras. Print and electronic media used the term 'Bodo ugrapanthi', meaning Bodo ultra; but 'Oxomiya ugrapanthi' was hardly heard of. Consequently, outside the predominantly Bodo areas of Assam, distressing vibes of either being a militant or espousing militancy, irrespective of age, profession, gender and political inclination or non-inclination, choked every Bodo. Spiteful looks sliced through the Bodo's confidence and feeling of oneness with the rest. Those were agonizing times for Bodos living among non-Bodo or Harsaa people, as the Bodos referred to non-Bodos. Likewise, non-Bodos found it extremely difficult to live among Bodos.

'It was the year 1988 and the Bodo agitation had gained intensity,' Apha recollected, his eyes fixed on the fire. 'One of my sons was in the final year of his post-graduation studies at the Gauhati University and he used to stay in one of the boys' hostels there. Tension was already mounting among the students, especially the boarders.'

Bandhs, which often went up to over a hundred hours at a stretch, crippled the state. Any kind of non-compliance or non-support gave rise to greater chaos and rioting. Bridges along the national highway were damaged to disrupt the movement of security forces and government officials. In those days, Kokrajhar was the only district with the highest concentration of Bodo people. The non-Bodos who could leave the district did so. But those who had to continue living there due to various reasons were left gripped with terror.

'Every morning, the newspapers would reach my son's hostel at the university,' Apha went on, 'and browsing through the headlines that invariably mentioned how many were killed, how many vehicles were torched, how many Bodo ultras were picked up by the paramilitary forces or killed in encounters, the situation would turn grim inside the hostel among the boys. They would look at my son, whisper among themselves and steer clear. Some would ask him, you are a Narzary, aren't you? Then they would look at their friends and say, "He's a Bodo." They stopped talking to him and all the other Bodos in the hostel. They didn't want to have anything to do with any Bodo. The situation had turned so volatile that the slightest offence or provocation would set the hostel raging. Amidst that stifling situation, studies had to be continued and the course completed. It was, after all, my son's final year and he could not afford to lose out. And the final exams were just around the corner. Till such time, Bodo students stuck to one another.'

As the exams began and then got over for Apha's son's Bodo hostel mates, one by one they began to vacate their hostels and leave. But they were anyway Bodos belonging to districts other than Kokrajhar, so they weren't looked at with as much disdain as those from Kokrajhar. Apha hailed from Gossaigaon in Kokrajhar, the hotbed of the Bodo agitation. Eventually, Apha's son was the only Bodo left in the boys' hostel.

'It was a traumatic phase for my son,' Apha said, 'he stayed all by himself because fellow boarders markedly showed their anger and contempt towards him, just because he belonged to a certain tribe. Just because he was a Narzary. He would walk into the dining hall all by himself, sit by himself and eat by himself, with no one to talk to or smile at, but also with everyone sending him vindictive glances that psychologically left him a total wreck. Unable to take the ordeal any longer, he left the university's hostel and shifted in with a friend in the Assam Engineering College (AEC) hostel, which was nearby in the same Jalukbari area. Meanwhile, his theory papers had begun.

At the same time, he had almost overstayed as a paying guest with the friend at the AEC hostel and had to once again change places. All this was happening while his post-graduation final exams were on, and he was emotionally and bodily insecure and apprehensive all the while. He could even be harmed physically, or his career could be jeopardized. You know,' Apha told her, 'there were so many like him.'

'So Apha, did he manage to sit for all his papers that year?' she asked.

'He could. Once again shifting from the AEC hostel, he went to stay with someone else at their quarters and just about managed to complete his papers, before rushing back home.'

The Bodo movement has left one of the deepest scars among the Bodos too, both in the individuals as well as in the community. Stories of atrocities by the police and other security forces abound, as they went looking for extremists in Bodo villages. When they couldn't find them, they left behind a trail of terror.

'The old were tortured to get them to speak, women were molested and granaries were ransacked.' Apha's eyes glistened with fresh tears of indignation that surfaced from stoking long-buried memories. 'Tell me now, why do you think all this madness began in the first place? Had the tribes received their rightful socio-economic, political and cultural dues from the authorities in the Centre and the state, had a spirit of brotherhood and fairness prevailed in the greater Assamese society, do you think things would have come to this? They wouldn't have!'

The night turned colder.

'Are you sleepy, Apha?' she asked.

He smiled, deepening the furrows between his wrinkles. Sleep had long forsaken him.

'Feeling cold?' she asked again.

'Could you please run along inside and fetch me my endi* shawl?'

She got up and cautiously walked across the moonlit yard into the hutment in the north. A mongrel lay curled in a heap of ash outside

---

* Eri/errandi silk.

the thatched kitchen. The Bodo homestead usually comprises of a neat mud courtyard with dwelling hutments all around it and a sijou plant in the northeastern corner of the courtyard. This plant is worshipped as an embodiment of Bathou, Lord Shiva. Look at the coincidence! And the irony therein! For the Bodos, their own northeastern corner is the most revered and despite being at the periphery, is central to their homesteads and to their lives.

The faint light of the kerosene lantern inside the hutment made her take some time to look around for the shawl that hung on an old wooden cloth horse. There were a few framed black-and-white photographs put up along the tree trunk posts that ran up the reed and mud walls. Turned crisp and yellow with time, one photograph showed a youthful Apha sitting next to a woman. His wife perhaps, she assumed. She pulled down the endi shawl and as she was walking away, a bright yellow dokhona slipped from a bar on the cloth horse and fell near her feet. She picked it up, folded it and hung it back, wondering whose it could be. Apha's wife was long gone, his daughters and daughters-in-law didn't live there, though they visited often. Walking back to Apha, she unfolded and gently wrapped the shawl around him. He was in no mood to get up and go to sleep. This lone walk down the corridors of his memory was perhaps long overdue, waiting to be taken. He needed to speak. About his people. And their tales of being Northeast Indian.

'Apha,' she hesitated, 'there's a dokhona …'

A flame leapt up as if signifying the one that did in Apha's ageing heart. It lit up the blush upon his hollowed cheeks.

'That's hers,' he said, coy and subtly embarrassed, as he fondly remembered his wife. 'It has memories.'

At the peak of the agitation, Bodo socio-moral police set a strict dress code that allowed no non-Bodo attire for the Bodos, especially the women, because traditional costume was considered an essential part of emphasizing their identity. Till before the movement, Bodo women who had lived, studied or worked outside would conveniently don the saree, salwar-kurta or even the mekhela sador of the Assamese. But later on, in their vengeance to dissociate themselves from all things Assamese or Indian, any Bodo woman seen in a saree or a mekhela sador was belittled and chastised, sometimes even in public.

'I can understand, Apha,' she said, 'I remember a friend's aunt, herself Bodo, once found the pallu end of her saree ripped apart in the marketplace in Bongaigaon, near Gossaigaon.'

In the socio-political framework of Assam, the significance of the Bodo movement lay in the fact that it could successfully mobilize pertinent tribal issues and questions and bring these to notice. Just as the Northeast had always remained in obscurity from the Indian heartland, so also the tribal areas of Assam remained in obscurity of the heartland of Assam. But once the Bodo movement began, more non-Bodos within the state of Assam became aware of Bodo culture, attire, linguistic identity and heritage.

Yet, even years after the Bodo movement ended with the signing of the Bodo Accord in 1993 by the Centre, the state and the ABSU and the formation of the Bodoland Autonomous Council, matters sadly remained mostly the same within Assam, just as the Northeast was and still is to India beyond West Bengal. Here's just one instance: many years later, at the 2010 Confluence: Asia International Literary Festival in Guwahati, a renowned writer and journalist had complimented a guest she knew, 'That's a very elegant costume you're wearing. Thai, isn't it?'

The guest had smiled, hurt. 'Bodo. Dokhona,' she had replied.

It pained the guest that her identity went unrecognized even in her home state, by someone considered knowledgeable.

It reminded the guest of all those times when Delhi-ites mistook something or someone Northeastern for Chinese.

'When the Northeasterner's spirit is mauled outside, they can always come back home. But when the Northeasterner's spirit is shattered in their own home, tell me, where do they go?'

'They will have to claim their rights and space within that home, Apha.'

A decade later, that same guest's son joined the National Law University and Judicial Academy, Assam. More than half of that university's students are from outside Assam, and some among them would often, though with good humour, call him, 'Hey Corona!' He seemed to just brush it aside, but the truth stung.

'We stand apart because of our looks, child,' Apha told her. All of us belonging to the East Asian stock get associated more with other East Asian countries than with our own homeland and sadly, even by those from our own home, our own state. Just as the harsaas in the Bodo areas were in the grip of constant fear, Bodos living outside the Bodo areas had a harrowing time during the Bodo movement. Some had roots in the Bodo areas but had to branch out elsewhere in Assam in search of work, education or so many other reasons. Some of them never got to learn their mother tongue. Of those living in Upper or Central Assam districts, most had even begun to identify themselves with the Assamese. They spoke Assamese, went to Assamese-medium schools, wore the mekhela sador and even went to the namghar, the Vaishnavite place of worship. But that was long before the Bodo movement had begun to raise a whole lot of buried, unsaid, significant issues that were till then only running as an undercurrent. Once the movement started, all of a sudden, the undercurrent gushed to the surface and people began to openly express that the Bodos were ethnically different from others in Assam. Consequently, those Bodos who had begun to identify themselves with the Assamese, found that the Assamese had never really accepted them as one among themselves. And the Bodos were wary of receiving those people back into their fold. Now tell me, where did these people belong? They were sitting on a fence running right across their own yard.'

Meanwhile, another son of Apha's had cleared the Union Public Service Commission exam and become an Indian Administrative Service (IAS) officer. He was allotted the home cadre of Assam–Meghalaya.

'He faced a whole lot of issues as a Bodo bureaucrat. His seniors and political heads in the state government suspected him of having connections with Bodo political leaders and extremists or both,' Apha said as he slowly got up and walked into the kitchen. The fire had now ebbed but the embers were still glowing bright. Apha returned with a few sweet potatoes and pushed those into the embers and let them roast. 'But before that, child, let me also tell you something. Remember the xotro that Lantha and Okon Chayengia had gone to visit but weren't allowed in to?'

She turned the sweet potatoes with a stick and nodded before looking up. 'Yes. What of that, Apha?'

'Coincidentally, my son's first posting was at Majuli as the sub-divisional officer (SDO), civil services. That was way back in 1992, when Majuli was still a subdivision of the Jorhat district.'

It was only in 2016 that Majuli was declared a district.

The SDO is to a subdivision what the collector or the deputy commissioner (DC), as is known in Assam, is to a district. So when Apha's son, and Lantha's nephew, landed at Majuli as its SDO, civil services, as a direct recruit of the IAS, the tables turned at the xotros. Apha laughed. He tossed one of the sweet potatoes. 'Done,' he said, dragging it out of the embers and dusting it between his palms as he blew into it to cool it. He peeled it, broke it into two unequal parts and gave her the bigger one. 'Some things are good when still warm,' he smiled, putting his share into his mouth.

While at Majuli, Apha's son visited most of the xotros, was cordially invited to many and was even received by the head of the xotro, the xotradhikar himself, at the Auniati xotro. Apha's son was led into the inner chambers of the xotro where he sat with honour opposite the xotradhikar himself and was served tea and snacks in baan-bati[*], which was considered to be an immense honour.

---

[*]   Brass metal bowl on a stand.

On 16 May 1996, when R.K. Singh, IPS, the superintendent of police (SP) of the Upper Assam district of Tinsukia, was brutally shot dead right in front of the SP's office during the peak of the ULFA's rebellious activities in Assam, the security set-up of the state's police and civil administrations got the rudest shock. Panic spread among officials of all ranks. Roads lay deserted and haunted due to bandhs, Section 144s and outright dread. Consequently, following an administrative reshuffle, the DC was transferred out. The government was in a fix because officers expressed their utter reluctance to walk into a seeming death trap and join as the succeeding DC, despite Tinsukia otherwise being a sought-after district.

'You see, they all feared for their own lives and loved their families,' Apha said. 'Finding no other officer, it was my son who was sent as the DC there at a time when Tinsukia and the whole of Upper Assam was burning under the fires of extremist activities. Might it have been because he was a Narzary? A Bodo? Might it have been that the powers at the state headquarters could do without a Bodo IAS officer, just in case of another eventuality in the turbulent region?' Apha looked up at the sky, as if wanting to know what the stars had to say.

'Yet again, in 2007, many of the Upper Assam districts witnessed a horrifying series of massacres of Hindi-speaking people. A region where law and order had been painstakingly restored, once again saw flames of hatred and resentment flaring up. And once again, it was my son who was sent into that violence to restore order. This time in the capacity of commissioner, Upper Assam Division.'

'Is it possible that both instances were regular postings, Apha?' she asked, genuinely concerned.

'Maybe.' He looked long and hard at the dying fire, as if it were the fire within his old heart. 'Maybe not!' He got up, picked up his khamplai and slowly walked into the house towards his room in the hutment in the north.

She followed him with her eyes till he disappeared into the darkness of his room and closed the door behind him.

Apha.
He could as well be her father or father-in-law.
Or mine.

Having been born, brought up, educated and having lived all my life outside the Bodoland Territorial Region but very much within the state of Assam—my own state, my own homeland—I am seen by the Bodos as nurturing a thought process, lifestyle and values that are not really similar to my Bodo brethren but exactly as those of the harsaas. When I travel to my ancestral home at Bhaulaguri in the Gossaigaon subdivision of Kokrajhar district, along the highway that glides through paddy fields, tall leafy trees, lily-filled ponds and picturesque wayside hamlets, which look the same all over the plains of Northeast India, I can't help but wonder, 'Where do I belong?'

Today, I find myself sitting on a fence that runs right across my own courtyard, my own homeland. Through all of it, I remain a Bodo proud of being a Northeast Indian, proud of being who I am and what I stand for.

That Was My Hometown Too

Easterine Kire

'Hi, this is Ashok here. Do you remember me? Class of '74. We were in the same batch in Baptist High School. Maybe you have completely forgotten me. I was one of the backbenchers, while you always had your nose buried in your books and never spoke to any of us.'

The Facebook friend request with a picture of a middle-aged north Indian man looked nothing like the boy I knew in school decades ago. But then who among us looked like our high school selves? If I looked closely enough, or if they showed me old photos, it helped me recognize former classmates. Ashok Kumar. Yes, I could picture him in his school uniform. Dark brown pants, white shirt and brown sweater with the obligatory school badge and necktie. He never came to school alone. Accompanied by two of his friends, they would walk up together from the town area, Ashok, Ravi and Rahul. Both Ravi and Rahul lived in the army camp in town. Rahul's father was a colonel in the army and Ravi's father was his subordinate officer. Sometimes, they were driven to school in an army jeep by a driver. Every term one of them would take away the prize for the most regular student.

'Tell me all about your life. What are your children studying? Do you keep in touch with our school friends?' Ashok's questions began to pour in and I answered them all as clearly as I could. None of our batchmates used Facebook, so I was not in touch with them there.

In the 1960s and '70s, Ashok's father owned one of the big textile shops in Kohima. All his goods came from Delhi by road transport. The shop offered tailoring services and mostly catered to men.

'The best period of my life was my childhood spent in Kohima,' he wrote. That surprised me, and roused my curiosity about how a non-Naga boy might have experienced my hometown.

'Don't forget, that was my hometown too. My grandfather came to Dimapur in 1930. Later on, he found a job when the railway station was built. My father did not want to follow in his father's footsteps. He married my mother in 1958 and they moved to Kohima in the '60s. In the early years of their marriage, they tried to get work as government suppliers, but there was a monopoly in that sector by a certain community. My father looked for other opportunities and it was then he realized that there were very few shops in Kohima. "I could start a textile shop here," he had told my mother. "This is a growing town with schools and offices. People need clothes for every season." My mother was very supportive. "Let's talk to your father, and get his blessings," she had said. People in Kohima liked to dress well. Even today, I know they still do. So, when my father started his tailoring shop, the orders kept coming, and he had to hire two tailors to fulfil all the orders for suits, trousers, shirts and school uniforms that poured in. People did not like to buy ready-made clothes. "Ready-made can't take the place of tailor-made clothes," they would tell us as they streamed into our shop.'

Ashok's memories took me back to the Kohima of my childhood, where the most exciting thing to do on a Saturday afternoon was to go to town with the excuse of shopping for some item or the other for our grandmother. Every step of the way was exciting, beginning from the path outside our house that linked up with the motorable road that curved its way down the steep Mission Road.

The route we used to get to town went past the Mission chapel that our school used every day for morning assembly. The paint was peeling off the walls and the doors were always kept open at school hours, with the result that students ran inside chasing each other and littering the floors with the roasted chickpeas that were sold by the woman who kept shop near the school. When we passed the Kevichüsa house with its rose-covered fencing, we always slowed down to admire the baby pink roses. The next stretch of the road found us walking beneath the canopy of rubber trees that had serpentine roots stretching all the way down to the street. The branches intertwined and arched over the street, offering shade on sunny days. But in the evening hours, the same branches dropped down caterpillars on unsuspecting pedestrians. My uncle had once brought home a great, hairy caterpillar that clung stubbornly to his leg. None of the careful efforts to remove it had worked, and in the end, it had to be peeled off bit by bit and thrown into the fire.

Further down the road were the houses that looked as though they had been built into the hillside, the way they clung to the steep slopes. The vertically built houses had no front yards because there simply was no room. You walked directly into the sitting room or the kitchen when you stepped inside the door. As the road snaked downward, old houses of tin pushed their way up, so that the road became very narrow, leaving space only for one vehicle to pass. The shops started after the crossing, where one road went toward the Choto Bosti colony and the downward road continued into town. There were very few cars on the road in those days, but we still took care to walk on the outer edge, remembering the jeep that had suffered a brake failure on that very road and ploughed into two women and a child. It was a dreadful business.

Along that slope was our favourite shop—the Kohima Bakery, which sold rusk, freshly baked bread and cakes. We always bought bread and cake on our way back from town. The bakery had a near-monopoly in baked goods as it was the only other bakery apart from Mr Jadial's. The first Kohima baker was Mr Jadial, who had opened a bakery along the same stretch on Mission Road.

Below the bakery were the yarn shops from where Grandmother bought yarn for the body cloths she wove. As the yarn shops ended, the road bifurcated into two and the main highway coming from the Ruzhukhrie High School area directly cut into town. On the right, there were a number of small shops of which one was a 'hair-cutting salon' and the shop adjacent to it sold pots and pans. On the left was the Peak Agency bookstore with its wooden floors and student customers. After the bookstore, there were two shoe stores and a glass bangles store owned by a Bengali man, who displayed his colourful bangles right at the entrance of his narrow shop. He used a certain technique on his female customers. If the customer said the bangles were small and asked for a bigger size, he would take the customer's hand and twist and push the bangle through until they were sitting prettily on her wrists. Since the customer could not remove the bangles, she would part with two rupees and show off her bangles at home.

At the turning into the Naga Bazar, Manipuri women sat on the roadside selling eggs, dried fish, chana and roasted peanuts. Next to that lane were three textile shops, where customers waited in line to get a pair of trousers or a full suit stitched. Ashok's father's shop was the middle one. It was bigger than the other two. The newly painted signboard above the shop said, 'Kohima Textiles'.

We rarely visited that shop, as they had only to men's wear. One Saturday, we accompanied cousin Avi who wanted to order a pair of trousers. 'Terylene or terry wool?' the attendant asked, as soon as Avi made his queries.

'Show me the terylene,' Avi responded. The salesman pulled out four or five spools of fabric with a flourish. The terylene fabrics shone in the light of the lone bulb. The most eye-catching was a dark green fabric with silvery threads running through the cloth that glittered when they caught the light.

'What do you think?' he turned to me. I was too embarrassed to reply. My cousin sister who was four years older was also with us. He could have asked her. Why did he have to ask me?

'Come on,' he insisted, 'I will buy your choice.' There was no getting out of it. Avi enjoyed teasing me, more so in public when he saw me getting flustered. He pulled up the green fabric and asked, 'Shall I take this one?' Feeling very awkward, I nodded to indicate a yes.

'You really like it?' Avi persisted. I wanted to run out of the shop, but my feet had turned to lead.

'It's nice,' I managed to say. The salesman had his tape and scissors ready and he quickly measured and cut enough fabric for a pair of pants. We waited while the tailor took Avi's measurements, then he paid an advance amount and was given a pink receipt. On the date of delivery, he went back to the shop and showed them the receipt and paid the rest of the money. Avi was very pleased with the results and wore the new trousers teamed with a leather jacket, which was the rage then. Ashok was nowhere to be seen on both days, and I was inwardly grateful because we never talked to each other outside the school. In fact, we had never spoken to each other at school either. The boys and the girls sat apart, and except for the times when the naughtiest of the boys would pester us by trying to steal our books or to pull our braids, we had no interaction.

'I am surprised you remember me. You never spoke to anyone in school,' Ashok had written. That was not true, but fourteen-year-olds never have much conversation, do they? Maybe they do in today's world. Again, he asked after classmates who had passed out of school with us, and I tried to answer as best I could. Three of them had died since leaving school.

'Do you have Kuto's number?' he asked one day, out of the blue.

'What do you want it for?' I was curious now. Kuto was the class bully. We were all scared of him. He once forcibly took my textbook away. For the next five minutes, he got a thrill out of pretending to give it back to me and snatching it away every time I reached for it. I was afraid my book would get torn if I pulled too hard. And I was near tears. Finally, he threw it on my desk when he saw the teacher entering the classroom. I still remember the day I had tied my hair in a ponytail only to have it pulled by Kuto who stole up behind me. It had hurt. Most of my encounters with him had involved physical pain or mental stress. Even after all these years, I had no wish to contact Kuto.

'I just want to greet him and tell him what I am doing with my life,' Ashok replied. Surely there couldn't be any harm in connecting the two former classmates now that we were all living as adults. My brother had Kuto's number and I passed it on to Ashok. He thanked me and said he would phone Kuto in the evening. A few minutes later, I was racked with guilt. I really should not have given Ashok Kuto's number. What was I thinking? What if they got into a terrible fight? It would be all my fault. Ashok was a grown man now. He must have many things on his mind to tell Kuto. I imagined a messy confrontation between the two men and felt sick to my stomach. I needed to stop the fight! Quickly I logged into Facebook and messaged Ashok. 'Boys, please don't start fighting! I can't let that happen. You simply must not fight.' Images of schoolboys with bloodied noses raced through my mind's eye. I didn't even realize I was constructing their telephone conversation on my own. In the middle of that, I recollected that Kuto, now sixty-four, had suffered a mild heart attack six months ago. If Ashok were to upset him, who knows what could happen to his weakened heart?

'Don't be silly, E. We are grown-ups now. We are no longer schoolboys. We won't get into a fight. What are you thinking!' Ashok's reply came instantly. He ended with a smiley emoticon. After that, I felt too embarrassed to ask how it had gone. But Ashok was eager to talk. 'You know, Kuto used to bully me a lot. He must have seen that I was scared of him. He was bigger than me and he would give a deadly look that made all his victims squirm in their seats. I could not bring myself to tell my parents about it.'

'Why not?' I asked.

'Well, you know my mother …' he began then he stopped mid-sentence. 'No, you never knew my mother. She rarely left the house, except to go shopping or to the gurdwara. She never came to the school for the PTA meetings. If I told her about Kuto and all the trouble he gave me in school, Mother would have nagged my father every day and given him no peace until he went to see the headmistress about it. And if Father reported the incidents regarding Kuto, the headmistress would call him to her office and give him a proper dressing down. Then it would be all over for me. Kuto would never rest until he had clobbered me.'

Ashok was right. But back in the day, he was not on his own, all of us were Kuto's victims. The times our parents reported the class bully to the headmistress were the most dangerous times for us. We could not be seen alone at any time. Older siblings picked us up after school, we hung around with friends at recess, and in the last period, we hurriedly stuffed our bags with our books so we could follow the teacher out of the classroom. All these were tactics to keep the class bully at a safe distance from our persons. Sometimes it worked, and at the end of the school week, we went home feeling we could put it all behind us. But not for Kuto. He seethed through Saturday and Sunday and would be waiting on Monday with a vengeful look.

I was unlucky enough to be in the same Sunday school class as him. My mother had reported him two days before one such class. When I came to Sunday school, I caught a glimpse of him glowering at me. For the hour-long class where a young woman read and acted out stories from the Bible to us, I studiously avoided looking in his direction. Later, when we were trooping out of the room, I felt someone kick me on the shin. Hard. It caught me by surprise. I thought my friend Mesaü had tripped and kicked me accidentally. I instinctively reached down and rubbed the area above the shin because it began to throb. I could already see the beginnings of a bruise. Where was Mesaü? I looked for my friend but she was talking to another girl at the back of the room, too far away to have made any contact with me. Then I looked to my right and froze. Kuto was standing next to me. Somehow, he must have managed to kick me while I was absently trooping out with the rest of the children. I will never forget the look he had on his face. The resentful, glowering look had been replaced by a self-satisfied expression as he nodded very slightly at me. Then he turned around and left. I don't remember how long I stood there looking at his retreating back. He had hit me! He had somehow managed to kick me in the shin without me noticing. He had got his revenge on me for reporting him. I squatted and rubbed my shin, but the rubbing only made it hurt more.

'What happened to you?' Mesaü asked with concern when she saw me. 'You have hurt yourself!'

'Oh, I … I must have hit it on the edge of the bench there,' I replied lamely. 'It's okay. It looks terrible, but it doesn't really hurt. Not much.' No way was I going to tell my closest friend what had happened. I couldn't say if Kuto would try something again if he heard me mentioning his name.

'Oh. Do put some salve on it when you get home. It doesn't look good to me.' Mesaü was the sweetest of friends and was the one girl that Kuto never picked on. We walked home together because her house was a few metres from mine.

Back at home, I hid my bruise from my mother and wore knee-high socks all day. The next day I wore cotton pants that reached to my ankles. I did that the whole week until the bruise was no longer visible. At school on Wednesday, I came face to face with Kuto when I was running back to the classroom after recess. He was standing in my way, but when he saw me, he stepped aside to let me pass. He even mumbled a sorry as I went past. I was not sure if it was meant for the shin attack or for blocking my way. I mumbled an okay or thanks and rushed to class.

I mentioned it to Mesaü when we were going home. I still had not told her about the shin-kicking.

'I was surprised because I have never heard Kuto say sorry to anyone.'

'Maybe he is changing his ways.' Mesaü would always look for something positive to say about people, even the ones who were not nice.

'I guess we will be free of him only when we leave school next year,' I said.

Mesaü looked shocked. 'Do you hate him that much?'

I felt ashamed then. I stammered and could not reply. It was not that I hated any of my classmates, but Kuto had a way of getting under my skin and making me feel worried, fearful and exposed all at the same time. And it was not a good feeling. An image of the boys whom he bullied came to mind. Did they also feel the same way? It must have been very unpleasant to have such feelings when you were a boy and were expected to defend yourself.

I would ask Ashok about it the next time.

Weeks went by without any messages from Ashok. I, too, was busy looking after a sick family member. Then he resurfaced and sent me greetings for Christmas.

'I miss Kohima at Christmastime,' he wrote. 'I mean old Kohima, the Kohima we grew up in. My father used to receive so many gifts at Christmas—cakes, biscuits, sweets and gifts for us children. Both Naga and non-Naga friends used to bring gifts. In those days, we never thought of Christmas as a Christian festival. It was a festival for everyone. My mother gave me new clothes on Christmas and my sister got a new Christmas dress every year. We went out in our new clothes to dinners at friends' houses. It was wonderful!

'We lived in town so we would hear carols being played from the Choto Bosti area. When the carol singers came out at night, my sister and I chased each other up the stairs to stand on the balcony and watch them as they marched to specific locations to stop and sing. The Naga hospital was one of their first stops. I remember there was one year when we watched a group of carol singers standing outside the jail singing many songs. They often carried lit candles so we could see them clearly. Some of those groups were invited to sing at Raj Bhavan for the governor. But there were many times when they would just stand on the road and sing for passersby. It was very moving. "Hark the Herald Angels Sing", "Silent Night", "Joy to the World", "Away in a Manger",

"Deck the Halls with Boughs of Holly"—all the popular carols. My sister and I would sing along because we knew all the words and my parents never minded. In fact, my father would join us with his big booming voice and my mother hummed some of the tunes. Imagine that, a Sikh family in the heart of Kohima town, celebrating the birth of Christ and singing Christmas songs! You'll never see the likes of that again. We had a Jim Reeves' Christmas album that we played during the Christmas season on my father's gramophone.

'And my mother would prepare many Indian sweets—jalebis, laddoos—you know, to give to people who came to the house with gifts for us. She could not let them go away empty-handed. It just was not done in our culture. Our neighbours, who were Christians, used to be the first recipients, and friends of my parents coming with cakes would be given my mother's wonderful laddoos. They laughingly called it a gift exchange. And that was not all. We would put up a plastic Christmas tree that my father had bought from Khan Market, Delhi, and hang lights on that tree. We always spent a whole day decorating our house for Christmas. The kids from the neighbouring houses often asked to see our tree. It was probably the first plastic tree in town.'

It sounded wonderful, but this was the first time I had heard that people like Ashok and his family also celebrated Christmas along with other citizens of Kohima. How strange that was. I always thought it was only Naga families who took Christmas celebrations seriously. Our own Christmases were all held at my grandfather's house. We decorated the house with coloured paper that my cousins cut into different shapes—triangles and star shapes to be hung on jute strings all around the house. The church was also decorated with coloured paper tied on long strings that were wound around the beams and the platform in front of the pulpit. The church youth would bring thorny boughs of holly and green ferns to decorate the church interior. The ferns and holly died in a week but that was fine as they lasted until New Year's Day, after which the decorations were all removed.

'You are bringing back many memories of childhood for me,' I wrote to him.

'But they are all good, aren't they?' he countered. 'Do you know the last time I went back was in 2001? And so much had changed. Our shop was no longer there, of course. We had sold it before we left, and in its place was a textile store being run by a Nepali family. Our neighbours were very shocked to see me. They said I looked like a young version of my father. The two of them, the man and his wife, had become very old and frail. I told them my father died in 1998, and they were so sad to hear the news that both of them wept and wept. When her weeping subsided, the wife went and fetched an old photo album and she made me sit beside her so she could show me photos of me and my sister as children and a formal photo of my parents taken in the Kohima photo studio. You remember that studio where you could take photos with a background of Taj Mahal or some grand Mughal garden? She said my mother had given her that photo and they had kept it in their album along with all their family pictures.

'"Where is your son?" I asked them. They had only one son who studied in a boys' school in Shillong and lived in the school hostel. She began to weep again and I felt bad for asking. I wondered what had happened to him. "Our son died. He came back after finishing his schooling from Shillong. He was admitted to a college in Guwahati, but the day before he was to leave he died in a motor accident. Your uncle and I are all alone now." I felt so bad for them. At the same time, I was very glad I had called on them and shared my news with them. Life is so hard as an adult. I am glad we had the opportunity to grow up in Kohima when life was still innocent and good. I am telling you, even Kuto could not spoil that for me. It is only as an adult that I appreciate my childhood years afresh.'

'Why did your parents leave Kohima?' I asked. I partly knew the answer to that. In the 1980s, factional killings took place in the heart of the towns and continued for a long time. Some non-Naga businessmen sold their shops and left the state. Businesses closed down and new shops came to replace them. The new Naga nationalist groups were coming down heavily on the business community in the urban areas, imposing taxes and extorting money. The traders dared not fail to pay because the new recruits had no sympathy for the businessmen who pleaded sickness in the family or trading slumps. Rumours were rife, and one rumour claimed that they sometimes sent a bullet in an envelope to shop owners who were lagging in payments.

'I left in 1987. I had got a job in Delhi in the government sector. My parents did not want me to return to Nagaland. They sold their shop, too, and left Nagaland. For the first year, they lived in our native place, Kapurthala. Later, I bought an apartment and brought them to Delhi and all of us lived in that house for the next two years. But one day my parents made a trip back to Kapurthala, where my maternal grandmother still lived. They never returned to Delhi, but bought a farm area adjacent to my grandmother's house and lived there quite happily. My wife is also from there.'

'I am sorry your family had to leave,' I wrote back. 'Things were not any better for the local people, and the worst part was we had nowhere to go. The extortion and demands for money made life very difficult. The nationalist movement was taken over by some unscrupulous people who saw it as an easy way of making money. It spoiled life for everyone.'

I expected someone like Ashok to be quite bitter against the Naga people for ruining his father's business. He had not said anything about it. But a few days later, I heard from him.

'You and I have to understand that the people who came onto the scene in the '80s and '90s and introduced violence into our lives were not real Nagas. I know that without a doubt. I grew up in Kohima and never had to worry that I was from another state. But when the troubles started in the late '80s, my father said it was a different generation from what he had known in all his life in the hills. "They are very different," that was the first thing he had said about the new nationalists.

'"They understand nothing of friendship and mutual respect. On the other hand, they only want to take what they can get for themselves. They are not doing it for their people. It is all about themselves." I understood what my father had meant. We loved Kohima because it was a place where people took care of each other. A place where people knocked on their neighbour's door so they could give them a cake or a plate of meat or even a bundle of vegetables. It was love passed on disguised as food. Suddenly all that came to a stop. Everyone was imprisoned by fear, fear of the new young men and what they could do. They all carried guns, of course. We left because the Kohima we knew had disappeared. They stole our Kohima, E, they stole our Kohima!'

I was a bit shocked at how emotional Ashok's message had become. Back then, I had felt the same way, but that was understandable because I was a Naga. He was not. He was from Punjab, for heaven's sake. How come he felt the same or almost the same as I had felt about Kohima? It was incredible. But then, why should it be so strange? We had both seen a different Kohima. We had both lived in it even though we had never even socialized while we were both living in it.

In his latest message, he was calm. 'I do know that things have changed since that terrible decade. I heard how different associations and groups worked for peace and were successful. But I can no longer return because the old Kohima is long gone. That is what makes me very sad, E. I could have taken over my father's business and brought up my children in my childhood home! I guess it was not my destiny. Yet, even today, a corner of my heart will always belong to Kohima.'

'I think you are a Naga in your heart, and not a Punjabi alone.' It had come out in a rush. 'I mean, the way you understand our people so well, it's almost as if you were one of us.' It was clumsily put but I hoped he would understand. He did.

'I am a Naga-Punjabi. I always will be.'

Could there be such a thing? Perhaps. Why not?

Outsiders in an Insider World:
The Migrant Workers in Nagaland

Nona Arhe

One morning in 2020, at the peak of the Covid-19 lockdown, a group of distraught locals surrounded a truck loaded with sacks of rice in the heart of Kohima town. It was a crowd of interested—or perhaps, desperate—buyers. There was a problem: Who would unload the sacks of rice? There were over fifty rice sacks to unload, each weighing 100 kilograms. Due to the lockdown and the uncertainty about their future, most of the labourers in Kohima had returned to their homes in other parts of the country, causing a severe labour shortage. After a bit of distress, customers were relieved when the truck driver and three other people offered to unload the rice sacks.

On a typical day, two labourers, commonly referred to as 'deshwalis', would have promptly done the work for a minimum wage. Nagas have become accustomed to the constant presence of such labourers from north India and Muslim labourers from neighbouring Assam in most of the town's commercial areas. Since these labourers do all the manual work, Nagas have become overly reliant on them. The Covid-19 pandemic highlighted this reality and challenged the Nagas to see how crippled they had become without their easily available services.

There is a substantial and reasonable demand for the services of migrant labourers in Nagaland. While this need is well-accepted, Naga society is far from sharing equal social or cultural rights with them. Regardless of how long they have lived in Nagaland and how much their services contribute to the economy of the state, they will always be outsiders, desperately seeking work in the state and constantly vulnerable to those around them, the insiders. The pandemic exposed the sad reality that when their services were not needed, they were viewed as intruders and treated with suspicion. There are districts and localities in the state that even have strict rules limiting which 'outside' communities or outsiders can and cannot work in their jurisdiction.

For many years now, Nagaland has recognized that the state is a popular migrant labour destination. As the need for construction workers grows, there is also an awareness that migrant labourers are now spreading across various districts, including in the most remote villages of the state. The state's economy could not have grown and developed without the flow of migrant labourers. Both the state and the migrant labourers are aware of this notion, but it is never discussed beyond the basics of paying them what they are entitled to and allowing them to work legally.

Migrant labourers in Nagaland come from Assam, Bihar, Rajasthan, Jharkhand, Chhattisgarh, Uttar Pradesh, West Bengal, Karnataka, Kerala and some from the neighbouring states in the Northeast. They are a common sight, working in construction, transportation, trade, domestic work, as daily wage earners and in education, among many other sectors.

The rapid change from wooden or cottage-type housing to concrete multi-storey buildings, both in urban and rural areas, has opened massive opportunities for labourers, who are needed for loading and unloading materials and labour work on construction sites. There is unprecedented demand as a result of the rise in urban population and related infrastructure development projects. In the last two decades, the demand for labourers in this sector has been at its peak, and there is a huge gap in the supply of these services.

The skyline of Kohima, the capital of Nagaland and the second most populous district in the state, is rapidly transforming, as an explosion of unplanned concrete structures coincides with the town's expansion. Rapid urbanization has led to the replacement of verdant hills by mushrooming concrete structures. Each one of those concrete buildings was most likely built with some contribution from migrant labourers because building concrete structures is not one of the Nagas' many common skills. Naga building traditions include woodwork and aesthetic stonework. Naga architectural skills are mostly based on using locally available materials such as bamboo, wood and stone. Hence, the sight of all those concrete structures on sloping hills is a clear indication of the presence and work of migrant labourers.

Although migrant workers have made significant contributions to the development of the state of Nagaland, they continue to remain outsiders in every aspect of the term.

Twenty-nine-year-old Binda Yadav, a native of Bihar's Motihari district, is a second-generation head loader migrant labourer in Kohima. He apprenticed under his father for a few years and learned the trade. After years of working as a head loader in Nagaland, his father returned to their village, passing on his trade and contacts to his son. Binda Yadav makes about Rs 10,000 a month unloading trucks from 2 a.m. to 10 a.m. every morning. He believes the rapport that his father had built over the last thirty years enables him to take on the job smoothly and with ease, which gives him an edge over other new labourers in his area of work. Since his father was already working in Kohima, he was able to get all of the necessary documents for his son, making his arrival in Nagaland much simpler than it would have been for other first-time labourers coming into the state. When Binda first arrived in Kohima, a completely different environment, he did not feel lonely or afraid because familiar faces surrounded him. But he also admits that his situation is exceptional because he was under the watchful eyes of his father.

Moti Kumar from Uttar Pradesh, on the other hand, believes that times have changed for the better. Back in the mid-1980s, when he first arrived in Nagaland to find work as a labourer, he was terrified to venture out on his own even during the daytime, for fear of being beaten for no reason and robbed of his hard-earned money by rowdy boys. From the mid-1980s until the signing of the Naga ceasefire agreement in 1997, there was a temporary lull in labour demand. This was due to, among other things, the political unrest and the drug use crisis that Nagaland had witnessed during that period. Young, boisterous boys would frequently swindle the daily wagers, steal their money and even physically attack them, leaving them with little choice but to avoid such encounters. Moti Kumar is now well into his fifties. He speaks Nagamese fluently and has a working knowledge of several Naga languages. After living for several years in the state, he claimed to have developed a taste for the local cuisine that would have surprised his relatives and friends back in his hometown. Among his favourites are the local rice beer and pork dishes. He recalls vividly how significantly the town has transformed in the last few decades. Reflecting on his journey, Moti Kumar notes that there are families who have seen him mature from a youngster to an adult. He has also witnessed the ageing and death of his first employers, the birth and upbringing of their children and the start of their new families. Moti Kumar has a deep affection for Kohima, the city where he has spent most of his life, but his energy is waning and he fears he will be worthless in Nagaland if he is unable to work and earn a livelihood. He is already making plans to move back to his hometown permanently.

His plight, and that of others like him, is better than that of the migrants who do the bulk of the agricultural labour work.

Dimapur, Nagaland's commercial capital, is rapidly expanding both in terms of space and population. Many well-off families in Kohima and other highland areas in Nagaland own second homes as well as vast areas of agricultural land slated for agricultural development in and around Dimapur. Due to the stifling humidity and high temperatures during the summer, people from other districts avoid living in Dimapur during the hot season. However, when winters in the hill towns become unbearably cold, many of them flee to Dimapur, where the temperature in winter is pleasant. During the rest of the year, migrant labourers from Assam, from a community known there as Miya Muslims, wind up working in these fields with temporary settlement arrangements. Miyas are generally among the most impoverished groups of migrant labourers living in these outlying farms and fields, where they tend to the surrounding estates, raise livestock and cultivate food, which they share with the landowners as a means of subsistence. A significant group of the Miya migrant population coming to the state have a poor image and are commonly viewed as 'illegal' Bangladeshi immigrants. There is a perception that they cannot produce permanent address proofs or government identification cards.

Aziz Rehman is thirty-eight years old. He moved to Nagaland from Karimganj district in Assam with his parents and three siblings when he was in his early teens. When they first arrived in Nagaland, they were taken straight to a field located roughly an hour and a half away from the Dimapur city centre in an auto rickshaw. Their new home area was a complete jungle, with the nearest shop almost six miles away. They first constructed a single room with a thatched roof where the whole family slept on one side and made a kitchen at the other end. After a few years of developing the area and making it habitable, the landowners built a private home, so Rehman and his family moved to another field, almost similar to the first house, and started just like when they had first arrived in Nagaland. Since then, they have moved homes seven times. Today, Rehman and his siblings are all married and live in similar fields spread out across the Dimapur area. They are given free housing in exchange for clearing the area of weeds and other unsightly vegetation. When they have access to paddy fields, they split the harvest with the owners. To sustain themselves, they raise livestock and cultivate vegetables.

Field after field near Dimapur, bordering Assam, has Miya families as caretakers. They all live in similar sheds with very basic amenities. All of them typically rear livestock, plough fields and have flourishing vegetable gardens, enough to get by each day. Landowners who want to avoid paying higher wages and want fewer workers in their area often provide temporary housing and farming land to the Miya families. In addition, the use of agents who can supply inexpensive workers is on the rise. For these Miya families, life is full of temporary arrangements. They do not know where their future will take them. As the local population grows and the city expands, it won't be long before these open fields and jungles are developed and turned into vacation homes and recreational areas.

Amongst the most at-risk groups of migrant workers are, perhaps, housekeepers and domestic workers. A large number of these employees come from neighbouring states, with Assam being a key source. Often, they include juveniles. Several cases of both psychological and physical abuse have been reported in the past. Most of these children come from extremely poor families and, as a result, they are completely ignorant of their rights or what their minimum wage should be and, hence, are grossly underpaid for the work they put in. Workers in this industry, most of whom are migrants but also include Nagas from low-income households from remote villages, face challenges in expressing their grievances due to a lack of awareness regarding their rights, limited access to labour unions, and the absence of proper wage regulations for domestic workers in the state. In recent years, however, the availability of domestic help has decreased considerably as higher-paying alternatives have spread throughout their communities.

Meena was twelve years old when her uncle brought her from Assam to Nagaland to serve a local family as a domestic helper. For the past nine years, she has diligently worked as a domestic servant. Meena receives Rs 3,000 each month, which is paid to her mother in three annual instalments. Her uncle received a commission in the first month as the agent. Beginning with a lower salary, her pay increased as she aged and gained experience. When Meena was seven years old, her father died, leaving the family in dire financial straits. Her mother sent her out to earn money to support her younger siblings, as she was the oldest child and the family needed cash. But she is not alone in her predicament. Many young children, particularly those from impoverished backgrounds, are recruited and brought to Nagaland to work as domestic help. Usually, a relative or an acquaintance is responsible for recruiting these children. Meena has worked for the better part of her adolescent years but has no savings because her mother gets her entire pay well in advance to cover the family's expenses. Her future is uncertain. The only thing she is certain of is that when she leaves Nagaland permanently, she will be carrying a couple of bags filled with her clothes.

The United Nations Charter begins with the recognition that all human beings are born free and equal in dignity and rights, irrespective of where they live or what status they hold. All member states of the UN endorsed this charter and pledged to abide by the principles laid down in this charter. However, we are all aware that the application of these ideals is only possible in a true sense and real in a society where there are no hierarchies or where there are no insiders or outsiders.

Migrant labourers all over the world are frequently subjected to hostile treatment and denied fundamental human rights simply because of their status as outsiders and their propensity to bend the rules to find employment. How we speak about migrant labourers and the narrative we promote often plays a fundamental role in ensuring their dignity and human rights. Similar to migrant labourers throughout the world, in Nagaland, they are often disproportionately vulnerable to discrimination and marginalization. Although there is clear evidence that their contribution to the economic growth and the daily lives of citizens of the state is invaluable, they are often compelled to live and work in the shadows, hiding their grievances, afraid to complain, and denied rights and freedoms that other citizens often take for granted.

The movement of migrant labourers across borders is a worldwide phenomenon. Due to unprecedented economic growth brought about by globalization, free trade and massive infrastructural development, demand for migrant labour is a growing trend around the globe. While there is a growing demand for services from migrant labourers, there is also a growing resistance and social unease amongst the locals in various places, including Nagaland, towards the continuing influx of these workers.

As an increasing number of migrant workers enter the state, younger generations of locals, especially those unemployed and living in rural areas, are starting to view migrants with distrust and disdain. There is also a concern among the local community that the migrant workforce may bring outside values that undermine the traditional way of life. As a predominantly Christian state, it may seem low through the lens of morality that migrant labourers who play a vital role in the day-to-day lives of the people are treated poorly. Besides hazardous working conditions, their living situations are often considered unsafe due to a lack of basic necessities. Every day, a migrant labourer in Nagaland is reminded in one way or another that he is an outsider and does not belong. Interestingly, in the rest of the country, those who feel unsafe or oppose authority are often told to 'go to Pakistan', but in Nagaland, according to Moti Kumar, a native of Uttar Pradesh and a long-time resident of the state, if they ever protest, the normal response is to tell them to 'go to India'. He considers such comments cruel and upsetting. However, the good weather, numerous job opportunities and steady earnings in Kohima have prepared him and numerous other migrant workers to cope with occasional abuse and prejudice.

In the local language, there are words specifically used to refer to outsiders. Some might be a rough translation from their place of origin, like 'people from the plains', while others may have a pejorative ring to them. For years, the term 'deshwalis' referred to any migrant worker who relies solely on their physical abilities to make a living. The term originated to describe the head loaders who do the most physically demanding work, but it has since come to refer to a more disparate group of labourers who rely on brute strength to make a living. Deshwali labourers are perhaps among the most important, yet the least compensated, least appreciated and most harassed migrant labourers. Their services are needed in a wide range of domestic contexts, from delivering cooking gas to constructing houses. For example, deshwalis are indispensable to communities that lack the human resources to move large, heavy items on foot, particularly in hilly terrain with limited access to paved roads.

Migrant labourers face major challenges while settling in towns like Kohima. There is constant pressure to double-check that they have all the proper identification and documents with them before setting out every single day. Anyone unable to present the required updated papers when randomly checked by multiple authorities faces the prospect of being imprisoned or made to pay fines.

The Inner Line Permit (ILP) is the first document that must be obtained to enter Nagaland. This permit can be obtained with a guarantee from a local citizen and a payment of Rs 300. The permit is valid for three months, and migrant workers are required to renew their papers a few days before the expiration date. The next step for them would be to apply for a proof of residency certificate from the colony chairman, along with confirmation from their landlords and a fee of Rs 100. The local district student union issues a supplementary permit for a yearly charge of Rs 200. The application for a student union permit in Kohima comprises a series of checkboxes that the applicant must tick. Workers are required to not only name their places of employment but also their religious affiliation. A work permission slip from the parallel government of the Naga political groups costs Rs 200, and depending on the town, migrant labourers may need to pay more than one group. With the Naga political group, checking is done at random and paid in cash on the spot.

For unskilled migrant workers, applying for the ILP is the most difficult part of the process. Many of them have trouble finding guarantors because most local employers, except for big contractors, are reluctant to furnish personal documents to guarantee migrant labourers, especially the daily wagers. It is even more difficult for new labourers coming to the state for the first time with no local contacts. As a result, many of them delay applying for an ILP until they have made contact with a local guarantor. Following the outbreak of the pandemic, it became mandatory for all migrant workers to carry a vaccination card. Those who were unable to provide their vaccination card when requested were not hired, and this was especially true for those seeking jobs in government facilities or other institutions.

Due to the lack of a legal and regulatory framework for migrant labour recruitment and employment, some migrant labourers illegally enter the state through the porous border with Assam. Sometimes individuals flout the law and hire labourers directly from their home state when urgent or low-cost labour is needed.

Through the state government, there are several social security advantages available to those who are registered for the welfare of the daily wagers, such as insurance coverage, medical aid, child support and maternity benefits. Throughout the year, the Nagaland Building and Other Construction Workers Welfare Board under the Department of Labour, Government of Nagaland conducts regular events to disseminate information to workers who are not registered. This benefit, however, is restricted to labourers working for the government or private companies and does not reach independent labourers.

Migrant workers in Nagaland, like everywhere else, face difficult living conditions and frequent social isolation. Being cut off from their usual support systems, unable to communicate in the local language and unfamiliar with the local customs—all put them at a higher risk of being exploited and abused. Most such workers rely on inexpensive, sparingly prepared meals as they make every effort to stretch their limited incomes. However, there is little they can do to save costs in the event of sickness, accident or injury. For the great majority of migrant workers, having access to high-quality medical care that is also reasonably priced is at the very top of their wish list of things they would want to have.

Many migrant workers, regardless of their current circumstances, are willing to embrace uncertainty in pursuit of future benefits. One such labourer is Bihar's Rampur Mathiya village native, Umesh Ram. Umesh has been living in Kohima for over three decades. When he was seventeen, he visited Nagaland with his uncle, who had opened a tea stall in Dimapur. Umesh struggled very hard throughout his first few years, which began in the late 1980s. His inability to speak the language and comprehend the customs of the locals caused him a great deal of trouble, including being physically assaulted on a few occasions. Nonetheless, he is pleased with himself for having persevered and has made every effort to adapt to local conventions, including learning the language, to ensure a steadier income.

A young man in his early teens came to Kohima from West Bengal in the late 1980s through a contractor from Odisha. Jiten Das was promised Rs 30 a day, which was Rs 20 more than what he used to get paid working as a helper on a construction site in Karimganj district in Assam in 1987. Untrained in any line of work, Jiten was willing to do any kind of labour work—he did it all, from working as a helper at construction sites to selling tea at a bus stop. He said he first saw the 500-rupee note in Nagaland. Jiten was one of the many migrant labourers who worked in far-off villages until he made Kohima his base in the early 2000s. More than two decades later, married with two sons, Jiten continues to live in Kohima. He proudly boasts about the number of buildings that he has taken part in constructing, the first few years as a helper and later, after working for over a decade, becoming a foreman in construction work. Jiten has been involved in many construction projects, including churches, cemeteries, residences, schools and hotels. In contrast, he lives in a house made of tin, from walls to the roof, which gets unbearably hot in summer, while the winters can be brutally frigid. The only earning family member with a family of four to feed, Jiten, cannot afford a house of over Rs 3,000 per month in rent. He depleted all of his savings when his younger son was diagnosed with a heart ailment. Like many of his peers, Jiten survives by working every day. A day without work would imply a reduction in one of their monthly expenses. Although the cost of living in Nagaland is nearly double that of most migrant labourers' native states, the availability of consistent employment for those with the necessary credentials and skill sets means that working in Nagaland is still a preferable option to staying in their home states.

While the state attempts to regulate migration in accordance with the demands of its population and established norms, there is insufficient data on the exact number of migrants and the kinds of jobs they undertake for the state to implement effective migration regulation. No formalized system of labour management is in place to deal with the insensitivity with which migrant labourers are treated, notably in cases of delayed or no payment after finishing a task, harassment, accidents and injuries sustained on the job. Data from the few available surveys point to the pressing demand for migrant workers. Take, for instance, the results of a survey on hotels and restaurants in Nagaland in 2020 carried out by the Directorate of Economics and Statistics.[1] According to the survey, migrant workers make up 31.70 per cent of all employees. The percentage of male migrant labourers is 24.36 per cent, while women account for 7.34 per cent. These findings highlight the undeniable fact that migrant labour is in demand even in areas where locals have the relevant abilities. A fascinating aspect of the report is its categorization of hotels by religious affiliations and gender of the hotel owners. The data reveals 78.75 per cent of hotels are owned by Christians; Christians & Hindus (Partnership) own 3.94 per cent; Christians and Muslims (Partnership) own 0.79 per cent; Hindus own 14.96 per cent; and Muslims own 1.57 per cent.

An important point to consider with the state of Nagaland is that Article 371 (A) of the Constitution of India grants Nagaland specific protections to preserve the state's indigenous way of life and the provision that no act of Parliament shall apply to the state of

Nagaland regarding Naga religious or social practices, customary law and procedure, the administration of civil and criminal justice involving decisions according to Naga customary law, or the ownership and transfer of land and its resources. As a result, except for Dimapur, Nagaland's commercial centre, no outsiders have a legal claim to land or property in the state. The hotel industry data is a good example of the impact of the rule that outsiders can only legally run businesses in the state when they form a legal partnership with a local resident. Similar trends can be observed in a wide range of other areas of economic activities.

Psychologists have long recognized the beneficial effects of social connection. A sense of belonging comes from being accepted by and contributing to a larger group. A sense of belonging arises when an individual feels rooted and accepted in some community and committed to fulfilling some role within it. Belonging is fundamental to human well-being because it confirms the individual's significance. On the other hand, without belonging, people can begin to feel worthless, shameful, lonely and resentful. All the negative emotions that make people isolated are sometimes even disruptive to social harmony. One cannot feel a sense of belonging or stay loyal when constantly reminded of his or her status as an outsider. Recognizing and appreciating the contributions put in by others is a great way to foster a feeling of togetherness and oneness for the greater good of all.

Divisive language, which stigmatizes and categorizes migrants using racialized descriptions, is one way of determining the non-belonging reality. The notion of belonging underscores that it is something that must be subjectively experienced; it cannot be determined from one's objective social or cultural status. Migrant workers bear tremendous personal sacrifices but they are also invaluable to the economies of both their home and host states.

The International Organization for Migration (IOM) states that human rights violations against migrants can include a denial of civil and political rights such as arbitrary detention, torture, or a lack of due process, as well as economic, social and cultural rights such as the rights to health, housing or education. In law, policy and practice, many migrant labourers lack an adequate standard of living, social security and other favourable conditions in which to work. Legal and practical obstacles that prevent migrants from effectively enjoying their rights include lack of identification or proof of residence, financial services barriers, lack of information, linguistic difficulties and fear of being reported to law enforcement agencies, which can cause detention or deportation.

With the strong presence of identity politics, which is so emotionally charged, any suggestion for social or cultural integration of migrants can lead to massive social and political unrest. However, the 'sense of belonging' required for good mental health, referred to as 'happiness', is rooted in the following elements: due recognition of their contribution to society's growth; positive interaction; access to basic health and housing services; and freedom of movement and worship. Meeting such basic human needs can break down the barriers between insiders and outsiders and enable a healthy coexistence.

Finding common ground can help us increase mutual understanding and empathy, build bridges, identify the core issues that cause resentment and hatred, and pave the way for the voices of underrepresented groups to be heard. When we promote stories, we realize that the values we hold in common are stronger than those that divide us, and we will find a space where we can meet as equal human beings. In that space, we can replace the dominant narratives of fear, division and exclusion with those of hope, inclusion and the change we want to see, one story at a time.

Many Complexities of a 'Simple' Tribal Identity

Ranju Dodum

Twenty years ago, as a young undergraduate student in Delhi, I found myself at a meeting of people from the Northeast. In attendance were several prominent members of the Northeast diaspora living in Delhi who had spent considerable time trying to build awareness about the issues plaguing the region. One by one as we tried to discuss some of the issues and find possible solutions, one of the delegates made a remark that has stayed with me to this day.

On the question of identity, the delegate said: 'When I'm out of the country, I am an Indian. When I land at Indira Gandhi International Airport [in Delhi], I'm someone from the Northeast. When I land at Lokpriya Gopinath Bordoloi Airport [in Guwahati], I'm somebody from Arunachal. When I cross the state boundary and enter Arunachal, I'm somebody from a particular district, I become someone from a specific village. And when I go to my village, I'm from a particular clan, and within the clan, I'm from a specific family.'

The delegate's point was that identity is fluid and changes as per our circumstances. That who we are is often related to where we are.

Since then, whenever I'm asked about the question of identity, I hark back to what I had heard a long time ago about its fluidity and relativity, physical and/or otherwise.

~

It was perhaps my third stint at a call centre job in Delhi, or rather, Gurgaon—sorry, Gurugram. Like many of my colleagues, I was in the queue for a meal at the office cafeteria. Suddenly, someone tried to jump the line, saying that his break was ending soon and asking if we minded. I had no issues; I still had twenty-five minutes on my break.

Somebody else in front of me (who knew the person who was trying to cut the line), did not share the same sentiment as me or was perhaps in a jovial mood. What he said next, on that day fifteen years ago, is seared into my memory.

He objected to the person cutting the queue by very casually asking, '*Arrey yaar, tu SC/ST hain kya?*' Hey, do you belong to a scheduled caste/scheduled tribe? It was a snide reference to affirmative action policies.

When I heard those words, as a young twentysomething, I felt it best to not react.

It is years later, like now, that I think maybe … just maybe I should have said something.

I remain clueless about the ethnicity and caste of that person who tried to jump the queue. I had not seen him before and never saw him again. He may have been SC/ST or not. But was that why he was trying to jump the queue? And did it give the other guy, dripping caste privilege, the right to make that comment?

But I sheepishly stayed mute.

And I stand ashamed.

~

I am from Arunachal Pradesh. You know, the state that dominates your news headlines for a few minutes when Sino–India relations are discussed. Or when a rain-induced climate disaster occurs in the Himalayan belt.

Arunachal Pradesh is home to at least twenty tribes and more than a hundred sub-tribes who live in an area roughly the size of the state of West Bengal. The entire state's population of 18.2 lakh, however, is less than that of the average district in West Bengal. But even within this relatively small population exists a plethora of ethnicities and cultures, tribal perspectives and identities, all of which, somehow, are bound together in the constructed Arunachali identity.

This essay is an attempt to try and understand what it means to be an Arunachali from my perspective. A little background, however, is necessary.

I am a child of mixed ethnicity. My father was one of the first people from his village, alternately spelt as Meora/Mlorang/Meyora (pronounced with a 'ñ' between the 'm' and the 'o') to step outside the confines of his ancestral home and seek a living outside. Stories of his adventures and misadventures (some real, many concocted) are enough to fill the pages of this book.

His younger brother, my uncle, also ventured forth. Their escapades together are the stuff of legends of the kind we do not publicly talk about.

My father's father, like his father before him, was a simple man who lived and died working his field, living the way his ancestors had for centuries. They hunted when it was hunting season; they fished when they could; they tilled the land when it was time; and they made merry throughout the year. That was, and in some ways still is, the Nyishi tribal way of life.

On the other hand, my mother is from the plains of Assam. She is from the Mishing tribe, who, although they trace their origins to the hills of present-day Arunachal and beyond, have grown accustomed to life in the plains.

Mishings have their own interesting history, which can be best described by members of the community. While I am no expert, having grown up in the shadow of my mother, I can at least say that they are generally more easy-going people as compared to my Nyishi 'brethren'.

Even as a child, I knew that we (my siblings and I) were of mixed heritage. I was more aware than my sister and brother because I looked the least 'tribal'. That is to say that I did not fit into the idea of what a Nyishi person is supposed to look like. For some, I still don't.

I was told I had 'big eyes' or that I didn't speak like a tribal person or have the domineering attitude that a Nyishi man should have. (Unlike our tribal brothers and sisters from the Chota Nagpur Plateau who have been subjugated by the upper castes of Indian society, the tribals in the Northeast never had to overtly live under the rule of an outside force, historically.)

Even though I grew up hearing such things, I never questioned my identity as a Nyishi. For me, my father is a Nyishi, so that naturally makes me one too. I do remember, however, as a pre-teen, asking my parents that if my father is a Nyishi and my mother a Mishing, does that make me a Bengali? The idea of ethnicity was clearly not as well-defined in my childhood brain as it is now.

Perhaps that was the only such moment of 'identity crisis' I've had.

I have never been anyone else other than a Nyishi man. That identity, which I have justified on several public platforms, comes from a sense of belonging to the land where my ancestors came from.

In the past, I have often said that I am Nyishi from a certain village because that is where my ancestors came from; and that no matter where I may have been born and raised, I can always claim my ethnic affiliation because we are tied to our land. That, I feel, is what gives a tribal or indigenous person their identity.

I say this because, in my worldview, a non-tribal or non-indigenous person can be uprooted from their home and blend into the ethnicity of the larger surrounding groups. It isn't like it hasn't happened. Several prominent families from western and central India or the Gangetic plains of north India whose ancestors migrated into present-day Assam are as important to the fabric of the Assamese identity as a Bodo person is.

After migrating to Assam a little over a century ago, many families have 'become' Assamese. But generally, in most tribal societies, becoming tribal is not tradition. You are either born a tribal or not.

Can you imagine the roles reversed, however? Can you imagine a Bodo tribal in Gwalior operating a successful hardware store or a petrol pump, while the family retains its tradition of marrying exclusively within the community? Can a tribal living in such a place whose traditional food includes beef open a restaurant serving beef to its patrons, mirroring the 'pure veg restaurants' run by settlers in tribal-majority areas?

We often forget to acknowledge that tribal indigenous people are the colonized today.

But I digress.

~

I had agreed to write this piece, but it was only after a long staring contest with the blank white page on the computer screen that I realized I was in way over my head. So, I approached a renowned author to seek some guidance.

'How should I approach the subject?', 'What should I even explore or write about?' were among the questions I asked to gain some clarity from the writer. 'Why should it be insider–outsider? Why should identity be about us and them?' the writer replied. It made me think back to a conversation I had had with a senior university professor some years ago about how all identities are made-up constructs, to which I had argued that not all are made up and that some become distinct organically.

Over the last few years though, I have noticed a growing practice amongst some tribes of the state who have changed their tribal affiliations. Friends and acquaintances who once identified as belonging to one tribe now identify as being part of another. Some tribal clans with the same surname identify as members of different tribes. In some such cases, meetings are held, seemingly lost kinship affiliations are rekindled, and it is then declared that henceforth no marriages are to take place amongst the people of the clan.

This happened recently with my clan—when a small number of clans from two other tribes, Aka (Hrusso) and Miji (Sajalong), were declared as being our brethren. There always existed lore that a few men from our clan had ventured out of their village many generations ago and had adopted different surnames and the identity of the neighbouring tribes. A couple of years ago, this was acknowledged at a village meeting and it was decided that members of those 'rediscovered' clans would not marry anyone from our clan.

The prohibition is common amongst tribes in the region, which often practice clan exogamy, i.e., not marrying someone who has been identified as a member of the same clan.

Exceptions, however, do exist.

I know of at least one clan in one tribe where those sharing the same surname are permitted to marry if it has been established that there exists a significant generational distance between the two individuals. This means that even if two people in love share the same surname, it is socially permissible for them to be married if their families have been separated by large distances for generations. While this is a rare instance, another tribe practices an extreme form of exogamy where a person is prohibited from marrying anyone from either side of their family going back at least seven generations.

This shifting nature of clan and tribe can lead to complications. There was one example where several clans/surnames of a tribe were subsumed under a larger clan and were henceforth said to be kin. In many cases, couples who had been married for years suddenly found themselves related not just through matrimony but apparently also by blood. They stayed married of course, but the clan heads/elders declared that henceforth such things must not be repeated.

Such is the complexity of the 'insider' of Arunachal Pradesh. The idea of an identity is not always as clear and lucid as many would like it to be. It is often ambiguous, depending on where one is standing.

~

As seen in some tribal-majority states of the region (most notably in Arunachal Pradesh, Meghalaya and Nagaland), there have been many cases of mixed marriages between tribal women and 'non-tribal' men.

The outsider, typically a non-tribal from the Indian mainland, is known by many names that vary across the Northeast from state to state and tribe to tribe. There's the Khasi word 'dkhar' and the Meitei 'mayang'. In Arunachal, owing to the diverse set of tribal groups, there are different names. The Nyishi term is 'hareng/haring'.

While these words may not have necessarily started as terms of derision and insult, that is what they have morphed into today. But that again, like all identities, is fluid.

The term 'hareng' in the Nyishi language may not always be a term of endearment, but that does not mean it is a term of enragement alone. When used in anger, violence and juvenility, it is very much a racist term. In casual conversation when referring to a person of non-tribal origin, it is merely an identifier.

In an ideal world, we wouldn't speak that way where we distinguish between us and them. But we live in a world where we do.

Aren't indigenous people from the region referred to as 'the Chinky ones' outside of the Chicken's Neck region? Can anyone deny the racist etymology behind that term? Has the word 'Chinky' ever been used endearingly in the narrow lanes of post-Partition housing colonies of Delhi? Is there any historical-linguistic basis for the use of the term?

Apologists in the Northeast often try to compare the use of such words and indulge in whataboutery. They say: 'Oh, but don't we use this term? Do we not discriminate?' There are also those who have genuinely suffered at the hands of criminally inclined individuals and bona fide terrorists whose very agenda is to divide people, who say that racism also happens in the Northeast.

There is no denying that. These things have and continue to happen.

Such whataboutery, though, is an admission of guilt. It acts as a justifier of inappropriate behaviour that is meted out by locally dominant majorities to individuals who do not conform to racist ideas of how a person should look and behave. To say that 'racism happens there too' is to say that it is fair game.

Instead of indulging in whataboutery, we must work together to build a better place. That proverbial better place cannot exist if we deny the real-world issues of identity and close our eyes to the fact that these identities, as constructed as they may be, have existed for centuries and one cannot simply wish them away.

In a utopia, we wouldn't have these barriers, these differing languages, philosophies and concepts, these differences in how we approach subjects and principles. But the world we live in allows us to differ, it makes us question and not conform to diktats.

In an ideal world, we would all live under one large metaphorical roof running across the globe. There would be no borders and passports and visas would be redundant. But we must realize that in such a scenario, that long-running global roof would collapse in on itself, with no pillars to stand on.

From 1964 to 1969, thousands of Chakma and Hajong people fled their homes in Bangladesh's Chittagong Hill Tracts following the construction of the Kaptai dam and religious persecution. While their natural areas of refuge were Tripura and Mizoram—which share borders with Bangladesh, and where ethnic Chakmas already lived—the government of India also settled around 5,000 of them in parts of Arunachal Pradesh, most of whom were pushed to the eastern districts. As their numbers increased over the decades, a fear of demographic change grew in the state. It has been alleged that there has been an unnatural growth in the population of the Chakma people in the state owing to illegal settlement and migration from other states.

Most Chakmas in Arunachal live in miserable conditions. This is a fact that no one can objectively deny. The areas where Chakma populations exist are economically backward and lack many basic facilities for modern-day living and hygiene. This is not to say that their lives are beyond liveable, but they could certainly be better. Efforts must be made to ensure that every individual has access to a respectable form of living. This is an essential that every human must desire for another.

However, when it comes to the Chakmas, the fear amongst the indigenous people of Arunachal is the same that people have about other non-indigenous population groups—that the insider will one day become the outsider.

In the international advocacy circuit, the Chakma lobby has the strong backing of eloquent individuals who have received modern formal education for generations but the second-generation of post-Independence educated Arunachalis is not so well-represented.

Human rights experts and lobbyists fight for the refugee rights of the Chakma in Arunachal Pradesh but say nothing of the rights of indigenous people. A constant argument given is that the Chakma population is minuscule when compared to the other tribal groups of the state. This argument conveniently forgets to mention that in the places where the Chakma population is concentrated, they are a significant minority. This fact bears mentioning because, in tribal societies like ours, every mountain, forest and stretch of river is owned by tribes and clans. This practice effectively means that those outside of the tribe and clan are not permitted to use the land or forage from it unless the owner allows it.

These rules and laws are still in practice today. Tribes that have lived with each other for centuries have been forced to change their ancient ways to accommodate settlers because someone in Delhi said so.

I wonder what would have happened if my parentage were flipped on its head. I have good friends of mixed parentage where the equation is reversed, with the father being an 'outsider' and the mother an 'insider'. Does the child become an 'insider'?

While the matrilineal system in Meghalaya allows it, none of the tribes in Arunachal Pradesh have traditionally followed that system. Yet, today, we find that many are of such heritage and have taken up their tribal mother's surname and become invaluable parts of their society. More often than not, such individuals tend to be 'more tribal' than those to whom the title of 'indigenous' is given at birth. They appear to play a relatively more active role in the tribe's societal activities. This is in contrast to others in the same economic conditions who may become complacent as they feel that what they want is a birthright, while the others may feel it is something that they must work hard to earn.

Perhaps such thinking lends itself to jealousy amongst men in societies that are not matrilineal towards a person who has adopted their mother's surname and progressed in life. In recent years, there have been growing calls in the state for an end to the adoption of tribal mothers' surnames by children born of non-tribal fathers.

During a conversation with a friend who comes from such mixed parentage, I sought his opinion on the matter. He said that as long as his tribe's society accepts him, it is no one else's business. But what makes a society and what counts as a society's opinion? Even if one person opposes it, does it still count? Would it not count if the one person opposing it happens to wield economic strength?

Such questions will likely remain unanswered for years.

Perhaps, identity cannot be categorized into insider and outsider alone. Many of us breathe in the middle.

Belonging and Unbelonging
in Sikkim: What Does
'Sikkimese' Mean to Us?

Karma Paljor and Naresh Agarwal

The skies are blue, perfect for mountain viewing. We watch in familiarity and awe as Mount Kanchendzonga, the guardian deity of Sikkim, starts changing colours as the morning sun hits the slopes. Two of us from Sikkim, and both living far away from it, are meeting at Ganesh Tok, which is at a higher elevation than Gangtok town and about five kilometres up hilly roads. During our conversation, we reminisce and discuss what Sikkim and Sikkimese mean to us. What was it like growing up in Sikkim? What do insider and outsider, belonging and unbelonging mean? What bothers us? What are we hopeful about? We invite you to partake in our conversation and take our views as those of two individuals who love and feel for Sikkim. You, as the reader, are free to either nod in agreement or disagree, because respecting individual opinions and human differences are what life and democracy are all about.

The two from Sikkim

Naresh Agarwal left Sikkim for Singapore in 1995 to pursue computer engineering and has since visited home once, or sometimes twice, a year. As he travels up from Bagdogra Airport, the vehicle goes around the hills and a cool breeze welcomes him. 'You feel a sudden drop in temperature—from the heat of Siliguri to the sort of natural air conditioning that we have as we travel by the Teesta river,' says Naresh. He crosses the Rangpo truss bridge and smiles when he sees the 'Welcome to Sikkim' board. He is home. As he continues his journey up the hilly roads to Gangtok, he says, 'The excitement is high by the time you're going to reach home and meet your people.'

Karma Paljor arrived a few days earlier and attended an ancestral ritual in Barfung village of south Sikkim. It's a ceremony where his clan members, the Namchankopas, come together to pray to their ancestors and thank them. He also visited Enchey Gompa. 'Enchey Gompa holds significance to many of us because we used to go there to pray and seek blessings for our exams, when travelling out and even otherwise,' Karma says. Looking down from the side of the road near the monastery, one can see Tashi Namgyal Academy, the school where both Karma and Naresh had studied, with its bright new tarmac, the football ground and the science block, where they had spent many days learning from their favourite teachers.

Naresh (N) belongs to the Marwari community that settled in Sikkim during the late 1800s. His forefathers had moved there from Rajasthan. He grew up speaking Marwari with his grandparents and parents and Nepali with his siblings. With six generations in Sikkim, he has known only Sikkim as his home. He is part of the less than 1 per cent population of the state, numbering about 3,000–4,000 people, who are also referred to as 'old settlers'. 'When I reach home, I try not to come out for a day or two because I just want to "be",' Naresh says. 'After being everywhere, I want to feel being home, being back. After a day or two, I feel more ready to meet people. When I start walking along M.G. Marg, I see many familiar faces and I stop at almost every juncture, with people saying hellos and asking *"Kahile aayo? Kasto chau? Apooi!"* When did you come? How are you? Oh my God! What I also notice is that some of the little boys and girls that I have seen growing up are now grown. I see more wrinkles on people's faces, more greying hair and sometimes, I see older people turned into photos on the walls.'

Karma (K) belongs to the Bhutia community. The Bhutia kings of the Namgyal dynasty ruled Sikkim from 1642 to 1975, when the state became a part of India. The land area of Sikkim was much larger previously and included parts of eastern Nepal and Bhutan. Present-day Indian towns of Darjeeling and Kalimpong had later been 'gifted' to the British. Some historians have recorded three founding races of Sikkim—Lho-Mon-Tsong. Lho refers to the Bhutias, Mon refers to the Lepchas and Tsong are the Limbus.

Context

In January 2023, a Supreme Court ruling granted income tax exemption to the 'old settlers' of Sikkim, who include Marwaris, Biharis, Punjabis and Muslims who had settled in Sikkim before it became a part of India in 1975, at par with Sikkim subject and Certificate of Identification (COI) holders. A remark in this ruling categorizing Sikkimese Nepalis as individuals of foreign origin sparked widespread outrage in the state. Anger poured out in the form of protests online and on the streets. The Sikkimese Nepalis, who constitute the majority of the population, held the old settlers responsible for their being tagged as 'foreigners' and saw this as a conspiracy against their community. Calls were made to boycott business establishments owned by old settlers. The fabric that bound the peaceful Sikkimese people was torn. There was also protest against the inclusion of people of Indian origin who were residing in Sikkim before the merger with India in the definition of 'Sikkimese' for income tax exemption. There were fears that this 'expansion and dilution' of the term Sikkimese would put at risk the special rights and privileges enjoyed by Sikkimese people as sealed in Article 371(F) of the Indian Constitution when Sikkim merged with India, and that it might empower the old settlers to demand more rights and equality with Sikkim subject and COI holders.

We, Karma and Naresh, decided to meet and have a conversation during this difficult time for the old settler community of Sikkim—a time when they have been singled out for the perceived backstabbing of the Nepali population. The chilly, crisp mountain air hits our faces as we sit at Ganesh Tok. Naresh is grim. Apart from the hate for the old settler community on social media, following the Supreme Court ruling, he is hurt by attempts to rob him of his sense of belonging to Sikkim and branding the community he was born into as 'non-Sikkimese'. It's hard for a person who deeply loves Sikkim and has known no other home. With multiple generations and extended family, including great-grandfather's brothers' descendants in Sikkim, Naresh has been a proud Sikkimese—at least, he thought so. His brilliance in academics and discipline had made him a darling of his schoolteachers. He was a school captain, loved and respected by all around him. The turn of events in Gangtok has hurt his sense of identity, associated with the only home he knows, and it saddens him.

The dialogue begins

K: How did you feel when you started seeing the hate on social media post the Supreme Court judgment?

N: I went through the full cycle of emotions—surprise to shock to deep anguish. I don't think I have reached full acceptance of it yet. Sometimes, the anguish was due to the extent of hate or viciousness; and at other times, due to the people engaging in it, as some of them were people I held, and still hold, dear to me. I did realize though that my anguish was not mine alone. It was a collective and shared anguish for all those who grew up loving Sikkim, irrespective of race or community. While our arguments could be different, the anguish was of a connected people who were feeling the disconnect and then assuring themselves with reasons to justify the disconnectedness.

K: You felt more hurt because some of the people spreading hate were close to you?

N: I guess so. I try not to distinguish among people. For me, people are people—individuals trying to fit in as well as stand out in the world, trying to survive, belong, to be loved, accepted and respected. And people in Sikkim have always been and will always be 'my people'.

Growing Up in Sikkim

K: What was it like growing up in Sikkim for you?

N: Usually, when we say 'in Sikkim', you don't grow up in Sikkim. You grow up at home, on the streets where you walk and in your school. If you ask a fish, 'What was it like growing up in a lake?', the fish does not know the lake. It knows the plants that are growing in the water and the other fish around. We did not know anything outside of Sikkim. All that I knew were Gangtok and Mangan, where my father's elder brother and his wife lived. I knew Kalimpong of course, where my mother's family was from, and where my eldest sister got married. Most of my winters were spent in Kalimpong, a few in Mangan (Kalimpong is outside of Sikkim, Mangan and Gangtok are in Sikkim). That's what my world was. Occasionally, it would be Siliguri for things here and there or for somebody's wedding. It was only in 1995 that I first saw an airport in Calcutta, now Kolkata, and was later astounded upon seeing the Changi Airport of Singapore. For me, growing up in Sikkim was the small world of a kid. The outside world is what you see later. I think that's the same for any other child who grows up in Namchi, Lachung or Geyzing, but does not know Mangan, Gangtok or some other parts of Sikkim. What you know are the surrounding hills. There is this hill that we see from Gangtok when one looks from M.G. Marg beyond Lal Market. It has a particular curve. There's a small dent on the left side.

That hill, to me, was Sikkim because I saw it throughout my childhood. When the weather was clear, you could see the Kanchendzonga above that. You get different views in Mangan and from the roads. Also in Gangtok, Deer Park was a big part of growing up. Whenever anybody visited, we would hike up the trails that we called 'shortcuts'. I loved the old Buddha statue there, with the lamp in front of it. Though it's still there, not as many people go to see it now. They have put a glass casing around it. I felt close to it while growing up, as with Chorten and Rumtek gompas.

K: How was family?

N: I got a tremendous amount of love from my grandmother, sisters and parents. My grandfather died early, when I was in lower kindergarten in Tashi Namgyal Academy, but my grandmother lived until I was in class four. I did well early on in my studies and was noticed. The teachers liked me. I worked hard to earn their appreciation, which I got from home as well. I think much of what I did was for that sense of connectedness and belonging throughout. I also had loving friends at every stage. How was growing up for you?

K: I think I was born to be a journalist. Growing up in Sikkim, I was always a curious child. I had so many questions. Sometimes, my dad's friends would run away because of them. I was a good student initially, but by the time I reached class ten or eleven, I lost interest because I started questioning. They were not teaching me what I wanted to know. For me, when I was growing up, and even now, a place is always about people. I try to know people. In this process sometimes, I may have offended people also.

When I remember my first fantastic trips, they are of me running up to the paan (betel leaf) shop, slightly above the then chief minister's house. That used to be the only paan shop where we could get paan for the elders, cigarettes, sweets, twenty-five-paise chewing gum and, importantly, Parle-G biscuits for fifty paise. Sugar was rationed; sugar tea was a luxury and I used to love it. Parle-G with tea in the morning was a dream come true, which my granny used to hide sometimes and treat us to. Both my parents worked in the government. My first interactions were with the paanwala (the person who sells betel leaves). His name was Sipai and he was a Muslim from Bihar. He would say 'Hello' and smile at me. What I loved was the respect he used to give my father. I always felt my father was an important person because he had a government jeep and all that.

In class one or two, my sister and I started walking to Tashi Namgyal Academy from Arithang (three kilometres away on hilly roads), which I still consider a big feat. There were few cars back then. Everybody knew everybody, so you felt safe. On my way to school, my first stop would be Metro Point, where we would get special treats or a softy ice cream. As a child, I found Metro huge. But the grocery shop next door, run by two brothers, also sold all kinds of stuff. We used to get five rupees for our lunch money, which we divided into two rupees fifty paise each. I loved Amul cheese. We used to buy a cube from that shop for fifty paise. My sister used to fight with me when I would give her two rupees and some change. I remember the people selling those and I remember people saying that they were Marwaris. I didn't know where they were from. I didn't know anything about them. I didn't find them to be any different from everyone else. When we went to school, we had such fantastic teachers, many of them from outside Sikkim. Our school was great. In my childhood, over dinner or otherwise, I never heard a discussion about 'us' against 'them' or being run over by people from 'outside'. I never heard those things, especially against the Marwaris.

I also remember my other favourite, Student's shop, where we used to get all kinds of stationery, books, and colourful stuff for our school projects. I remember the 'father', the patriarch who started the shop, speaking in perfect Bhutia and Lepcha. It was fascinating. It was later that I started hearing some local people talk about threats from outsiders, about Sikkim getting taken over and all that.

'Indian' and other labels

N: I also don't remember any of these terms like 'outsiders' or 'influx' while growing up. I started hearing these more in the late 1990s or early 2000s, when I used to come home from Singapore. Growing up, the terms that I had heard of occasionally were slurs like 'dhoti' or 'kaiyan'—not personally, but I was aware of them. It was mostly used when you saw two people in a conflict. But another word that was used more was 'Indian'.

K: Yes, yes!

N: I remember, as a child, sometimes if I'd be called Indian, then I would feel like retorting, *'Mo Indian ho bhani, timi ko ho?'* If I'm an Indian, then who are you? A Nepali friend of mine, two years older than me, told me that people used 'Indian', but they should be saying plainspeople, as that's what they're trying to say.

K: I heard 'dhoti/kaiyan' many times, but I never thought of them as racist slurs. I always thought them to be something you say when you pull somebody's leg, along with other terms like 'bhotey' or 'bahun' (used for other communities). I never looked at it in a racist kind of way. But later, when I was in class nine or ten, it clicked. I understood, 'Oh, this is racist!' Another term, 'madhise', was a natural term that my granny used without malice. When she grew up in the kingdom of Sikkim, 'madhes' meant the plains and 'madhises' (or 'madheshis') were people living in the plains.

N: As is used in Nepal as well, right?

K: Yes. As for the term 'Indian', I think many of us used it while growing up. We would say, 'Oh, you're Indian,' without realizing what we were saying, just because our grandparents or parents used it. We didn't get as many tourists then, but instead of asking them, 'Are you from Mumbai, Delhi or Bengaluru?', we would ask, 'Are you Indian?' I think it was so because we were growing up not long after the 1975 merger of Sikkim with India. It's been forty-eight years now, so I think it has finally sunk in fully that we are a part of India.

N: I think you touched upon something important. A few words had nothing to do with the community, but were used when boys fought. And sometimes, these community-centric words would come as a part of that. I think people were getting offended then, but, at the same time we did not even know what racism meant or that it was bad to be racist. Nor did we know anything about diversity and inclusion, which we know now.

K (laughingly): And don't forget 'Bhotay-kaiyan' (used for Bhutia-Marwari), which you would be called if you were stingy. Which community should take offence?

N: When people speak in Marwari and say *'Kistra karoon?'* or *'Kaiyan karoon?'*, they're asking 'How should I do it?' When the Marwaris arrived in Sikkim around the late 1800s, more than 120–130 years ago, the locals heard that different language for the first time and being spoken by people who looked different—men in turbans and dhotis, women with long 'ghoongats', veils, over their heads—and had come from faraway Rajasthan to do business. I see images of people like these in some of our old family pictures from the 1950s or '60s or earlier. People heard the Marwaris saying 'kaiyan-kaiyan' in their conversations. When you don't understand a people or a language, you start calling them with what you hear. I think that's how this term came into being.

I see problems with labels. Even the terms 'Sikkimese', 'Indian', 'kaiyan' or any other term can mean different things when used by different people. What I see happening a lot lately is politicization of terms. You take a term, throw it up in the air and ask people to catch it—turning people into jugglers. The terms mean nothing more than the differing meanings attached to them by different people at different times.

Language

K: When I went to Bengaluru to study, a brilliant lecturer taught the economics class I took. But every so often while teaching in English, he would just break into Kannada. I used to feel alienated then because I wasn't able to understand what he was saying. The whole class would laugh, but I would suddenly feel alone. Did you ever feel like that, since starting school? You did know the language, however.

N: Language was never an issue for me. You and I both went to Tashi Namgyal Academy. We studied in this elite school founded by the Chogyal (Sir Tashi Namgyal, king of Sikkim from 1914 to 1963) and, as you know, speaking in Nepali was frowned upon there. Kids had to speak in English and were punished for speaking in Nepali. For me, there was never this question of a language in terms of Marwari or Hindi. During the first week in class one, you had to choose a second language to study, apart from English. I went to the Nepali class and there somebody asked me, 'Are you sure you want to take Nepali as a second language? Maybe you should take Hindi.' I had no idea why they said that. Nepali was, at least, a language I spoke at home. We all spoke Nepali among brothers and sisters. And I had absolutely no idea about Hindi.

K: Wow! Wow! I took Hindi, by the way.

N: Yes! After that, I came home and asked my mother about it. I told her that Hindi is not our language—we speak Marwari or Nepali. My mother said, 'Why not? Hindi is our official language. You should learn Hindi.' I said, 'Okay, fine.' And from the next day, I switched to Hindi as a second language. I eventually took Nepali as a third language a few years later.

Nurtured by different communities

N: When anyone in Sikkim called me 'Indian', I saw myself as no different than them, as I was born in the local STNM (Sir Thutob

Namgyal Memorial) hospital and grew up in Gangtok. The only difference was perhaps that I spoke another language apart from Nepali or that my mother wore a 'sari pallu' over her head—many older Marwari women do that.

Naresh (centre) with Tikamaya didi (left) and Manju didi (right), Gangtok, Sikkim, late 1970s.
Photo courtesy of Naresh.

My sisters studied at Paljor Namgyal Girls' High School and all their friends were mostly Nepali, Tibetan, Bhutia or Lepcha. There's a childhood black-and-white photo of mine that I love. My oldest sister, Manju didi, who was fourteen years older than me, and her closest friend, Tikamaya didi, are both holding my hands. Manju didi is wearing a 'bakhu', which was royal blue, the colour of their school uniform, and Tika didi is wearing a kurta-pajama. I'm this little kid, about three or four years old. I think that image, for me, is Sikkim—a Marwari girl wearing a bakhu and her Nepali best friend holding the hands of a little boy who is a brother to both. The picture is also special because Manju didi passed away in 1988, when I was in class six.

My other sisters' close friends were also from different communities, and they called me 'bhai' and treated me as their younger brother. We were close. It was not just a visit-once-in-a-while kind of relationship. They were just there as a part of you, like family. I used to go to their houses, and they would come to ours often. We celebrated 'bhai tika' (brother-sister festival). Even now, they're close and present in good or bad times, as we are for them. There was never this separation in terms of communities. The only thing that we thought about was whether 'this person is nice or not'. That person could be from my family, a Marwari, or a neighbour who was Nepali, Bhutia or Tibetan. My own close friends were from different communities. When I was in class two, my friend, Sangay Dathup, and I used to pray together. He would bring images of the Buddha and I'd bring images of Hindu gods. We'd put them inside our shared desk. At times, incense smoke could be seen coming out of the crevices of the desk, hahaha!

K: We were great friends, of course. We went to each other's homes. My Marwari friends and I were close-knit, and still are. We were there for each other through thick and thin.

N: Right. We were always there for each other's weddings and funerals. My wedding pictures and videos have my local friends from all communities. Many classmates and teachers came to my wedding in 2003, which was held in Deorali, Gangtok. I have gone to my sister's friends' weddings. Our communities have always been there to support each other in times of illness and death. During the class ten and twelve board exams, my friends stayed at my place and we studied together. There wasn't this idea that you only go for your own community's events. Community was based on friendship, kinship and location.

Inter-community marriages

K: I do wonder though as to why I didn't see too many love stories between the Marwaris and other communities. Why didn't I see inter-community weddings? What was it that brought us close enough to eat together but not marry?

N: Inter-community love stories were there but were frowned upon. I can think of at least four examples of Marwari–Nepali weddings in my extended family itself, including during my father's time, and their children born of mixed heritage. The reason why these were infrequent is because across India, I think, elders encouraged their children to marry within the community. For the Marwaris, it was probably to do with vegetarianism to a large extent. What you ate or not was an important consideration for marriage.

K: Growing up, I did not see inter-community marriages, but you did. I guess it was slowly getting there.

N: Yes. In our generation, there are many more inter-community marriages, including those of some of my cousins. There is much more acceptance now. These love stories and marriages did happen, and are happening. Irrespective of these, one shouldn't need to have an inter-community marriage to be recognized as equal. One can be distinct and still have equal rights.

Contributing to Sikkim

K: Absolutely. We were comfortable. We had no problems. The Marwari community began migrating to Sikkim in the 1800s. The community, since then, has settled in Sikkim with no or little connection to their roots. They have been pioneers in establishing trade ties with Tibet.

The community had contributed so much—to the growth of business, trade, banking and economic development of Sikkim. Rajesh Lakhotia has been my mentor, and I learned a lot from him. His father, Motilal Lakhotia, was a pioneer of the Indo-Tibet trade. They went through tremendous hardships trying to break down cars, bringing them here by carrying them on bamboo stilts across the 15,000-foot Nathula Pass, and reassembling and selling them. These are amazing stories of resilience.

N: My uncle Deepchand Agarwal, my father's sister's husband, used to go to Tibet as well. He and Motilal Lakhotia were buddies in the Indo-Tibet silk route.

K: I guess it's because of their efforts and resilience that the Marwaris uniquely found a seat at the Chogyal's table. The Namgyal dynasty was always open to communities who brought prosperity and trade to Sikkim. And the reason Marwaris were close to the Chogyal was because they had something to offer. There was value in Indians settling down in Sikkim, leaving everything behind in Rajasthan. I don't know if any of the Marwaris invested the money that they earned in Sikkim back in Rajasthan.

N: That money was spent in Sikkim. I remember even in the Thakurbari in Gangtok, after my grandfather died, my family donated money for a room there in his name. I never saw Thakurbari solely as a Marwari place. It was a Hindu place, a mandir. It belonged to various communities. There was a Bihari pandit called Akhilesh, a Nepali pandit and a Marwari pandit as well. Rumtek was also a place of reverence for us. All these places were yours to go to whenever you felt like, including Enchey Gompa, Chorten Gompa, etc. I never saw them from the lens of any caste or community.

Marwaris follow culture and tradition, with various rituals for childbirth, weddings, etc. To carry those out, we had pandits from different communities coming to our house all the time. They would call my grandmother 'Aama'. I don't recall my family looking for a pandit from any particular community. There was never this kind of apparent malice or viciousness that we saw in some of the social media comments in the aftermath of the recent Supreme Court verdict.

Not taking up Citizenship

K: Now, let's talk about the elephant in the room. These were people who spent their entire lives in Sikkim and were even there when we were a kingdom. Then why did they not take up citizenship when the Chogyal offered it to everyone in 1961?

N: I asked my mother about this. She got married in 1960. Her parents were from Kalimpong and my father was from Gangtok. She used to have this ghungto (veil) over her head in front of my grandfather and speak to him facing elsewhere. She said she asked my grandfather, '*Log nagrikta lewen lagra hai. Aapan bhi lewan.*' People are taking on citizenship. We should too. My grandfather told her, '*Aapan ne kembi chiye hai?*' Why do we need it?

I can understand his thinking now, as I went through a similar sentiment. I lived in Singapore for fourteen years but did not take up its citizenship. Some of my classmates did, as that would help them apply to American MBA programmes from a smaller pool of Singapore applicants compared to Indian applicants. You could also travel visa-free to most countries that way. It is a pretty powerful passport. I didn't feel I needed to give up my 'Indianness' or Indian citizenship for the sake of visa access or just to get college admission. I see my grandfather's argument from that point of view.

I also read the 1961 Sikkim citizenship eligibility requirements. One of the requirements was giving up any property that you had elsewhere. That property had to be disposed of or given away, along with any live interests that you might have had.[1] I find that to be a difficult clause. I don't typically see such a clause in the naturalization requirements of other countries where you have to dispose of or give up inheriting any property in your country of origin. My family had a house in Rajasthan—a traditional haveli, which was shared between my great-grandfather and one of his brothers. I think it would have been a difficult decision to give up all property rights and family ties there. Now, some of the arguments that I read when the Supreme Court verdict issue happened is that if many families tore up their land 'parchas' (documents) in Nepal to become Sikkim subjects, why didn't families with origins in India do that. The sense in those arguments was that when the Chogyal gave an equal opportunity to everyone to become citizens, our forefathers made the choice by giving up ties and yours did not; now live with it, bear with it—it was a choice you made.

Equal rights

N: My problem with that line of argument is that my grandfather was given that choice and let us say, he made an error in judgement. Maybe my grandfather made a mistake in 1961 by not taking on Sikkim citizenship, but apart from that, he and his kin's entire lives were spent in Sikkim until death. My question is this: Why should that one decision of your forefather become a barometer for subsequent generations being denied rights until now, even after your family has lived in a place for 120–130 years, or being called an outsider after all this time? How many generations does it take to be considered an insider? Are five or six generations not enough? Or do you need to get plastic surgery to change your features to make yourself look a certain way—to be accepted as equal? Or do you need to give up being vegetarian totally? Or stop marrying within your community in all cases? There are many mixed families now in Sikkim. And many of them do not have the COI.

K: Maybe you do need to change your features to be accepted. Let us accept that there is racism all around us. We divide, divide and divide more, based on everything from your religion, physical features, place of origin, food habits, etc.

N: The fact that fails me is that it is such a small community. There are 400-odd old settler families in Sikkim. If you give them the full rights that every other Sikkim subject holder has, rather than losing, you will help integrate a people who have been on the margins for a long time. You will help strengthen your multiracial society. It's only some 3,000–4,000 people. You can serve as an example of diversity and inclusion and show other Indian states and the rest of the world that while they might indulge in 'us versus them', we take everyone along, including people who might look different from us.

K: I don't see that happening.

N: Yes, especially because of the prejudice and viciousness that we saw recently. But it would be a worthy move. The Chogyal saw it. He saw the people on the fringes of society, and he offered the Sikkim citizenship in 1961. He offered it to everyone. It was the right thing to do. In my view, rather than the old settlers fighting for their rights, other people in Sikkim should be arguing to give them equal rights. It is such a natural thing. I don't even understand why the old settlers had to go to the Supreme Court by themselves to fight for their rights—to get income tax exemption which the rest of the Sikkimese have? You don't become weaker by giving equal rights. You only get stronger. Even in the context of countries, you see that in Singapore, which transformed from a Third World to a First World country by embracing multiracialism. Despite being a Chinese-majority country, they have had Tamil-Indian Presidents in S.R. Nathan and Tharman Shanmugaratnam, a foreign minister in Vivian Balakrishnan and various other examples.

K: But the funny thing is you're talking about a different country. That is the paradox. This is happening with people in a state from the same country, which is strange.

Foreigner Versus Foreign Origin

N: Yes, it is ironic. Even in the aftermath of the Supreme Court verdict, many things happened. There was a major misrepresentation all around that the old settlers called the Sikkimese Nepali community 'foreigners'.

In reality, as I understand it, the word 'foreigner' was never used for any of the current people of Sikkim. There is a major difference between 'foreigner' and 'foreign origin'. When you say someone is of a foreign origin, it means your forefathers—your grandfather, great-grandfather and others—came from a foreign land. When the huge uprising happened, one of the major reasons for mass anger was that '*Hami lai foreigner bhanyo!*' They called us foreigners. When you say you're a foreigner, you're saying that you don't belong here or that you are an outsider. And that is hugely offensive to anyone. That foreigner argument was widely floated at the time, which rightly angered the majority Nepali community of Sikkim but was clearly a misrepresentation.

I don't like the term 'foreign origin' either, which was there in the Supreme Court verdict (and, thankfully, removed after the protests). It was clearly wrong and childish of the petitioners to argue for their rights by terming their brethren community as one of foreign origin. It is like a child going to a teacher and asking why their friend got more marks than they did. As far as the anger based on the 'foreign origin' term is concerned, it is rightful and justified. Just that a vast majority did not make this important distinction between the two terms. If a person is of foreign origin, that does not make them a foreigner at all. Several American Presidents traced their family origin to foreign lands. I have no shame in saying that my great-grandfather came from Rajasthan. My grandfather, his three brothers and cousins died in Sikkim. My father was born in Sikkim and died here. I was born in Sikkim. I lived in Singapore for fourteen years and have lived in the US for another fourteen. As far as I am concerned, I am from Sikkim. The fact is, in 1961, all those people who chose to become Sikkim subjects became citizens of the kingdom of Sikkim. This is what the term 'Sikkimese' meant until 1975.

'Sikkimese' identity

N: Now, in the current context, when you say Sikkimese or non-Sikkimese, what is it that you mean? Do you mean erstwhile Sikkimese?

Sikkim subject meant 'citizen of the kingdom of Sikkim', right? But Sikkim became a state of India in 1975.

K: Yeah.

N: I see the term 'Sikkimese' as someone who was born in Sikkim, grew up in Sikkim and loves Sikkim. That is Sikkimese to me. Look at it from an Indian point of view. People from Sikkim are Sikkimese. People from Rajasthan are Rajasthani. People from Gujarat are Gujarati. Your identity is linked to whichever state you come from. And people from each state could be of different communities, including ethnic minorities with origins in other states.

I know I'm not a Sikkim subject or COI holder. Personally speaking, I am okay with having limited rights. That does not matter too much to me, even though it would not be ideal from Sikkim's point of view. Rather than me wanting it, ideally, you would want your people to have equal rights. The Marwaris of Sikkim are Sikkim's people. They're not Rajasthan's people. It's good for a region to give equal rights to its people, so that there is an equal sense of belonging, and nobody feels lesser. Irrespective of limited or equal rights, the term Sikkimese matters a lot to me. It's linked to my identity. The question is if I am not a Sikkimese, then who am I? I am not a Gujarati, I am not a Manipuri, I am not any other term. I am a Sikkimese without being a Sikkim subject or having a COI, but I am not a non-Sikkimese. Basically, today, the Sikkimese are people from Sikkim, where Sikkim is a state of India. If you're calling yourself Sikkimese as citizens of the kingdom of Sikkim, I think you can distinguish that by saying 'erstwhile' Sikkimese, which is Sikkim citizens before 1975. Yes, my family was not Sikkimese before 1975, though they had lived here since the late 1800s, and thus, is not 'erstwhile' Sikkimese. But my family is Sikkimese today because we are from Sikkim.

People made fun on social media about what 'Sikkimese of Indian origin' means. This means 'erstwhile' Indians in Sikkim or Indians who were in Sikkim before 1975. There is confusion between pre-1975 people and people now. Pre-1975, my family was Indian and did not take up Sikkim citizenship in 1961. But post-1975, the people of Sikkim are all Indians.

Whether you were a Sikkimese or not in 1975 matters to the extent that people who were Sikkim citizens then are given special rights now. I am okay with the term 'Sikkim subject or COI holder' versus not. But 'Sikkimese' is a term I am not willing to say doesn't belong to me. It's funny because now that I live in the US, I'm not looking for any privileges or jobs in Sikkim, but the term 'Sikkimese' matters a lot to me emotionally.

The need to safeguard rights

K: You don't have to be physically here. For me also it does not matter. I pay my taxes like anybody else. I have not taken any special privilege or scholarship meant only for Sikkimese people or for scheduled tribe people. I have done none of that. I have been selected and have fought on my merit for educational seats and jobs. But, I guess, you and I are different from the rest. As I grew older, I associated myself with different people, including Sikkimese sub-nationalists, and could understand their sense of insecurity. I was drawn into this idea that we needed to protect our people and safeguard our rights and our land from encroachers. The issue of fake COIs is also there—people who are said to have procured COIs using illegal means. What has now happened with the income tax case is that it has united the Sikkim subject and COI holders of Sikkim, who are now suddenly feeling threatened by outsiders. This is being echoed more than ever. Who are these outsiders? Speaking for myself, I never saw Marwaris as outsiders, nor Biharis as outsiders.

From here, I don't know where this is going. I want the Sikkim youth to be prepared and ready for challenges. I want them to be able to conquer the world. I want us to be a community of survivors because we are such a small community (six to seven lakh people). I want us to thrive. It's nice to look up at the Parsis—how they arrived in India, created businesses, and built one of the biggest business conglomerates in India, the Tata Group. Can we do the same? Will the people of Sikkim be able to thrive in the new India? It is easy for us to be overrun. Ideally, I would want us to train our youngsters to thrive. But is it even possible when we still have many issues such as alcoholism, learning disabilities in children related to alcoholism, and an education system not aligned to prepare our children to face the world? These are the questions that, sometimes, worry me.

N: These are legitimate questions. Unemployment and mental health are major issues. We have the dubious distinction of having one of the highest suicide rates in the country. I completely understand this insecurity. It is somewhere correct. Sikkim largely depends on funds from the Central government to run the state. There are Sikkim quota seats in colleges and universities across the country for students from the state, with sub-quotas within those reserved for various communities. Article 371F and the protection it provides are important for the people of Sikkim. The way it works with rights and privileges is that once you get them, you never want to do away with them. This has been the case for many other kinds of reservations and privileges across India. I think what has happened, especially since the removal of Article 370 in Jammu and Kashmir, is that there is deepened insecurity in Sikkim, and maybe also in other Northeast states of India that are protected. We've seen people expressing fears of their rights being taken away. Personally, I don't think these will be taken away at all. They were the special terms given to Sikkim as a part of its merger with India in 1975. People need these rights and privileges. I do not think we are yet prepared to compete with the rest of the country on an even keel. I think the fear of being overrun is also legitimate. There is the danger of big industries and people who do not love the Teesta coming and taking over. When I see the changed colours of the Teesta, I feel disheartened. Deforestation is happening. The flash floods of October 2023 brought death, destruction and calamity to so many people, especially in north

Sikkim. We saw how everyone living along the Teesta could easily be endangered. It was heartbreaking for all of us. We do need to protect our environment and natural resources.

Addressing racism against 'outsiders'

N: I think the Marwaris feel the same way as the Nepali, Bhutia or Lepcha communities in terms of these concerns. My concern is that the increased use of terms such as *Bahira ko manche*, person from outside, and so on gives rise to a racist mindset in the younger population. I am troubled to see these terms being used easily by young people now, because you must see human beings as human beings first. You have special rights, that is fine. You need to protect those rights. But that should not give you this kind of viciousness to start looking at other people with malice. And that was never there in all our years growing up.

K: It was already there!

N: It was not there the way we see it now, right? Not to this degree. Maybe it has to do with social media. People have their rights and privileges, which is fine. But there is this sort of policing that we see—trying to guard identities strongly with statements like 'Why is this hawker who does not have the COI over here?', 'Residential Certificate (RC) holders should not have these rights', etc. Permanent residents of Sikkim are anyway lesser people than the Sikkim subject and COI holders, in terms of rights. These are pre-1975 people in Sikkim without the same privileges. They are not post-1975 people in Sikkim. Whatever limited rights permanent residents have, any talk of removing or lessening them is unnecessary. When you are given special rights, you should hold on to them. But don't be vicious against people who do not have those rights.

K: Isn't racism present across India? I have seen this 'insider–outsider' debate in other states as well.

N: It is. But whoever does that is being foolish. For instance, if you call Amitabh Bachchan an outsider in Maharashtra, it is absurd. Amitabh Bachchan has contributed more to Maharashtra than he might have ever contributed to Uttar Pradesh. To limit him to Maharashtra is again myopic. He is a global icon. If you try to limit Mahatma Gandhi to being a Gujarati, you are doing a disservice to the legacy of a person who has impacted the whole world. Having a limited sense of identity means that you live a parochial life. This limited outlook might be intrinsic, but it happens when we don't understand people as people first. It's just stereotyping. Our sense of identity must always be in a space where we include the person we are speaking with. You and I have a shared kinship in terms of growing up in Sikkim, a shared history of our school, etc. With every person we meet, we have similar shared values. While we might have forms of identity that differentiate us, the sharedness is what should connect us. Things that divide and things that unite both coexist in people. It's about what we choose to focus on. And I find much focus on the dividing part right now, rather than on things that unite us.

K: I find many of the current discussions centred around the insider–outsider debate. Do I want my son to also start discussing such issues? I don't know, because he's been brought up in Delhi and now Guwahati—he doesn't know what it is like to be a part of a community or how to seek protection. I don't even think he knows that he's protected or what his rights are. Should I be telling him that as a tribal, he enjoys special rights? Should I be sending him back to Sikkim? These are questions that haunt me sometimes.

N: Whether you tell him or not, he will get to know about these to a certain extent. But as parents, we don't want our children to be limited only by rights and privileges. The problem I see happening is that people are depending heavily on those rights and not equipping themselves adequately to face the world. It is important that we adjust, we live, and make our place in the world, and that happens when we don't limit ourselves to privileges, which can be a double-edged sword.

Stereotyping based on facial features

K: Is this insider–outsider issue of Sikkim, apart from what has happened with the income tax verdict, mainly about the way you look and your facial features? A Nepali from Nepal who has come in recently, settled down in Sikkim, and is driving a taxi or running a business has a greater chance of being accepted as he doesn't stick out like a sore thumb. Compare that to a Marwari who might have lived all his life in Mangan and suddenly decides to move to Gangtok and is looked at as an outsider.

N: I think you've hit the nail on the head. What is funny is that the Marwari girls and boys from Sikkim, or even from Kalimpong and Darjeeling, are mocked for their Hindi. Even my wife, who is from Darjeeling, uses phrases like, '*Adua kahan hai?*' (where is the ginger?) when talking in front of other Indian friends. I then need to explain to my friends, 'Adua is adrakh in Nepali', the Nepali word for ginger. Their Hindi is often mixed with Nepali. Marwaris of Sikkim and surrounding regions are intrinsically more Nepali than one would think.

K: That's funny. If I were to go to Delhi or Mumbai or Bengaluru, I would stick out like a sore thumb because of my looks. People sometimes ask me if I am from Malaysia or Singapore, and I laugh in response. Once when I was anchoring a show, they would say it made the channel look international, like Singapore TV. It has a lot to do with the way you look.

N: You've got it absolutely right. The stereotyping and prejudice that we experience, whether as a Marwari or a Bihari person in Sikkim, or as a Bhutia or a Nepali person in the rest of India, are, in large part, about the way you look. In the US, it often has to do with skin colour— people are seen as White people or Black people. In Sikkim again, when I was called 'Indian' growing up, it was about the way I looked. But that is only on the surface. As soon as you spend some time with someone or talk over a cup of tea or coffee, the initial prejudice starts diminishing. Stereotyping comes from a lack of information. Looking at the colour of my skin and facial features, a person in Sikkim might think of me as an outsider, and looking at you, a person in Delhi or Bengaluru might think of you as an outsider, but as soon as they talk and get to know us, they realize that we are from their state or country, much like them, and an insider just like they are.

Seeing through 'us versus them'

Why I call what is happening in Sikkim 'vicious', especially with certain people, is because they are knowingly indulging in prejudice. This is not about people who do not know you—that you're not from Malaysia or Singapore, and are an Indian like them. If a person knows that and still calls you an outsider, that is where I see a level of viciousness. Here, I know that it is coming from fear: that today the old settlers have asked for parity in income tax exemption; if you don't indulge in this vicious attack by calling them 'non-Sikkimese', then tomorrow they might ask for more social, economic and political rights, a COI, and a claim into the privileges that are meant only for us.

Any person who does 'us versus them' is making you believe that they are fighting for your rights but is basically trying to be in the limelight or gain political mileage or power for themselves by dividing people. We need to realize this clearly. This has been going on for centuries and is a common game, playing on your fears and emotions. If we see Hindu–Muslim, north-Indian–south-Indian, Sikkimese–non-Sikkimese kinds of statements anywhere, we know that the purpose is to divide society. These people are either victims of propaganda or are spreading propaganda themselves. Once a narrative settles, it is difficult to wash away. They will pretend to care about the land, but basically care only about themselves. That is how they bring relevance to themselves. We will vote for them, clap for them or like and share their social media posts, getting a moral victory over the 'other', but we are not doing any service to our place. Look at what happened to Germany. The Jewish people suffered when there were atrocities against them, but Germany itself got hugely destroyed in the process. Now, we see human rights violations in the Israel–Palestine conflict, in turn. If we see anyone doing Sikkimese–non-Sikkimese, insiders–outsiders or indigenous–settlers, we are not helping Sikkim or the cause of the Sikkimese. We are only dividing society and causing disharmony.

If we really care about our state and our nationalism, it must be an integrative one that takes every single person along, and not sow the seeds of division within our own place. No wise person would want to make siblings inside a house fight or call each other names. 'Divide and rule' was a tried and tested British policy when they ruled India. But this policy is widely used even today. People in Sikkim need to realize that anyone who is trying to divide us, in the garb of uniting the rest by creating a small 'other', is simply wanting to gain limelight or power, nothing else. A polarized people are easy to influence and rule over. If anyone talks about uniting all the people based on one religion against people who follow another religion, they are creating the 'other'. Similarly, if anyone talks about uniting all 'Sikkimese' against 'non-Sikkimese', they are still creating the other. So, we need to understand this game.

When you take less than 1 per cent of the population who have been with you for over a century, and you tell them that they are outsiders, second-class citizens or that they deserve to be called non-Sikkimese, when you alienate any part of the population, then you're not doing Sikkim any good. There should be an expiry date for calling someone an outsider. By accepting people on the fringes and making them mainstream and giving them any rights that they might not have had, and that too to a small number of people, you actually make Sikkim stronger. You don't weaken it in any way.

To the question of influx or the fear of being inundated by people from the rest of India, we already have Article 371F as a protection. Population increase is a reality in any place. People need to think about the right way to manage those coming to Sikkim from the rest of India, seeking opportunities. So far, the talk has been about the pre-1975 people—'the Sikkim subject and COI holders' versus 'the old settlers and/or RC holders'. How do you deal with the post-1975 people? Let us say, somebody's family came to Sikkim in 1976, they don't have permanent residency but have lived in Sikkim for forty-eight years now. Should they belong to Sikkim? Should they have certain rights, or not? On the one hand, you have certain rights and privileges that others don't have. But we also must be human. We must think about ways to protect our environment, resources and jobs, but how do we prevent creating a parochial society, and create one where we do not look down upon other human beings. These are not easy questions. I don't see people discussing these things often. There is a limited lens through which many people are talking.

Into the future

N: To summarize, all I would say is this. For me, Sikkimese is any person who loves Sikkim, who cares about its environment—rivers, mountains, hills and walkways, and its people. You should not try to lessen this sense of belonging in anyone who feels this belonging to Sikkim. And that would be the biggest service to Sikkim when you call the land, 'Sikkimey aama' (Mother Sikkim). A mother doesn't like to see conflict in her house. Embracing everyone is what you do if you really love Sikkim.

K: My summary would also be this. Only a community that is forward-looking, opens itself up, works hard, sets its priorities straight, and can do 'jugaad', improvise, will survive going ahead. It is the survival of the fittest. The more you try to protect yourself, build a wall, and get into a cocoon, the more you weaken your seed. For you to thrive, you need to be bold and you need to seek. That said, I don't worry about people who have privilege and money and can educate their children outside. Many Sikkimese now send their children to expensive boarding schools. I worry about the children who are studying in government schools and struggle with finances. I worry about that section. And I feel that until our infrastructure, education and healthcare systems are up to the mark, until our society becomes better and without alcoholism, drug abuse, and so on, we need a certain kind of protection.

N: I agree. I think the most important thing that you said is about protecting people who are economically weak. There was a big argument made about the Marwaris of Sikkim being rich, taking over resources, and controlling the economy. People don't know that there are many Marwaris in Sikkim who are financially weak, including some of my own relatives. There is this whole level of economic disparity. I think the divide should be between 'rich people of Sikkim' and 'not-so-rich people of Sikkim', instead of dividing based on community or insider–outsider. Economically stronger people, no matter which community they come from, could take some of the onus to uplift those not doing so well, and educate or provide better opportunities to one child from Sikkim, apart from one's own children. That is where the focus should be. We need to help those who are economically weak, underprivileged or marginalized in different ways; help people succeed—whether in fighting drug abuse, overcoming mental health issues or gaining employment. Everyone can serve as a mentor to someone else and be mentored by someone.

I feel that this talk of '*hamro manche, bahira ko manche*', insider–outsider, does not make for a strong, resilient person. You want to prepare a person to see the world as it is, equipping yourself with the skills and the knowledge to take on opportunities and overcome obstacles, and seeing people as individuals capable of both good and bad, and not from the lens of community because you have good and bad people in every community.

K: Absolutely. There are different communities here, and we've been living together for many years. That's what makes Sikkim unique. We've seen good times and bad. It is important for us to remember that we all love Sikkim, and we are here because we are a part of this place. We need to stand together and face whatever challenges come our way, as one people.

Epilogue

It has been a long morning. The day is sunny and Mount Kanchendzonga still shines brightly. The guardian deity has witnessed many conversations over the centuries and will witness many more in the future. It will always be ready to inspire, to guide and to protect. Karma and Naresh get up and slowly begin walking down from Ganesh Tok towards Gangtok. They both smile and are glad that they could meet and talk.

Notes

Scan this QR code to access the detailed notes.

Notes on the Contributors

Indira Laisram is a media professional based in Melbourne with seventeen years of experience in Indian mainstream media. She holds a master's degree in English from NEHU, India, and one in social policy from the University of Melbourne. Indira is actively involved in community journalism within the multicultural ethnic media landscape and was a recipient of the Judith Neilson Institute Grant in 2020.

Makepeace Sitlhou is an Emmy award-winning independent journalist, a Fulbright fellow, who has reported on human rights, social movements and about culture and travel in national and international publications. Her work on borders and indigenous issues spans from India's Northeast to Tanzania to the American southwest. She has been the recipient of several awards and fellowships both in India and abroad.

Veio Pou discusses literature, culture and society in the department of English, University of Delhi. Academic engagements aside, he also writes occasionally at the popular level on everyday issues. His debut novel, *Waiting for the Dust to Settle*, won the 2021 Gordon Graham Prize for Naga Literature (Fiction).

Teresa Rehman is an award-winning journalist and author based in Northeast India. She has worked for *India Today*, *The Telegraph*, *Tehelka* and Thumbprint NE. Recipient of the Ramnath Goenka Excellence in Journalism Award for two consecutive years (2008–09 and 2009–10), she has written two books—*The Mothers of Manipur* and *Bulletproof*. She is a member of the Editors Guild of India.

Margaret Ch. Zama (born April 1955) retired as professor of English at Mizoram University, Aizawl, in 2020. Besides serving as dean and head of her department, she was registrar of the university in 2004–05 and director, Internal Quality Assurance Cell, 2009–14. Her publications, apart from academic works, include her translations of Mizo fiction and tales that can be found in edited volumes published by Katha, Oxford University Press and Sahitya Akademi. Her areas of specialization are fiction and critical theory, while her areas of interest are folkloristics, cultural and literary studies, particularly of Northeast India.

Pratap Chhetri is a fourth-generation Gorkha settled in Mizoram whose ancestors were foot soldiers of the British colonists, some of whom later took part in the First and Second World Wars. He is based in Aizawl and works on media matters and public communication.

Hamari Jamatia teaches English literature at Govt. Degree College Santirbazar, Tripura. She completed her PhD from the University of Hyderabad. She is a former journalist who worked with *The Indian Express*, *The Hindustan Times* and *The Pioneer* in New Delhi. Dr Jamatia has also previously worked as a digital writing trainer and a mentor to Adivasi/tribal content creators. She is deeply interested in analysing the history of Northeast India as well as understanding its contemporary political repercussions.

Subir Bhaumik is a former BBC and Reuters correspondent and author of four books on India's Northeast and its volatile neighbouring countries like Bangladesh and Myanmar. He is now contributing editor (South Asia) for *Eurasia Review*. Bhaumik is a former Queen Elizabeth House fellow at Oxford University, Eurasian fellow at Frankfurt University and Senior Fellow at East-West Centre, Washington. He is on the board of two successful Calcutta-based companies and is both a corporate political risk analyst and a business facilitator for foreign corporates looking to invest in India.

Ramona M. Sangma has authored three books, two of which are on the Garos and their heritage. She is also involved in the conservation of heritage through different channels and activities. Her areas of interest are folk art and crafts, traditional knowledge, music, literature and culture. She is currently associate professor and head, department of English, North Eastern Hill University, Tura Campus.

Patricia Mukhim is currently editor, *The Shillong Times*, one of Northeast India's oldest English language dailies. She was a member of the National Security Advisory Board between 2010–14 and also served on the board of the Indian Institute of Mass Communication (IIMC). Mukhim unapologetically calls herself a journalist-activist and sees no conflict of interest there. She writes regular columns on India's Northeast for the national media and news portals.

Vatsala Tibrewalla is a writer and business professional who was born in Shillong. She has a bachelor's degree in economics from Shri Ram College of Commerce, New Delhi, and a master's degree from London Business School. She set up the iconic Dylan's Cafe in Shillong where she took a keen interest in literary events and organized several book launches, readings and film screenings. Vatsala has also had a decade-long career leading strategy at some of the world's largest consumer technology firms in India and Singapore. She has recently relocated to London and will further both her literary and business endeavours there.

Abhishek Saha is a journalist and author. He is currently a doctoral researcher at the University of Oxford, studying citizenship in India. Born and raised in Guwahati, Saha studied civil engineering at the Birla Institute of Technology, Mesra, and print journalism at the Asian College of Journalism, Chennai. He reported from Kashmir for the *Hindustan Times* (2015–18) and the Northeast for *The Indian Express* (2018–21). He won the Ramnath Goenka Excellence in Journalism Award for his coverage of the Kashmir unrest of 2016. Saha's debut book *No Land's People: The Untold Story of Assam's NRC Crisis* was published by HarperCollins India in 2021. It was shortlisted for the Sahitya Akademi Yuva Puraskar 2022.

Sangeeta Barooah Pisharoty is a New Delhi-based journalist and writer. Native to Assam, a part of her journalistic interest lies in Northeast India. Currently associated with The Wire as its national affairs editor and the chief of the news bureau, Sangeeta is the author of two non-fiction books—*Assam: The Accord, The Discord* and *The Assamese: A Portrait of a Community*.

Rashmi Narzary is a Sahitya Akademi awardee for children's literature in English. Her forte lies in creative storytelling and the reimagination of folklore and legends. Recipient of the Prag Prerona Award for Literature (2020), her debut novel, *Bloodstone: Legend of the Last Engraving*, has inspired doctoral research, while *An Unfinished Search* has attained global acclaim. Her work is being taught in universities and is translated into other Indian and foreign languages. *Whistles of the Siphoong: Tales from Assam's Bodo Heartland* is her latest work. A dog lover at heart, an author by passion and an independent editor by profession, abundance of nature rules her otherwise simple, easy narrative style.

Easterine Kire is a Naga novelist, poet, writer of short stories and children's books. Kire has a doctoral degree from Poona University.

She is a founder member of the publishing company, Barkweaver, based in Norway. She was awarded the Free Word prize by Catalan PEN in 2013 and the Hindu Literature for Life prize in 2015. She won the Tata Lit Live Book of the Year in 2017 and the Sahitya Bal Puraskar in 2018 for her book, *Son of the Thundercloud*. In 2023, her book, *Spirit Nights*, won the FICCI award for best fiction. Kire regularly writes articles for a Naga newspaper.

Nona Arhe is an independent writer and storyteller with over fifteen years of experience writing about Northeast India. She is passionate about shedding light on the region's diverse cultures, traditions and issues through her writing. She lives between New Delhi and Kohima.

Ranju Dodum is a journalist based in Arunachal Pradesh, recognized for his contributions to bringing the region's issues to the forefront in both Indian and global media. Over the past twelve years, his work has largely centred around environmental and local cultural issues, including the protection of Arunachal Pradesh's environment and tribal beliefs in the region. He is a Pulitzer Center grantee whose commitment to journalism has been acknowledged with the inaugural Kalyan Barooah Excellence in Journalism Award in 2023, recognizing his impact and dedication in the field of print media.

Karma Paljor is the editor-in-chief of EastMojo, a digital media news outlet that plays a pivotal role in delivering digital news focused on Northeast India. The platform has a mission to represent the 'eastern opinion' and bring stories from this often underrepresented region to a wider audience. He brings a wealth of experience from his tenure at notable media houses, including five years at CNBC TV18 and a substantial twelve-year period at CNN News18. He has won the Ramnath Goenka Award for Excellence in Journalism twice. He is a fellow of the Kamalnayan Bajaj Fellowship and a member of the Aspen Global Leadership Network.

Naresh Agarwal, professor and director of information science & technology concentration at Simmons University, Boston, USA, and former president of the Association for Information Science & Technology, was born and raised in Gangtok, Sikkim. With a degree in computer engineering and a PhD from Singapore, he is a painter, speaker, learner and author of two books—*Exploring Context in Information Behavior* and *Engineering to Ikigai (South Asia)/You Know the Glory, Not the Story*. See nareshagarwal.com, projectonenessworld.com

About the Editors

Samrat Choudhury a.k.a. Samrat X is an author and commissioning editor, and a former editor of daily newspapers in India's major metropolises, Delhi, Mumbai and Bengaluru. His latest book is *Northeast India: A Political History*, published by HarperCollins in India and Hurst in the UK. Some of his essays and short stories have appeared in translation in German, Spanish, Italian and Portuguese. His earlier works include *The Braided River*, a travelogue following the Brahmaputra, and *The Urban Jungle*, a novel. He was one of the two editors of *Insider/Outsider: Belonging and Unbelonging in India's Northeast*, an anthology on that issue in Northeast India. His other interests include the Partition of India. Samrat was the Asian Leadership fellow from India at the International House of Japan in Tokyo in 2018 and a Chevening scholar at the University of Westminster, London, in 2019.

Preeti Gill is an independent literary agent who has more than twenty years' experience in the publishing industry as a commissioning editor and rights director. She has travelled extensively in Northeast India and written on issues of conflict and women. She is the editor of *The Peripheral Centre: Voices from India's Northeast* and *Bearing Witness: A Report on the Impact of Conflict on Women in Nagaland*

and Assam. Her writings have appeared in numerous journals and anthologies, including *1984 in Memory and Imagination* (2016). Her documentary, *Rambuai: Mizoram's 'Trouble' Years* (co-produced with Sanjoy Hazarika), was released in September 2016. She has edited *She Stoops to Kill*, an anthology of murder stories by women, and co-edited *Insider/Outsider: Belonging and Unbelonging in India's Northeast*, both published in 2019.

HarperCollins *Publishers* India

At HarperCollins India, we believe in telling the best stories and finding the widest readership for our books in every format possible. We started publishing in 1992; a great deal has changed since then, but what has remained constant is the passion with which our authors write their books, the love with which readers receive them, and the sheer joy and excitement that we as publishers feel in being a part of the publishing process.

Over the years, we've had the pleasure of publishing some of the finest writing from the subcontinent and around the world, including several award-winning titles and some of the biggest bestsellers in India's publishing history. But nothing has meant more to us than the fact that millions of people have read the books we published, and that somewhere, a book of ours might have made a difference.

As we look to the future, we go back to that one word— a word which has been a driving force for us all these years.

Read.

Harper Collins

HARPER FICTION

HARPER NON-FICTION

HARPER BUSINESS

HarperCollins *Children's Books*

HARPER DESIGN

Harper Sport

HARPER PERENNIAL

HARPER VANTAGE

हार्पर हिन्दी